D0105269

Radiant
Daughters

Radiant Daughters

FICTIONAL AMERICAN WOMEN

Thelma J. Shinn

CONTRIBUTIONS IN WOMEN'S STUDIES,
NUMBER 66

GREENWOOD PRESS

NEW YORK • WESTPORT, CONNECTICUT • LONDON

Library of Congress Cataloging-in-Publication Data

Shinn, Thelma J., 1942-
  Radiant Daughters.

  (Contributions in women's studies, ISSN 0147-104X ;
no. 66)
  Bibliography: p.
  Includes index.
  1. American fiction—20th century—History and
criticism. 2. Women in literature. 3. American
fiction—Women authors—History and criticism. I. Title.
II. Series.
PS374.W6S55 1986   813'.54'09352042   85-27196
ISBN 0-313-25197-5 (lib. bdg. : alk. paper)

Library of Congress Catalog Card Number: 85-27196
ISBN: 0-313-25197-5
ISSN: 0147-104X

First Published in 1986

Greenwood Press, Inc.
88 Post Road West
Westport, Connecticut 06881

Printed in the United States of America

The paper used in this book complies with the
Permanent Paper Standard issued by the National
Information Standards Organization (Z39.48-1984)

10 9 8 7 6 5 4 3 2 1

Acknowledgments

Sections of this book have previously appeared in earlier forms. For permission to
reproduce materials, we are indebted to the following sources:

"Flannery O'Connor and the Violence of Grace," *Contemporary Literature* (Winter
1968), 58–73. Reprinted by permission of the University of Wisconsin Press.

"Women in the Novels of Ann Petry," *Critique: Studies in Modern Fiction* 16 (1974),
110–20. Reprinted by permission of the publisher.

This book is dedicated to my "glittering sons and
radiant daughters": Ramona, Rebecca, Joe, Jim, and Rachel.

What bright babes had Lilith and Adam!—
(Eden bower's in flower.)
Shapes that coiled in the woods and waters,
Glittering sons and radiant daughters.

Dante Gabriel Rossetti, "Eden Bower"

Contents

Acknowledgments

Papers based on this material have been read at meetings of the Rocky Mountain Modern Language Association, American Association of University Women, and the Conference on Sexism in Education at Arizona State University.

I would also like to acknowledge thanks due to my classes in Women and Myth, Contemporary American Women Writers and Women in Society at Arizona State University for the insights they have contributed and generated which have greatly enriched this work. Acknowledgment of the contributions of writers and scholars has been given in the endnotes and bibliography.

Preface

"Literature," Joyce Carol Oates quotes herself as saying through her character Maureen Wendall in *them* (1969), "gives form to life." But whose form is it? "What is form? Why is it better than the way life happens by itself? I hate all that, all those lies, so many words in all those books," Maureen responds. In her response is a particularly female challenge to the literature she has known. In the nineteenth century Ibsen had projected a similar attitude through Nora in *A Doll's House* as she claims the right to individuality: "I know quite well that most people would agree with you, Torvald, and that you have a warrant for it in books; but I can't be satisfied any longer with what most people say, and with what's in books. I must think things out for myself and try to understand."

Although I had always shared Oates's belief in literature as a key to understanding ourselves and our lives, I became aware over the years that literature itself had been divided along the same lines as other aspects of our lives in dualistic, sexist Western society. There was LITERATURE, which most often was written by men about men. Then there was "women's literature," the romances that women devoured and continue to devour in incredible numbers.

While fiction is the literary genre designed to explore the self in a social context, neither the mainstream fiction nor the romantic novels concerned themselves with the individuality of the female self. Even when I read that LITERATURE approved by men, I found in its women characters at best a mirror image, which placed me in my social context but which lacked depth. On the other hand, the romances, as Kay Mussell has shown in *Fantasy and Rec-*

onciliation: Contemporary Formulas of Women's Romance Fiction (Westport, CT: Greenwood Press, 1984), "rarely challenge the social
order, and they do not urge women to recognize oppression or to
revolt: instead, they reinforce the value of traditional roles in a
changing society" (xi).

While my formal training even in graduate work in American
literature introduced me to few women writers, the circumstances
described above led me to seek them out. As an individual and as
mother of three daughters as well as two sons, I sought the female
self in the fiction of my time and place, hoping with Oates that it
would "give form to life." As I slowly discovered women writers
of serious fiction, the female self did take on new dimensions through
their women characters. The social context as well was challenged
by new questions, and "the way life happens by itself" rather than
the way it is defined for us by "all those lies" became a subject for
exploration. This initial interest led first to my dissertation on
"Women Characters in Contemporary American Fiction" at Pur-
due University (1972).

Studying and establishing a growth pattern for today's woman
through what women had to write was exciting and revealing. I
discerned many patterns similar to those Annis Pratt would discuss
in her 1981 study, Archetypal Patterns in Women's Fiction, patterns
which could help Nora discover the self she sought, and those
patterns will be discussed in this study. Yet, what Pratt's research,
which encompasses three hundred years of women's fiction, suggests most strongly is the endless repetition of such a pattern. That
the pattern of maturation for women has been different from that
for men in our society is important to note, and that will also be
addressed in this study.

Even more important to me was that the growth cycle reflected
in women characters in contemporary American fiction since 1940
led as well to a consideration of the growth pattern of the society
itself. Inasmuch as the traditional values of American society were
being challenged by the contemporary crisis, so too was challenged
the polarization of the sexes, which had resulted in a denigration
or rejection of characteristics and attitudes associated with women.
"Women are the heroes of dead lands," John Updike claims in The
Poorhouse Fair (1958), and Norman Mailer in particular decries the
"womanization of America" in the same decade. Both are reacting

to the undercurrent of change that was already threatening to over-turn the "feminine mystique" which Betty Friedan so convincingly diagnoses as the prevailing attitude of the day.

An examination of the women characters, I discovered, not only revealed the contemporary realities of growing up female in Amer-ica, but it also indicated the social and individual imbalances created by what psychologist Dr. Karl Stern would call "the flight from woman" in his book of that title (1965). The final effect of the suppression of growth in women emerged in reality as the suppres-sion of half of the self for every individual, male or female. Con-sequently, women characters were often presented as internal as well as external threats to the male characters; such writers as Jean Stafford and Carson McCullers even seemed to suggest that survival of one sex might necessarily be at the expense of the other, as Chester E. Eisinger has noted in *Fiction of the Forties* (1963).

Even on the level of individual development of women charac-ters, therefore, it became necessary to examine the women created by male as well as female writers to achieve a composite of that growth in the social context. Adding this dimension made the social questions more prominent as well. The "flight from woman"—the denigration of that half of life which our society has identified with the "feminine" in humanity—can perhaps define the schizophrenia of our contemporary world.

On the other hand, I have selected a disproportionate number of women writers to discuss in this study, especially in relation to the total number of contemporary writers receiving critical notice in the period, to reflect how contemporary woman sees herself and her relationships. Since, as John W. Aldridge points out in *After the Lost Generation* (New York: Noonday Press, 1951), a writer depends on the self as a source of information ("This amounts to no less than everything he is or has become up to the moment of writing," Aldridge affirms, "and that part of everything he is which he is able to communicate in language to the reader"—231), I have chosen women writers who provide a wide variety of perspectives from which to view the contemporary American scene, while con-fining myself to mainstream writers rather than including the more experimental works. Eudora Welty writes from a rural Mississippi region still somewhat protected from the contemporary disinte-gration of traditions; Carson McCullers takes memories of a more urban Georgia home with her to the loneliness of New York City; Shirley Ann Grau reveals Southern life in Louisiana from the isolated Creoles to the surviving aristocracy. Two other Southerners, the Kentuckian Caroline Gordon and the Georgian Flannery O'Connor, suggest the richness of the contribution of the South to contemporary fiction.

Gordon and O'Connor share with the Northerner Mary McCarthy both her Catholicism and her intellectual orientation through college and teaching experiences. Equally a part of the intellectual community—if there is such a thing—are the Eastern writers represented here: Jean Stafford, transplanted from Colorado to New England; Shirley Jackson, another transplant from California to Vermont; Hortense Calisher and Susan Sontag, both native residents of New York City. Moving in the opposite direction, Nebraska-born Tillie Olsen has spent most of her life in San Francisco, although she has also taught in Massachusetts.

Two other Eastern college professors chose different genres: Grace Paley utilizes her knowledge of New York City in the first of what has become three volumes of short stories, while Sylvia Plath had expressed her often suicidal vision through poetry, writing only the single novel we will examine. So too has Gwendolyn Brooks, a black poet raised in the slums of Chicago, offered only one novel so far to her readers. New York's ghetto is one of the locations for the work of another black novelist, the New Englander Ann Petry, while the slums of Detroit and the shanties of poor whites in the South contrast sharply with the equally unhappy mansions of the nouveau riche in the fiction of Joyce Carol Oates, herself an upstate New Yorker from near Niagara Falls who is a college professor and one of our most prolific contemporary writers. Finally, an international perspective is offered by Texas-born Katherine Anne Porter, who has often written from her experiences in Mexico and Germany.

Such a richly varied background should, and I believe does, give a fairly thorough view of contemporary American women, since I have chosen writers of realistic rather than speculative fiction (even O'Connor's grotesque characters, Jackson's gothic horrors, and Sontag's existential dreamers are trapped in the world we know). The male writers I have included are those who serve as foils for the women or who are representative of intrinsically interesting views of women in their observations of the same realistic surface. The women created by each of these writers must attain their growth and survive in or be destroyed by the contemporary chaos which has undermined the traditional values by which they would have been defined in earlier periods. These values have certainly not disappeared; in fact, the decade of the 50's reasserts them with a vengeance, as do Phyllis Schafly and Marabel Morgan in the 70's. Yet fewer and fewer contemporaries believe what Wendall considers "all those lies" and more and more are searching for something to believe in. This examination of women characters in our fiction reveals that they have some suggestions to offer as they take on adult responsibility for themselves and for the world around them. If a woman character can be seen as a human individual with whom any reader can identify, then too those characteristics which have been associated particularly with women might also begin to be recognized as human and not only acceptable but perhaps even essential if we are once more to "give form to life" and to a fragmented and destructive present.

If "man" has been a generic term for people male or female, it has also carried connotations of specifically "masculine" characteristics—to be a man is to be active, aggressive, strong, rational, etc. On the other hand, another generic term has always been available which is not limited by those connotations. In fact, "human" has included what might be considered the "feminine" connotations: compassion, sensitivity, mercy, intuitive understanding, for instance. To be human is even to have the right to make a mistake, because to err is human. Even Eve, blamed as she was for Adam's fall, survives as well as the mother of humanity.

The evolution of women revealed in the fiction of our time and place does go beyond the individual. Perhaps it is time that our role models become "human" and that our social definition comes more in line with "the way life happens by itself." That is what this literature reveals through its women characters. In these troubled times, if the next generation is to "succeed" both its women and men must take adult responsibility for the survival of a human society. "Those children are such lovely examples of what may well be the last generation of humankind," Grace Paley's narrator warns their fathers in "Anxiety" even while she assures them that each of them is "about a generation ahead of your father in your attitude and behavior toward your child." It is not only women who have come a long way and still have a long way to go, this story published in her 1985 collection, *Later the Same Day*, suggests.

Among the people who deserve special thanks for this study are Chester E. Eisinger; Charles and Barbara Bickford, the late Maloa Faurot and William Joseph O'Brien, and the entire Women's Studies faculty at Arizona State University, who have given encouragement, information, and incentive. Particular thanks go to Nancy Russo, ASU's Director of Women's Studies; to librarians Ann Regner and Deborah Blouin; and for the financial support provided by a summer grant and a sabbatical from ASU. Final thanks go to those closest to the project: my students, my children, my husband, and my former secretary, Judy Drake.

Radiant
Daughters

Introduction

> Each age, it is found, must write its own books; or rather, each generation for the next succeeding. The books of an older period will not fit this.
>
> Ralph Waldo Emerson, "The American Scholar"

Emerson's defense of the contemporary American literature of his time takes on double meanings when applied to literature written by women. Not only has each generation felt the need to reinterpret the human condition in the light of its own experience; each generation of women has felt isolated from the "books of an older period" because so few of those given the privilege of surviving were written by women. This is not because women had not written; even in the relatively short history of American literature women have been incredibly prolific. Nor is it always because the products of these "scribbling women," as Nathaniel Hawthorne called them, were not deserving of preservation. Buried in the past until 1969, for instance, were the works of Kate Chopin, including her classic *The Awakening*, which had to await a renewed effort in women's studies research to be brought to the attention of the reading public. Because of the prejudices of the time against her subject matter, perhaps also because of the traditional dominance of male critics and male literary historians, Chopin was discouraged from writing a sequel to this fine novel.

Few of us will make the effort to rediscover these lost works; most have been convinced by the virtual exclusion of early women fiction writers from the anthologies of American literature that women had little to say, or at least little worth listening to, in the nineteenth century. Yet the stories of Mary E. Wilkins Freeman are not only brilliantly written but also offer insights into the oppressed lives of women that should have motivated social change; the short stories of Chopin present women choosing revolutionary life-styles and succeeding in them; even the more romantic works of Harriet Prescott Spofford decry the unrealistic attitudes toward women and finally with delightful humor (in "Mrs. Claxton's Skeleton") present and admire the woman of equality.

It is a truism that those who do not know their history are doomed to relive it; equally true is that those who do not know their literature are doomed to rewrite it. Nearly every generation of women writers in America have had to rediscover their own oppression, to reexamine the alternatives open to them, and to redefine their lives. The necessity to define, or redefine, the self has played a particularly important role in our literature since 1940, especially for those members of our society who had in one way or another been oppressed by that society. The average American might have experienced a frightening sense of insecurity when he saw his world and his values breaking down in the wake of a second world war, but the same social collapse for a Black or Jewish American, and for many women, meant as well that the stereotypes which had predefined their characters within the society were also disintegrating. For this reason and Emerson's, this study is directed at that period of our literature. I would like to believe that we could trace the growth of women through our literature beginning with Anne Bradstreet's cautious desire for a little credit for women in her "Prologue" culminating in Denise Levertov's mature assertion of the value of selfhood and womanhood in "Stepping Westward." Poets, however, can discern the direction we must take long before our social selves can make the move. It is in the fiction, which must realize personal growth within the social context, that we find the accurate if not the ideal picture of our lives. In contemporary American fiction we can discover the pattern of growth common to women, a pattern that has been reproduced periodically by other generations. Hopefully, each repetitive cycle has spiraled us somewhat nearer a realization "that woman is man's equal—was intended to be so by the Creator, and the highest good of the race demands that she should be recognized as such."[1]

The impediments to the maturation of women in America have been many; their struggle for personal and social growth has been constant at least since Bradstreet penned her early protest in 1650. Spofford would start it even earlier; in her version of the love story of Priscilla Mullins, John Alden, and Captain Miles Standish, she sees more to the gentle Priscilla than a simple romantic:

> But perhaps she was not so very gentle. Was there a spice of feminine coquetry in her famous speech to John Alden, for all her sweet Puritanism? Or was it that she understood the dignity and worth of womanhood, and was the first in this new land to take her stand upon it?[2]

The early feminists, small in number, were easily dismissed by many as "emancipated neurasthenic women," "alien" to their own class.[3] Even in 1848 when they met together at Seneca Falls for their first national convention, these women were only ridiculed by the media (the exceptions, such as Frederick Douglass's supportive editorial in *The North Star*, only proving the rule[4]). Surprisingly, Hawthorne gave one of the strongest feminist statements of the time through the character of Hester Prynne in *The Scarlet Letter*, a description of the position of women which acknowledged their oppression but which also clarified why so few women publicly protested by showing how few alternatives were open to the women of the time. Hester was in many ways a prophetess, as she mused on woman's life: "Indeed, the same dark question often rose into her mind, with reference to the whole race of womanhood. Was existence worth accepting, even to the happiest among them?" The only solution to the problem which she can discern sounds very contemporary:

> As a first step, the whole system of society is to be torn down, and built up anew. Then, the very nature of the opposite sex, or its long hereditary habit, which has become like nature, is to be essentially modified, before woman can be allowed to assume what seems a fair and suitable position. Finally, all other difficulties being obviated, woman cannot take advantage of these preliminary reforms, until she herself shall have undergone a still

mightier change; in which, perhaps the ethereal essence, wherein she has her truest life, will be found to have evaporated. (Chapter 13)

Hawthorne has recognized that the position of woman is determined by the whole structure of the society, is reinforced by the identification of certain qualities as "natural" to women or to men alone, and is perpetuated by the lifelong habit of women of accepting their assigned role and therefore willingly sacrificing their rights. But the alternative to a continuation of these inequities—the total restructuring of society and of its concept of the individual—seems to him not only unattainable but even undesirable. In the process, he is afraid, women would become less spiritual. The women in his stories are therefore offered a "higher" solution: "A woman never overcomes these problems by any exercise of thought. They are not to be solved, or only in one way. If her heart chance to come uppermost, they vanish." By devoting herself to a man and living through him, or to the spiritual sacrifice of a higher love, woman could forget her untenable position on earth and ascend to the top of the pedestal (which often meant actual death).

Most women of his time seemed to agree with Hawthorne's solution. Just as the slaves had recognized that they were better cared for than those blacks who achieved freedom in a slave society, so too women instinctively recognized that they were protected and cared for by their masters (husbands and fathers) within the traditions of their society. Their position had been clearly defined in the Victorian period as well by what William O'Neill calls the "conjugal family system":

"the cult of true womanhood," as one historian calls it, which made central virtues of piety, purity, submissiveness, and domesticity. Almost the only form of activity permitted women was religious work, because it did not take them away from their true "sphere." "From her home woman performed her great task of bringing man back to God."... But woman was also physically weaker than man, inferior to him in cognitive ability, and wholly unsuited to the rough work outside the home.[5]

Yet, although they didn't join the ranks of the militant feminists, what these women did do was purchase, read, and demand more and more fiction written by women. The often condemned sen-

timental domestic novels, most of which were written by women
and which led naturally into the admirable realistic novels at the
turn of the century, were seen by one critic as a lethal weapon in
the war between the sexes. In *All the Happy Endings*, Helen Waite
Papashvily suggests a subtle rebellion implicit in these novels:

> Nonetheless the quiet women revolted, too, and waged their own devious,
> subtle, undeclared war against men—their manual of arms, their handbook
> of strategy was the sentimental domestic novel they read for half a century.
> The pages reveal the tactics women adopted, the weapons they chose, the
> victories they sought—and finally won.[6]

Less subtle was the oppression of women revealed in the realistic
fiction of such writers as Mary E. Wilkins Freeman, the lack of
communication between the sexes revealed after the turn of the
century by Susan Glaspell, the untapped strengths of women ad-
mirably depicted by Willa Cather. Generation after generation, each
woman writer told her story for her generation.

The cycle of woman's growth, both public and personal, reached
a high point when women were granted the vote in 1920. The
freedom of the 20's, the aspirations of the 30's, the accomplishments
of both decades by women bespoke a new maturity; women had
come of age and were entering colleges, professions, and public
life in greater than ever numbers. Although the depression slowed
their accomplishments, it affected both sexes fairly equally and the
unity produced by common problems at least perpetuated a type
of equality.

However, the war years changed the picture, both personally
and socially. Men and women were sharply separated in every way;
the individual was subordinated to the needs of the social crisis.
Although superficially women seemed to be freed from traditional
roles as they began filling factories and taking over as heads of the
household while their men were at war, everyone was aware that
such changes were temporary and artificial. The gains women had
made as individuals in the years between the wars were held in
abeyance; they would be virtually destroyed after the war by a
wave of conservatism and a desperate attempt to regain lost innocence by hanging on to dying traditions.

The war years can be seen as beginning a new cycle of growth, for women as well as for the world in which they lived. The new generation birthed by World War II is one with which we are still trying to come to terms. The violence of that birth is evident in the fiction of the period. Nor will the perpetual childhood promised by the media in the next decade long assuage the need to discover the self and to understand the world in which that self must exist. And if the seemingly doomed rebellions of the 60's seem adolescent in retrospect, they are often adolescent in the finest sense of the word—an expression of values, a refusal to compromise, and an attempt to embody those values in their society. By the end of that decade, women as well as men in our fiction turned their concerns outward from the self to the society as adults responsible for the future.

Writers from many fields have reflected these changes in each decade. Particularly revealing of the attitudes of the 40's we will see reflected in the fiction is the psychological study *Modern Woman: The Lost Sex* by Ferdinand Lundberg and Marynia F. Farnham (1947), which sought to treat the "illness" of the modern woman by returning her to the home and motherhood where she belonged.[7] Yet "Mom is a jerk," Philip Wylie asserted in his 1942 attack on "momism," *Generation of Vipers*.[8] Clearly, women needed to begin again, and they could perhaps start with the anthropological studies of Margaret Mead, which could help them realize that the way we define *Male and Female* (the title of her 1949 study) has always been caught up in social roles: "every known society creates and maintains artificial occupational divisions and personality expectations for each sex that limit the humanity of the other sex."[9]

The 50's would open with Josephine Lurie Jessup's literary study of Ellen Glasgow, Edith Wharton, and Willa Cather in *Faith of our Feminists*, but her search for easy victories by strong women characters seemed more wish fulfillment than a heritage of strength for the contemporary generation. Most agreed more quickly with Simone de Beauvoir's assertion in her 1952 study that women were still considered *The Second Sex*. De Beauvoir even reminded women that the war between the sexes continues precisely because they as well as the men try to perpetuate femininity: "Woman, who is being emancipated from it, wishes none the less to retain its privileges; and man, in that case, wants her to assume its limitations."[10] The literature of the 50's certainly seemed to support her contention.

Despite the history of *Sex Variant Women in Literature* published by Jeannette H. Foster in 1956, most of the fictional American women of the decade were descended from those examined in Papashvily's 1956 study of the nineteenth-century sentimental novels in *All the Happy Endings* and William Wasserstrom's *Heiress of All the Ages* (1959). Wasserstrom's heiress is also descended from a long line of fathers' daughters: "And yet devotedness is what men admired: in part because they valued this quality so highly, fiction is preoccupied with daughters trained by fathers to be passionate but docile wives."[11] However, both authors were also perceptive enough to note that the surface passivity of these women characters was deceiving. Papashvily recognized in the novels she examined a quiet assertion by the "silent majority" of women; Wasserstrom sees a twentieth-century evolution of his heiress. Although he couches this evolution in romantic terms, he clearly recognizes that they might be central to an understanding of contemporary reality: "If you want to know the forces that create men, children, and culture, you must first know the secret of a woman's force. Her secret is the clue to the secret of love and her love, the source of life itself, is the best definition of the quality of being itself."[12] Wasserstrom's application of this romantic formula to twentieth-century literature reflects the difficulty his male writers (Fitzgerald, Warren, Morris, Bellow) have with seeing both love and women in a new light: "But when the sexual revolution occurred, the American dream of love lost its enchantment; the American myth lost its cogency. . . . And nausea came into being. Following nausea, today we have terror. . . . " If he too is referring to the loss of Hawthorne's "ethereal essence" here, fortunately he moves beyond the nineteenth-century stereotypes to see, for instance, Robert Penn Warren's characters (particularly Anne Stanton and Amantha Starr) as women who "lead us not into evil but deliver us by showing that the way to salvation is through the door that Kafka feared to enter, that Malraux's Kyo allowed May to open for him and anyone else, that Bloom and Molly open for Dedalus. . . . As they themselves learn how to live, so they show us how to shed our innocence, and if we do not respond the fault is ours not theirs."[13] Woman is still the heiress, saving her man. Now, however, she seems to promise that salvation by changing rather than by reinforcing his stereotypes.

Studies published in the 60's confirmed that women were quite ready to initiate the changes Wasserstrom predicted. No longer accepting the stereotypes of the past, Betty Friedan set the tone by rejecting *The Feminine Mystique* (1963). While Louis Auchincloss tried to reaffirm through a study of nine American women novelists that women continued in their social roles as *Pioneers and Caretakers* (1965), Katherine Rogers came out the next year with *The Troublesome Helpmate*, which attacked misogynistic literature throughout history. Leslie Fiedler as early as 1960 had published *Love and Death in the American Novel*, decrying male immaturity in our fiction, and he would follow in 1968 with *The Return of the Vanishing American*, which showed male characters again following Natty Bumppo and Huck Finn into the freedom of the woods and leaving the responsibilities of and the blame for society with the women. In *Thinking About Women* (1968), Mary Ellman offered an insightful classification of the types of women characters that had dominated our literature. Each work seemed to be clearing the decks for the flood of new women who would fill the literature of the 70's and 80's and particularly pointing out the reflection of social problems found in these fictional American men and women. A final literary and ideological struggle between extreme points of view on the war between the sexes as embodied in our literature can be traced through Kate Millet's *Sexual Politics* at the end of the 60's and Norman Mailer's response in *The Prisoner of Sex*.

The period since 1970 is filled with ideological and literary examinations of the social and individual questions raised by the maturation of women and the reassertion of human values in contemporary American society, but I will save this discussion for my Afterword and Bibliography. As we examine the fiction written since 1940, then, we not only find a formula for individual growth embodied in the female self but also discover possible alternatives for social growth. Focussing on the women characters inevitably focusses as well on those characteristics and attitudes which our society has associated with women. As these women mature, their assertion of self often evolves into an assertion of those values as well and a challenging of the "lies" they have been told. Potentially, therefore, this self-discovery of women promises the rediscovery of social balance opposing the destructive dualism of our present system. In the view of many still trying to come to terms with the Holocaust, the Bomb, and other atrocities of and since World War

II, some alternative to our present system is essential if we and our world are going to survive at all.

This study approaches the human condition in its social context through the fictional American women of contemporary writers because in them I have discovered the key to who we are and where we are going. Carolyn G. Heilbrun agrees in *Toward A Recognition of Androgyny* (1973) with Wasserstrom that women characters have been heroic since Henrik Ibsen and Henry James:

> The particular tension that exists between her apparent freedom and her actual relegation to a constrained destiny is a tension experienced also by men in the modern world. . . . Woman, serving as metaphor for modern man striving to express himself, to *be* himself within a mechanical society, discovers her greatest wish is to *live*, a wish for which she will turn aside anything and everything.[14]

Women are willing to realize and accept their own potential despite the impediments of social roles, of childlike dependency, of threatening insanity, of inescapable aloneness—which makes them symbolic of humanity's hope for a future in this absurd world. If male characters are fascinated, as Fiedler has observed, with death and escape, women embody our commitment to life.

"The novelist begins always with the meaning which he, as a unique sensibility, brings to the experience he has chosen as his material," John W. Aldridge reminds us.[15] Consequently, I have chosen to let the "unique sensibility" of women who began writing in the three decades since the beginning of World War II dominate this study, and have chosen to approach their works chronologically by the decade in which they began publishing their fiction. I have also purposely chosen realistic writers with differing frames of reference to broaden the scope of the study, hoping that the many similarities among the presentations will yield common, human concerns while the differences will reveal the subtler pressures exerted on special groups and regions within American society. In each decade I have sought to present a range of male perspectives as well.

These writers utilize many forms and techniques, all of which must be taken into consideration; however, despite distortions in characterization and even action determined by these formal considerations—often, in fact, even because of these conscious distortions—the women portrayed reveal the psychological realities, not only of their own social and personal lives, but also of those ideas and values that our society has traditionally defined as feminine. This discussion limits the attention I can give to other aspects of the fiction, however, so my technical comments will be brief. If it seems that the disproportionate number of women writers will produce skewed or unreliable findings, I remind the reader of the words of John Stuart Mill:

The knowledge that men can acquire of women, even as they have been and are, without reference to what they might be, is wretchedly imperfect and superficial, and always will be so, until women themselves have told all that they have to tell.[16]

NOTES

1. "Declaration of Sentiments and Resolutions, Seneca Falls," in *Feminism: The Essential Historical Writings*, ed. by Miriam Schneir (New York: Vintage Books, 1972), 81.

2. Harriet Prescott Spofford, "Priscilla," in *Three Heroines of New England Romance* (Boston: Little, Brown & Company, 1894), 28, 31.

3. Christopher Lasch, *The New Radicalism in America, 1889–1963* (New York: Alfred A. Knopf, 1965), 62.

4. See discussion in Schneir's *Feminism*, p. 83.

5. William O'Neill, *Everyone Was Brave* (Chicago: Quadrangle Books, 1969), 4, 7.

6. Helen Waite Papashvily, *All the Happy Endings* (New York: Harper & Brothers, 1956), 40.

7. Ferdinand Lundberg and Marynia F. Farnham, *Modern Woman: The Lost Sex* (New York: Harper & Brothers, 1947), 202.

8. Philip Wylie, *Generation of Vipers* (New York: Pocket Books, 1958), 188.

9. Margaret Mead, *Male and Female* (New York: Dell, 1949), 349.

10. Simone de Beauvoir, *The Second Sex* (New York: Bantam Books, 1952), 677.

11. William Wasserstrom, *Heiress of All the Ages* (Minneapolis: University of Minnesota Press, 1959), 128.

12. Ibid., 129.

13. Ibid., 129, 131.

14. Carolyn G. Heilbrun, *Toward A Recognition of Androgyny* (New York: Harper & Row, 1973), 23.

15. John W. Aldridge, *After the Lost Generation* (New York: Noonday Press, 1951), 231.

16. Quoted by Germaine Greer in *The Female Eunuch* (New York: McGraw-Hill, 1970), 3, from chapter 1 of *The Subjection of Women* by John Stuart Mill.

1

Stumbling over Stereotypes:
Fiction of the 40's

Although the United States officially entered World War II after the Japanese attack on Pearl Harbor on December 7, 1941, Americans felt the real impact of the war more than two years earlier when Hitler attacked Poland and launched a blitzkrieg of mechanized warfare and indiscriminate bombing which overwhelmed Poland and shocked the world. Particularly for Americans, the political and physical ruthlessness of World War II put a final seal on the painful death of their innocence—what was left of it after the "war to end all wars," the jazz age, and what W. H. Auden describes as "a low dishonest decade" in his poem commemorating "September 1, 1939." Then the attack on Pearl Harbor made direct involvement in the war inevitable, and the nation's men were sent to fight on another continent.

The situation for the women left at home was complex. Deprivation is different from combat, and it demands different reactions. Women no less than men found themselves in a world whose values were crumbling; but, when we consider that one of the chief roles woman plays in our society has been as the "caretaker" of those values (a role which provides the basic assumptions behind Louis Auchincloss's study, *Pioneers and Caretakers*) as well as teacher of them (which John Stuart Mill defines as the "training of the affections," the "most indispensable part of education" provided by the mother in that "she makes her own character pass into the child"[1]), this loss of values shakes not only her security but also the very definition of her social role.

This psychological turmoil must have been increased by the absence of her loved ones, a concrete and immediate deprivation of love which paralleled the seemingly growing absence of love in the world. Although admittedly men at war were equally deprived of the presence of their loved ones, they did not have the accompanying fear that the women were in mortal danger, in a strange place inaccessible to them. Furthermore, they were united with other men, working and living closely in a brotherhood entirely sanctioned by our society. No similar sisterhood could boast social sanctions, although relations between women were not always defined along the competitive lines encouraged by their society. Still, unless they had full responsibility for a young family, women often found themselves unexpectedly isolated during the war years.

What this amounts to is that during the war most women were deprived of their social roles—teaching and preserving values, because which values should be taught or preserved was no longer clear; and protecting, loving, and caring for their sons and husbands while being protected and loved in return in the immediate, physical sense. They were thrust into an artificial public life, doing men's work not because they had chosen to but because an emergency labor force was needed; heading families hopefully only on a temporary basis; and generally functioning as extensions of society. If life at the front forced men to come face to face with often unattractive physical and political realities, "manning" the home front kept women from the realities they had known.

The other side of the coin to this psychological and social upheaval in the lives of American women during the war years, however, was that many found they enjoyed their new roles. New economic pressures also kept many of them at least part time in the work force. In 1940 only about 35% of married women were working in the United States; by 1960 that had increased to 60%.[2] The confusing changes which accompany any war were further intensified by the violence and inhumanity of this war. After the Holocaust and the Bomb, few could simply turn their backs on the war and return to "real life." In fact, many postwar writers began questioning the very nature of reality. The reality of six million Jews being eliminated in Europe, of the burning hell let loose on Nagasaki and Hiroshima, haunted the men who tried to return to a way of life they had thought was real before the war. Women, too, were forced to face a seemingly uncontrollable violence from which they had always been taught that men would protect them. In all aspects of their lives, the questioning began.

A significant feature of the novels of the 40's, especially those written by women, is that few of them directly reflected the war-torn world. An important exception is Norman Mailer's *The Naked and the Dead*, which only treated women in flashbacks from the men at war. The only novel we will be discussing which does combine war and women is *Guard of Honor* by James Gould Cozzens, and it is in this novel and Cozzens's other works that we encounter the first stereotype which women had to overcome to begin their growth.

TOO LITTLE OR TOO MUCH

It really never was that I didn't like men. I thought they were marvelous; and anyone could see that girls were just terrible—so silly and always a nuisance. . . . I wanted to be a man like that so much I could hardly stand it.

So says Clarissa in *By Love Possessed* (1957) by Cozzens. In his fiction, the woman is always an incomplete male, and the closer she can come to eliminating any differences between the sexes the more acceptable she will be. Cozzens is loyal to Freud's concept of penis envy; for him, in fact, unisex means male. Certainly, he seems to reason, a society built by and for males would be run best without the corrupting or at least upsetting presence of women. Although we might prefer to dismiss his attitude as the exception, an expression of the extremely conservative and rationalistic position, the immense popularity of this novel, lauded as "the great American novel" and selling 170,000 copies in seven weeks,[3] must make us reconsider.

In many ways, Cozzens reflects the dehumanization of the war years. His focus is social, not personal: many of his characters are representative of viewpoints rather than of individuals. Certain of his types recur in each novel, such as the mature, understanding man who reaffirms the value of maintaining conventions and traditions because they are the best structures available to order our disordered lives. Because of this social identification, the stereotypes he establishes for women are significant. They reflect a social attitude which severely limits female growth.

Cozzens obviously prefers in this fiction a competent, often boyish or even mannish woman; while his men are bewildered with, and often resentful of, the less rational aspects of male/female behavior. They perpetually seek order; and while the basic practicality of women impresses them and even their apparent intuition is praiseworthy when it contributes to a more orderly world, they are still frightened by the unpredictability of women and the irrational effect they seem to have on the men.

In his early novels, Cozzens expresses this fear first by dealing as briefly as possible with these "womanly characteristics" that bewilder and presenting instead the kind of woman he admires. Often as not, these women are first met as young girls, either a childhood friend of their future husband or at least many years his junior. In *The Just and the Unjust* (1942), Bonnie is "the quiet child who had lived several years in the same house with him, long ago. Bonnie had been too young—almost six years younger—to deserve actual notice." Similarly, Clarissa was much younger than her husband and had been a counselor at his daughter's summer camp; and in *Morning Noon and Night* (1968) Henry Worthington, attending church while home from college, sees the teenager Judith and the "chubby ten- or eleven-year-old" Charlotte who will become his first and second wives respectively.

All of these women except Judith are sisters to the efficient companion Mrs. Beal and the boyish pal Lieutenant Turck of *Guard of Honor* (1948). Turck defines herself as "on pretty familiar terms with a good many of the men—they used to stop at the library desk and kid me; they were really very nice to me. Women medical students often have a tough time; but they more or less adopted me." One might have hoped that a "woman medical student" would be more independent than the "adopted" child of her male classmates!

Not so in Cozzens's world, however. To win approval, a woman must be sexless or even male in the sense of "one of the boys"; if female, she must remain a child. In fact, Henry Worthington briefly recognizes the father/daughter connotations of his relationship with Charlotte:

Our sage head of HW Associates cannot be unaware that his employee, the relatively youthful Charlotte, almost from the start of her working for him, is possessed by earnest love, by daughterly deep feelings for Father that constitute . . . a "crush" on him. One guesses that little Charlotte has remained at heart the chubby child of the church steps, feeling in need of care, and needing to have herself needed.

This stereotype leads easily into keeping woman in a dependent and childlike position. Also, by choosing the woman who will be a devoted companion and daughter, grateful for what he has to offer rather than demanding, the Cozzens hero feels safe and protected himself from the inexplicable natures of women and from the irrationality of sex. The "other women" he encounters are terrifying, so either he totally rejects them or he dismisses them as unbalanced, schizophrenic: the apparently normal human being is periodically possessed by a "maenad"—as is Marjorie in *By Love Possessed*—or an "incubus"—as is Judith in *Morning Noon and Night*. When thus possessed, these women seek what to the Cozzens hero is inconceivable sexual gratification.

By dividing women in this way, Cozzens perpetuates a stereotype at least as old as Western society. The dutiful woman, properly subservient, is Eve's daughter; the "other woman" can be traced back to Adam's first wife, Lilith. According to the Kabbala, which refers to her as an incubus, Lilith was created Adam's equal and left him when he tried to dominate her. Then she became a symbol of female sexuality, seducing men against their wills and stealing their seed to create her illegitimate offspring—the *lilin* or night demons of Jewish legends, the "glittering sons and radiant daughters" of the poet Dante Gabriel Rossetti.[4] The free, independent woman is rejected by Cozzens. Preferred is the woman who remains dependent, denying her own sensuality in order to preserve the safe, asexual image of the child.

Female sensuality as evil is reinforced by or combined with the stereotype of female assertion as madness. If betraying the stereotype of the subservient woman is insanity, as Cozzens seems to imply, one must question the nature of such sanity, as does Phyllis Chesler. Chesler asserts that sanity is a social judgment. Those who don't conform are "insane." Women are caught in a double bind,

Chesler adds, between not fulfilling their "role" as women and fulfilling the "hysterical" definition of female behavior, which is also deemed mad.[5] Perhaps "much madness is divinest sense," as Emily Dickinson has written. The "madness" of women which is demonstrated by a failure to fulfill social expectations will be defined in this study in relation to the mythical figure of Undine, the stream that becomes a woman. Lilith and Undine, the free and free-flowing women of Western myth, offer models for future radiant daughters among our fictional American women.

Cozzens, however, dismisses these "other women" with his supernatural condemnation. Yet even those women he admires betray him through self-destructive, illogical acts. Turck perpetually abuses herself verbally, while Charlotte and Helen Detweiler in *By Love Possessed* both commit suicide. These women have literally sacrificed themselves for men.

Cozzens's men, of course, assert that the women cause their own misery by refusing their role. Helen, "on the world she never made, . . . imposed with all her strength a pattern of the world she wanted." Such strength will be praised by later women writers, such as Shirley Jackson in *Come Along With Me*. In truth, Helen's suicide seems to be a rejection of logic in favor of emotional reality. She is accused of "a want of principle, which is to say, too much feeling" and is pitied because she is "mad, possessed by love."

Helen fails to be male enough, fails to conform to the stereotype of male justice and rationality. Conversely, Cozzens' men reveal what Dr. Karl Stern has called a "flight from the feminine." Stern summarizes the condition as "an undue emphasis on the technical and the rational, and a rejection of what for want of a better term we call 'feeling' . . . with a neurotic dread of receiving, a fear of tenderness and protection."[6] Helen has denied her feelings for so long that when she does express them she is overwhelmed by them. Cozzens identifies the destruction, but not the cause.

Cozzens's men are further frustrated by their failures with their real daughters. They too must remain perpetual children to please their fathers. When by some "mischance" Arthur Winner, Jr.'s daughter Ann in *By Love Possessed* asserts herself and matures, Winner is frightened because the "long-known child was gone forever, the stranger was already arriving." Nor does Henry Worthington's daughter, twice divorced and well on her way to a third, seem very successful in her adherence to his practical, businesslike approach to human relationships. Since a female is more likely to be boyish before she enters womanhood, Cozzens's men are reluctant to see their daughters mature. Thus, growing into womanhood means courting yet another kind of rejection and disapproval for these women. The only viable option seems to be growing into manhood!

Despite the popularity of *By Love Possessed*, most men do not seem to share Cozzens's attraction to masculine women devoid of passion. Yet women are often told to be more logical, less emotional. "You think like a man" was offered as a compliment to the intelligent woman. It is the other side of the stereotype, however—that masculinity in any form is forbidden a woman—which intrigues two women writers of the 40's. Yet Jean Stafford and Carson McCullers echo Cozzens in that their children are allowed more freedom of choice and self-expression than are the adults and that even the adults feel a need to be protected from the intensity of mature passion—perhaps a reflection of their violent decade.

The young women in this fiction are reluctant to mature; as Annis Pratt has shown, maturation means sacrifice of self for girls. Boys grow up; girls grow down to their role.[7] In her first and longest novel, *Boston Adventure* (1944), Stafford introduces such a young woman in Sonie Marburg. A first-generation American with a controlled German father and an uncontrollable Russian mother, Sonie is one of the "strange children" who play such important roles in contemporary American fiction, roles discussed by Ihab H. Hassan. Hassan classifies Sonie among the "rebel-victims" as "the lonely adolescent or youth, exposing the corrupt adult world" where "dramatic emphasis is on the loss, the pain and bitterness of growth, the fall from uneasy grace."[8]

Sonie's father walks out on the family when Sonie is twelve and his wife Shura is pregnant with their ill-fated son. Shura, beautiful as a saint but bitchy as a witch, is estranged from the society she knew and understood, and the poverty of her new life in America so embitters her that she takes out her frustrations on her family, especially her husband. The difficulties of her early life combined with the constant and often disrespectful attention men have always paid her beauty lead her to hate all men, a hatred intensified by the desertion. Her passionate nature becomes a destructive force: her nagging drives away her husband, her hatred destroys her son, her

frustrations drive her insane, and her failure as a role model leads
Sonie to seek the protection of Miss Pride, a wealthy spinster, and
of a socially dependent role in order to avoid any recurrence of her
mother's weakness within herself. This female heritage of insanity
permeates the fiction of women writers, as Sandra M. Gilbert and
Susan Gubar have noted in *The Madwoman in the Attic*, finding
"images of enclosure and escape, fantasies in which maddened dou-
bles functioned as asocial surrogates for docile selves, metaphors
of physical discomfort manifested in frozen landscape and fiery
interiors" in the fiction of the nineteenth century which they
examined.[9]

Shura wants to protect Sonie herself—from men. "Not but she
couldn't have any man in the world for the asking even now and
only twelve going on thirteen," she explains of Sonie, "but what
kind of a mother would I be to let an angel like her be treated the
way my poor self has been?" While she is forced to see the dangers
of men, her father's desertion when she is twelve and on the thresh-
old of womanhood leaves Sonie in need of male attention. Besides,
she understands how Shura might have caused his departure: "My
father, his pride lacerated, his shame festering would, at this point,
retaliate. . . . What man on earth would *want* to work for a creature
like that?" She has seen her mother's attitude even destroy the joy
her father had tried to give her one Christmas by building her a
crèche: "I was delighted with it, until . . . I saw that my mother
had no interest in it and that my father had lost his. It was as if
some ungovernable force in her was determined to extinguish every
joy her husband might have." Sonie hopes to find safety from a
similar "ungovernable force" in herself.

Sonie turns briefly to her friend Nathan Kadish, but her mother's
teachings stand between them: "The desire for his companionship
was tantamount to a betrayal of my mother who for so many years
and so diligently had schooled me in the treacheries of men, although I believe that she assumed that I would marry in spite of
her warnings." Although Shura is an exaggeration of the problem,
generations of women have been raised to fear men, to dread sex,
and yet, "in spite of . . . warnings," to marry. The inherent contradiction in these attitudes could easily make a sensitive young
woman hesitate, could make her view maturity as a violent and
destructive period in which she would be the victim. Not only

would she be victimized by men if she allowed them into her life, but also her own passions—as Sonie could see in Shura—would be difficult if not impossible to control if she allowed them free rein. The awakening of sexual desire reminded Sonie of her mother's song, a lamentation of female vulnerability and "woman's sad lot!" which promised only pain.

Couched in such terms, maturity—especially sexual maturity and commitment—is too dangerous. Sonie chooses instead the security and sanity of a dependent position as the companion of Miss Pride. She and many like her were discouraged from full development by being taught that womanhood meant unhappiness and even victimization. Through Sonie, Stafford suggests that a structured society is essential to a woman, that its shortcomings are outweighed by the protection it offers. Sonie's choice precludes a home and marriage of her own: men, she knew, might go away; society is more permanent and will not abandon its children.

Stafford's traditionalism implies the inferiority of women and their need for protection at all ages. The society she pictures, at least for her women, is sterile and artificial, but it is inherently "safe"; reminiscent of the Victorian world of Henry James's *The Bostonians*, Sonie's Boston preserves the forms without the content for its shallow debutantes. Implicitly, therefore, Stafford challenges the social stereotypes as well as personal influences on the maturing woman. Only from the West does she detect a breath of fresh air, as Maudie, the cook for the Brunson family, breezes into the novel. Conspicuously masculine, this widowed mother of sons expresses the free Western spirit that Stafford might be recalling from her own Colorado upbringing. Reminiscent of Cozzens's masculine women, the Idaho-born Maudie

was a horsy, red-cheeked, raw-boned woman, nearly six feet tall. On her day off, she lounged in a one-room house, not far from the Brunson's, drinking whiskey and reading magazines called *Lariat*, *West*, and *Rio Grande Romances*. The combination of the liquor and literature produced in her a virulent homesickness which was contagious to her cronies—all men.

Maudie is honest, open, sentimental, and practical, accepting violence and passion as parts of life. Her honesty contrasts with the pretensions of the Brunsons, for instance, when she tells their daughter Betty about childbirth and is reminded that "here we do not discuss certain facts, or to put it in plain English, sex." Yet Maudie is atypical, rising "above her sex" and approaching the "completeness" of masculinity; as such, she only confirms the view that males alone can be independent.

At the opposite pole from Maudie is Miss Pride, who recognizes Sonie's duty to her mother as traditional: "One's first duty, after all, is to one's mother or to one's father, as in my case." Thus too had Torvald in Ibsen's *The Doll's House* reminded his wife Nora that her "most sacred duty" was "to your husband and children." Nora had disagreed: "I have another duty, just as sacred. . . . My duty to myself . . . I believe that before everything else I'm a human being—just as much as you are—or at any rate I shall try to become one." Fifty years later that news had still not reached Boston.

In the war years, when society took precedence over the individual, Stafford's women not surprisingly choose its limitations. Even Sonie's meager education is more than enough for a woman; as Miss Pride warns her, she "should concentrate on manners, my dear, not on ideas." Reading *The Atlantic Monthly* is better than reading Shakespeare, for instance. Sonie's allegiance to Miss Pride suggests her inability to walk out the door with Nora. Out there, she has seen, lies her mother's madness, a female heritage to avoid.

Even Hopestill, Miss Pride's niece, is only, as her name suggests, a stillborn hope. Her rebellion is superficial and crumbles when she is faced with an unwanted pregnancy. Marriage to Philip (not, as W. Tasker Witham mistakenly claims, suicide to escape Miss Pride's "ravenous maternal appetite"[10]) is her traditional solution.

Each woman in *Boston Adventure* either directly or indirectly reflects the dangers inherent in becoming a woman. Shura and Hopestill are victimized by men and by their own passions. Only the overtly masculine Maudie has the strength to survive the violence of maturation. Miss Pride and Sonie, on the other hand, seem much wiser to choose social protection despite its artificiality. They willingly limit themselves.

That violence which Sonie has sought to avoid destroys young Molly in Stafford's next novel, *The Mountain Lion* (1947). Molly is killed by her male counterpart, her brother Ralph, before she can become insane or destructive. Clearly too intelligent, too passionate, and too determined to be herself in a world which demands that she become more ladylike, Molly is destroyed before she can offer any alternative for Stafford's young women. Her very creation, however, as well as her violent end, speaks for Stafford's dissatisfaction with the limitations her other women find inescapable. Molly too is seen by Hassan as a "rebel-victim," as "a child who may stand for truth or Edenic innocence, and is victimized . . . by an ideal that society can never sanction or recognize. Innocence, it seems, can only reveal its face in perverse guises, and childhood recalls the demon world as few adults can safely remember."[11] Ralph and Molly are balancing precariously on the line between childhood and adulthood. As William Blake's children of innocence must face the tyger of experience, so too must they face the mountain lion, their symbol of sexual guilt.[12]

This encounter takes place in the freedom of their Uncle Claude's Colorado ranch, outside the parental and social restrictions of their upbringing. But the West is very much a man's world; here Molly, as Eisinger has argued, must be destroyed as "the feminine principle that stands as an obstacle to the full expression of maleness."[13] While Ralph is aided by this frontier environment, Molly is more vulnerable without the protection of her home: "a safe, cloistered, effete, respectable, merchant world." Although it is described by Eisinger as "a feminine, middle-class home whose air is stultifying to the two children,"[14] such a structure again seems necessary for a young woman's survival.

Molly is further fated to fail in her attempts to mature because of her "perverse" interest in "unladylike" pursuits such as hunting, and her equally perverse refusal to pattern herself after her pretty sisters Leah and Rachel. Even Ralph recognizes that she cannot fulfill her social role with her present outlook: "It was natural for her to want to be a boy (who wouldn't!) but he knew for a fact that she couldn't be." When Molly wears one of his old Boy Scout shirts, he must remind her to remove the "Be Prepared" badge because, as he told her "brutally," "Having that on a girl is like dragging the American flag in the dirt." Molly can dress like a boy, but she cannot claim male values. If she should happen to preserve that sense of freedom in herself, she is quickly reminded of her fault.

But Molly is determined to be herself, beautifully or irritatingly, despite the attempts of her mother and sisters to teach her a woman's

place. As their names suggest, Rachel and Leah are being raised for
the marriage market; Molly's intelligence will not help her to this
goal, as her mother is aware: "Everyone had said that she had the
brains of the family, but as Mrs. Fawcett was not interested in
brains, she thought this a handicap rather than otherwise." Even
Molly's name separates her from the Jewish tradition embodied in
her sisters, reminiscent of the Jewish daily prayers: Males pray daily,
"I thank Thee, Lord, that Thou has not created me a woman";
females pray submissively, "I thank Thee, Lord, that Thou has
created me according to thy will."[15]

As Louis Auchincloss remarks, Molly is still one "of the memorable children in American fiction,"[16] memorable as a girl with
many of the traits only boys were supposed to have: intelligence,
a lack of concern with appearances, and a taste for hunting and
roughhousing. While childhood can encompass the "tomboy," even
then, as Kate Millet argues, "any failure to conform to stereotype
reduced the individual, especially if a child, to an abysmal feeling
of guilt, unworthiness, and confusion."[17] Millet particularly refers
to sexual nonconformity, and Molly's problem reflects this as well,
her growing sexual awareness making her even more conscious of
her failure to fit into social roles. Hers, as Eisinger asserts, is "the
tragedy of the maladjusted personality whose journey toward selfhood will never be completed."[18] However, is an inability or unwillingness to "adjust" to the social image of women a crime
punishable by death? The failure is society's, not Molly's; but, as
usual, the guilt is foisted upon the individual, while the social code
is "right."

Molly cannot even pass on appearances, as could the beautiful
Sonie. She is unattractive, although she and Sonie do share intelligence, insight and isolation. Sonie protects herself by sacrificing
the first two of these in hopes of eliminating the third; Molly rebels
against giving up even her looks. As Ralph observes when he com-
pares his "scrawny, round-shouldered, tall" sister with himself and
Uncle Claude in whom "such ruggedness" was admired: "nothing
could be done to improve the features, nor, probably, would she
have permitted any alterations even if they had been possible, for
she took a vindictive pleasure in her plainness." Molly is a failure
for being born a girl with features acceptable only in males or
children. She cannot be permitted to enter adulthood or even to

"pass" for a woman as she is, so her legitimately male counterpart must eliminate her. Ralph is able to mature by overcoming the obstacle of his feminine self as embodied in Molly; Molly as herself must die. While Stafford may sympathize with her misfits, she faithfully reflects, as she must, the social realities she has experienced and observed. In reflecting its society accurately, fiction often runs the risk of helping to perpetuate the very stereotypes it has revealed.

Stafford is acutely conscious that growth in today's world demands violence—the violence implicit in the death of innocence—and exposes the individual to even more violence. This violence destroys Molly; it deters Sonie from risking independence. Carson McCullers shares the recognition of the violence, but her characters find no "safe" alternatives. Nor can they escape the isolation of the self, as does Sonie, by finding an acceptable niche in society. Although she chooses to concentrate on characters particularly handicapped by extreme grotesqueness, McCullers does so to emphasize her point. Each of us is grotesque; each of us is isolated. Like Molly, Mick Kelly in *The Heart is a Lonely Hunter* (1940) has two older sisters who seem to suit the stereotypes. A closer look, however, reveals that, unlike the perfect gentility and fragile beauty of Molly's sisters, Etta and Hazel have shortcomings as debilitating as their names. Etta longs to be a movie star and cries in the night because of her lack of beauty; Hazel is "plain lazy" and "thick in the head."

Society offers no protection or offers it to so few that its effect is negligible in McCullers's fiction. Writing at the beginning of the war, immersed in the social and economic inequities of the South, McCullers envisions neither social change nor social protection. Rather, as Eisinger argues, her "maimed half-people hope to make themselves whole by entering into a fructifying human relationship. She understands the need of an individual to define himself by something outside himself."[19] Few achieve such definition, however, because most relationships are not reciprocal. Caught in this frustration are two adolescents who share with Stafford's young women the particular problems of entering womanhood as well as with McCullers's own cast the universal problems of defining the self. Frankie in *The Member of the Wedding* (1946), whose parallels to Mick Kelly are indicated by their asexual names, joins Mick and Molly in the indistinct definition of childhood. If Molly dies, Mick and Frankie survive only by the sacrifice of self she refused. Annis

Pratt includes Mick and Frankie in her discussion of the limitations inherent in growing up female in America, and as do Stafford's women, they justify her conclusions that "the female hero who undertakes to adventure into a man's world finds herself confused and isolated at best and at worst succumbs to madness or an early death."[20]

Letting us see Mick from the points of view of those people influencing her growth as well as from Mick's own turmoil, McCullers takes an important step, as Witham points out, by including "the sexual thoughts and experiences of adolescent girls more frankly than women writers had previously done."[21] Although sensitive to the changes in herself, Mick needs external validation of her interpretation. She finds this in the deaf-mute John Singer and in her music—in the singer and the song. Even if both supports are somewhat illusory, they become a part of her reality to allow her time to discover which way to grow.

Illusions can dissolve, however, and external supports like the men in Stafford's novels can prove unreliable or even destructive. When Singer loses his own illusions and commits suicide, all those who had depended on him are once again vulnerable and alone. Mick ends up working in a dime store and cannot even discover why she is bitter:

Mick frowned and rubbed her fist hard across her forehead. That was the way things were. It was like she was mad all the time. Not how a kid gets mad quick so that soon it is all over—but in another way. Only nobody had cheated her. So there was nobody to take it out on. However, just the same, she had that feeling. Cheated.

Mick shares the fate and frustration of other characters who do not fit or resist stereotyping. As she is caught between childhood and adulthood, so too is Dr. Copeland caught between two races; Jake Blount is caught between two classes, Biff Brannon between two sexes.

In other ways, Mick faces unique problems of female adolescence. At her party, she dresses like a young lady, then races through the neighborhood like a tomboy. With Harry Minowitz, she loses her virginity, but Harry runs off because he cannot face his mother, and Mick is accused only of getting a sunburn when she comes home. "It was almost worse this way," Mick thought. "Maybe she would feel better if they could look at her and tell. If they knew."

Much of Mick's growth seems to be intertwined with the betrayal of her brother Bubber. As he withdraws from her and others after accidentally shooting a neighbor girl, Mick is conscious of her own part in hurting him by telling him he would be sent to jail. Like Molly and Ralph in Stafford's *The Mountain Lion* and Frankie and John Henry in *The Member of the Wedding*, one child seems to grow only at the expense of the child of the opposite sex—a frightening variation on the war between the sexes in which children are the victims.

If Mick can be said to mature, it is a maturation into compromise and unhappiness, a maturation by deprivation and sacrifice. To face "reality" for her is to accept limitations rather than to achieve independence. So too does Frankie sacrifice certain qualities to enter adulthood in *The Member of the Wedding*. To make this move she first rejects her childhood companions, John Henry and the motherly Berenice. She looks for an external support which would identify her with the adult world, so she naturally turns to her brother and his new wife-to-be:

But the old Frankie had no *we* to claim, unless it would be the terrible summer *we* of her and John Henry and Berenice—and that was the last *we* in the world she wanted. Now all this was suddenly over and changed. There was her brother and the bride, and it was as though when she first saw them something she had known inside of her: THEY ARE THE WE OF ME.

Again the support is illusory, but it enables Frankie to move from the ambivalence of adolescence to the sexual commitment of adulthood—to F. Jasmine. The romance that the new name indicates reflects the tenuous reality it initiates, one that will have to give way to a more practical Frances when Frankie learns that she cannot share another couple's marriage. Her loss of innocence, a brief moment in a hotel room with a soldier the night before the wedding, distances her with its violence from John Henry, who was too young to understand, and her father, who "did not take her seriously, so that her questions must be asked twice." By the time she is thirteen, Frances has lost John Henry to meningitis and is learning from a fifteen-year-old girlfriend how to be a lady. Only occasional nightmares of his suffering remind her of the cost of maturation.

But Frankie's ideal world would never demand that she define her sexual self: "She planned it so that people could instantly change back and forth from boys to girls, whichever way they felt and wanted." Adulthood means sacrifice, vulnerability, and unhappiness in McCullers's novels, and it can only be tolerated, or even survived, if it can be shared. In a short piece in *The Mortgaged Heart* (1971) called "Loneliness... An American Malady," McCullers discusses Frankie's need as particularly American, positing that our loneliness is "essentially a quest for identity.... After the first establishment of identity [we need] to belong to something larger and more powerful than the weak, lonely self. The sense of moral isolation is intolerable to us." Through love we gain support and security, avoiding the destructive fear which McCullers sees as its negative counterpart: "The bewildered soul can answer only: 'Since I do not understand Who I am, I only know what I am *not*.' The corollary of this emotional incertitude is snobbishness, intolerance, and racial hate." I would argue that women particularly are affected by this American malady. This "weaker" of the two sexes by tradition is even more in need of external support, especially when it doesn't even fit the stereotype. Furthermore, the insecurity experienced by each sex has manifested itself, as McCullers suggests, in an intolerance directed toward the other sex; and since men have traditionally had social power, that amounts to sexual discrimination against women.

Much of this pessimism is directly attributable to stereotyping. Frankie dreads giving up her boyish traits. Although Louise Y. Gossett would have us believe that McCullers is advocating a strong social structure which "defines what is acceptable in the stages through which the girls grow and also super-intends their progress,"[22] a more accurate assessment would be that McCullers has shown stereotypical remnants of just such a strong social structure surviving into a very different time and serving rather to impede than to encourage growth. Her young women protest being told "what is acceptable" in their own character and what must be abandoned because it is too "masculine." Mostly, however,

McCullers seems disillusioned with society in any form. It is resistant even to those changes which might improve it, as the workers resist Jake Blount and the blacks resist Dr. Copeland. Only among individuals do support systems seem to work, as does the family of Portia, Willie and Highboy in *The Heart is a Lonely Hunter*. Society offers them nothing but suffering, life is violent and unfair, but they love each other and survive as best they can. In *The Member of the Wedding*, Berenice offers a blueprint for a better world, but only the children are listening:

> First, there would be no separate colored people in the world, but all human beings would be light brown color with blue eyes and black hair... all human men and ladies and children as one loving family on earth.... No war, said Berenice. No stiff corpses hanging from the Europe trees and no Jews murdered anywhere.... Also, no starving. To begin with, the real Lord God had made free air and free rain and free dirt for the benefit of all. There would be free food for every human mouth, free meals and two pounds of fatback a week, and after that each able-bodied person would work for whatever else he wished to eat or own.... And, finally, Ludie Freeman would be alive.

Berenice's is a stereotypically female world: everyone is part of the family and is peacefully provided with food. Yet, although her pacifism and nurturing fit easily into social definitions and her rejection of the horrors of the war-torn world reflects the 40's, still Berenice is aware as a black woman that society can be destructively exclusive. This insight leads her to desire equality—of looks, of color, of race. Her ideal world lacks differentiation, individuality. Kate Millet would expand this to include sex as well, noting that the physical similarities between the sexes so far outnumber the differences as to suggest a need for "a synthesis of the two sexual temperaments."[23] Such a synthesis should be possible socially; pacific ideas dismissed as "effeminate" in the past could and must supersede the militaristic notion that "every generation needs its war." On a personal level, changing the stereotypes, avoiding the predefinition of each sex, would go far to allow each individual better to realize the self.

Sexual stereotyping can be devastating. Seeing woman as an incomplete male means that she can only be complete inasmuch as she resembles a man. Cozzens presents this view by approving only of boyish or childlike women who deny or repress their emotions. Stafford and McCullers indicate that such masculine-defined traits in women are socially unacceptable, that only in childhood is a female allowed the freedom of being herself. Consequently, their young women dread adolescence; to them, growth is sacrifice. The stereotypes block them from self-definition or force them to define themselves socially rather than individually. At the same time, this role stereotype helps perpetuate a host of others: to become male must be to become rational and active; to become female must be to become emotional and passive. Finally, to betray the stereotype is to court insanity.

TRIPPING OVER PEDESTALS

If some women were deterred from growth because they hesitated to invade a man's world, others were convinced that as women they were inherently superior and that their lives should be spent maintaining this position. The seeming contradiction is merely a change in perspective: since man is the standard of excellence in this world, woman is often offered preeminence in the next. She is seen as willing to sacrifice all earthly realities to the greater spiritual realities. So Hawthorne could decry woman's position in life as hopelessly desolate and unfair, but the only alternative he would offer her was losing herself in loving others or disdaining human existence to achieve spiritual perfection—and die. Even Kate Chopin, so eager to free women, seems to admit in *The Awakening* that only in death would the female self be preserved: Edna walks into the sea in preference to giving up what she had discovered or hurting her children by living the life she would choose.

These women who do live are allowed only half-lives, carefully defined and limited by the pedestal upon which they are placed. When they do not measure up to the impossibly unrealistic standards set by this stereotype, they are often the first to condemn themselves. In any case, the stereotype successfully obscures individual definition in favor of social standards. This is especially true for the Southern lady. Although one might expect that this stereotype would have passed with the Civil War, the fiction of Caroline Gordon belies that mistaken notion.

The three generations of womanhood explored in Gordon's *The*

Women on the Porch (1944) show how destructive this stereotype had become. When Catherine Chapman leaves New York City and her professor husband Jim, she temporarily returns to the traditional world of her Southern past—the world that her grandmother still lives in because of her senile isolation into illusions, and that her Aunt Willy is trapped in, able to relate neither to the past nor to the present. These two "women on the porch" of Catherine's home are traditionalists, seeing themselves as expressions of their society. Their insecurities reflect the decline of Southern society as they had known it as clearly as does the physical decline of the home itself. Willy is trying to run the farm alone while caring for the grandmother and for Daphne Passavant, but her own upbringing has not prepared her for this struggle. "It was hard for a woman to hold all those things in her head," she mused. "Sometimes she wished she were back in the old days when Jack ran the farm and she had nothing to do but wait on Mama."

Willy's values are consistently those of a Southern lady: "None of the women in our family have ever been coarse, whatever their failings." But the world has changed, and she exists mainly through good fortune and the advice of Mr. Shannon, whom she could never marry because he is not an acceptable partner by her mother's standards. She remains, as Dorothy Yost Deegan observes, "a provincial and stereotyped character. She is 'thin and pale' and 'had never thought of anybody as being particularly fond of her.' "[24] But the stereotyping is not Gordon's failure to create character; it is a reflection of the realities of limited lives.

Still, Willy tries to survive; she lives for Daphne and for grandmother. They, on the other hand, live only for the past. Daphne carefully avoids yet dwells on the memory of her brief, ill-fated marriage, which was perpetrated on her as a joke by her friend Charlotte. "I did not deserve that," she argues. "I am a good woman. I have always done my duty." Her bewilderment points up another reality of contemporary life: traditions (if they ever could) can no longer offer protection. The traditional woman is, in fact, the most vulnerable to the pressures of contemporary upheavals, because she cannot adjust to change. The woman who sincerely believes, for instance, that marriage is forever is shattered by divorce, which is a decision made by only one of the "members of the wedding" in most cases. Daphne's friend Charlotte reflects how the more liberated woman copes with such difficulties and is not embittered or disabled by them. She is left a penniless widow and supports herself by running a boardinghouse, an activity which would be too far below Willy's standards to be considered. The more traditional the woman, the fewer the choices that are available to her when she is finally forced to make choices.

Catherine cannot become another woman on the porch, but the choices offered her seem slim as well. Elsie Manigault, for instance, is an example of a woman who has abandoned the Southern lady image by going to the city. But "she was too energetic, too dominating, too *moneyed* for [Catherine's] taste." And neither Elsie nor her son Tom knows how to run their farm; they have severed their roots too completely to survive the transplanting. Elsie is a tired, unhappy woman living and fighting daily with the son she loves but has emasculated. In this latter detail especially, Gordon seems to be reflecting a prevalent attitude toward the developing independence of women, an attitude which argued that women were abandoning or destroying their men when they departed from their "natural" role. Lundberg and Farnham, for instance, would argue that Elsie is miserable because she has taken over the male role, consequently producing a neurotic, mother-bound son.[25] They cannot return to the Eden that the South once was; in fact, Eden is no longer Eden once it has been infested with those who have lost their innocence.

Nor can Catherine choose to be like Edith Ross, the woman who corrupts her husband Jim and commits adultery without even considering marriage until after Catherine has left him. Catherine is too well-trained as a Southern lady: she must always control her emotions, as is reflected in her signing the farewell note to Jim with a simple "Sinc'y"; as is implied in his description of her as "a cold woman, really, moody or subject to sudden inexplicable withdrawals"; as is implied in his projection that she, "even if she loved him—he did not know whether she ever *had* loved him—might stand up as straight as that poplar outside the window and tell him to go to hell." She was aware of her inability to express her emotions—because the ideal woman has none but spiritual emotions—aware that, before she would threaten Edith, her pride would have produced the opposite reaction and she would be accommodating instead. Trained to be subservient to her husband, she has never felt comfortable with the freedom of her New York City friends. Catherine has particularly blamed herself for not giving Jim a baby—as a perfect wife must do. Again Lundberg and Farnham provide us the clue to the conflicting attitudes of their time when they decry a contemporary society that belittles the importance of motherhood:

Significantly, our age does not seriously attempt to classify women, for example, as mothers and non-mothers, as successful and unsuccessful mothers, as adjusted and mal-adjusted mothers and non-mothers, and to draw conclusions from such breakdowns. These categories, obviously, are much more fundamental, invested with more human content, than... others.[26]

As these psychologists plead for a return to traditional lives for women, Gordon pleads even more eloquently through her fiction for the preservation or reestablishment of a similar ideal woman. Modern woman is even too immature for motherhood, the grand-mother seems to think:

It might be that women didn't have to do anything nowadays, that they didn't have the children in them. Catherine was thirty-five years old but she acted more like a girl than a woman. Perhaps when a woman didn't mature her seed didn't ripen either. In time there might not be any more children. The race might vanish from the earth.

Jim also echoes this problem, first indirectly when he dreams of swallowing the globe which churned within him, causing a pain "so exquisite as to be indescribable. Like child-birth, probably." This concern is evident as well in his memories of Catherine: "Did the woman who once truly received a man become the repository of his real being, and thence-forward, witch-like, carry it with her wherever she went?" Finally, he faces the problem directly, though possibly not recognizing the concomitant truth that his own lack of maturity is reflected in his unwillingness to share her womb with a life other than his: "They had considered having a baby but she had wanted to go abroad with him that summer and they had

decided against it. . . . It takes will to have children nowadays, he
thought."

It would appear, therefore, that Catherine's unhappiness really
stems from her failure to have a child and that this failure results
from her immaturity. Since Gordon is a traditionalist, she presents
Catherine's as a personal failure—she is immature and incomplete
because her alienation from her Southern heritage has caused her
to be less than the ideal Southern lady. She has lost her innocence
by immersion in the contemporary world of New York City, as
the South has lost its traditions by economic deprivation and Northern desecration. Neither Elsie nor Edith offers viable alternatives
for the future, and the "women on the porch" cling to a lost past.
While Gordon decries the passing of the ideal, she cannot realistically offer it to her women. Consequently, Catherine can only
return to Jim, to at least the structure of a marriage, a socially
approved institution, as the closest alternative a woman can still
reach to the traditional world she has lost.

The women in other novels by Gordon reflect this heritage as
well, the extreme example of the ideal, satirized in the title character
in the short story "The Petrified Woman," attesting to the mori-
bund state of the tradition. Cousin Tom describes this sideshow
freak as a woman "that had real charm": " 'Some women are just
petrified in spots,' Cousin Tom said. 'She was petrified all over . . .
She just lay there and looked sweet,' he said. 'I like a woman to
look sweet. . . . Hell, they ain't got anything else to do!' " The
humor of this story indicates that, while Gordon may lament the
loss of security and beauty implicit in the Southern lady, she is also
conscious of the emptiness of the stereotype.

Like Gordon, another Southern writer of the 40's—Robert Penn
Warren—often turns to the past for subject matter, but not to
mourn or to eulogize it. Rather, it supplies him with a context in
which he can examine human action. His aim is to study inner
quests which are only indirectly affected by the time in which his
characters live. This is a creditable aim, but the very assumption
that individuals can be considered entirely outside the social and
historical context leads to a perpetuation of stereotypical roles. The
roles of Southern women have been particularly well-defined; these
are never really questioned in Warren's fiction. He is enlightening,
however, in his perception of the reactions to and expectations of

these roles. A significant example is the interaction between Percy and May Munn in *Night Rider* (1939). May is an ideal lady, frail and beautiful, gentle and dutiful; yet periodically Percy has a desire to hurt her and finally does rape her (for one *can* rape his own wife), and she leaves him. His anger is produced by what she is and by what she does not do. She is separate from him, a person in her own right—although only minimally so—and he, losing sight of his own identity through his involvement with the night riders, resents her for this. After all, a woman is meant to be a reflection of her husband. Furthermore, May fails to help him understand himself, and this too is her role. He hurries home to tell her when he joins the tobacco growers' board "because her words or expression, even her mere presence, might help explain himself to himself." He makes no attempt to discuss his feelings with her; rather, he expects her to react intuitively by being and saying the very thing that will "give him the clue to understanding."

Because of his faith in the ideal, Percy sees other wives as succeeding where May fails. Because of the "secret integrity and purity of her passion," Buck Trevalyan's wife has supposedly "set him off from other men"; because of the "secret warmth and fullness and steadfastness" that he reads into a look which Cordelia MacDonald gives her husband, Percy is filled with pain for "something which he had never had. He felt cheated and impotent and was filled with envy of the other man, to whom, apparently, it had come so easily."

Little does it matter that May always appears to love him, assures him of her love, and worries when he is upset; the lack seems to be in his own inability to face himself. David W. Noble argues that Jack Burden in *All the King's Men* is the "first Warren hero to accept the responsibility of a woman's love."[27] Certainly Percy cannot accept what May has to offer, but at least part of the reason lies in what his society has taught him to expect from her. He looks for the feminine mystique and misses the female love.

Repeatedly, the women in Warren's fiction find themselves trapped by or at least defined by the concept of the ideal woman. In *World Enough and Time* (1950) Warren shows that the betrayal of such values may be destructive and suggests as did Gordon that motherhood can be the redeeming experience. Maria Hopeby Jordan has not benefitted from her fine Virginia heritage because she has always been disloyal to her husband, deriding him to her daughter and rejecting him herself because she feels that he is not good enough for her. The daughter Rachel then turns to the fatherly Colonel Fort after her own father's death to try to salvage her life by conceiving a child: " . . . nobody's fault, and if he had lived, if he had been in my arms, then everything—then everything. . . . " She has a stillborn son, then a miscarriage. Finally her insanity near the end manifests itself in her stealing another woman's child repeatedly and rocking and coddling it as if it were her own.

Even twenty years after he wrote *Night Rider*, in *The Cave* (1959), Warren's plea for acceptance of a woman as an individual still contrasts sharply with the attitudes of his characters. One character, Monty Herrick, objects to discovering anything common about his girlfriend Jo-Lea: "Any of those things she might do was, in fact, a defilement—and a betrayal—like going to the toilet." While most of Warren's men will tolerate bodily functions in a woman, her role is still to lead her man to a better life (no longer because she is saintly but because she has suffered and survived), and her happiness and fulfillment still come only through him and her children. John M. Bradbury even protests that in *The Cave* "so many of these East Tennessee women, young and old, fall flat on their backs at the least male touch, so many illegitimate child-births bring redemption to old people, and so many failures of the young to complete their affairs lead to frustration that one can only conclude that a freely copulating world is happy."[28] Warren's men repeatedly agree with Ibsen's Torvald that woman's first duty is "to your husband and children" and that female identity lies in love and procreation. If the purity of the original Southern lady is somewhat tarnished, her redemption still lies in traditional roles.

Another idealization of women which has naturally influenced our image of ourselves comes from myth. Religious, folkloric, and other mythical definitions of women have given us standards of beauty and behavior by which we unconsciously measure ourselves and against which we must inevitably fall short. The perfect faithfulness of Penelope has been held up to us since Homer; the ideals of Ruth in the Old Testament and the Virgin Mary in the New are just a few of our models from Jewish legends. These women and others show us not only how we should behave but also how we should *not* behave, as was discussed earlier in relation to Lilith and

Undine. These external definitions of woman form the framework for the fiction of Eudora Welty. Welty's underlying archetypal patterns serve further to emphasize the rebellion implicit in the attempts of any of her women to break the social pattern and seek their own identity. For instance, in *The Golden Apples* (1949), both King MacLain and Virgie Rainey share the archetypal unrest of the isolated wanderer—the Odysseus in search of his identity. Since the archetype is male, however, the community tends to excuse, even to expect, such behavior in King while they reject it in Virgie. Not only through its males but also through its females, myth defines correct behavior for women: women do *not* fill the same roles as do men; women follow the models of those women approved of by the men if they are good women and try to control or crush those characteristic weaknesses in themselves which they share with the women not approved by the men. It is interesting to note that in most myths men are defined individually; in negative instances, however, women are defined collectively: for instance, when Odysseus visits in Hades and learns of the crimes of Clytemnestra, he learns as well that because of her no woman should ever be trusted again. Penelope's great loyalty, on the other hand, benefits only her. Nor in Christian myth can women attain or benefit from the purity of the Virgin Mary, while each must suffer from the fall of Eve.

Welty recognizes the surviving influence of myth and of the structures it establishes. Most of her books written in the collapse and disillusionment of the 40's reveal a world that does not collapse, or a world that has learned to continue the business of living in the very rubble of the current collapse. But survival is not growth; Welty's world fits the given, unchanging patterns of Western myth. Women are automatically limited to traditional roles in that world.

Welty's rural Mississippi women accept their wandering men, for instance, as godlike, fructifying forces to which any woman would gladly offer herself (perhaps because, as Yeats suggests in "Leda and the Swan," to which Welty refers in *The Golden Apples*, she might share "his knowledge with his power" through the experience—authority denied the traditional woman). Her short stories "Asphodel" and "At the Landing" in *The Wide Net* (1943) and "Sir Rabbit" in *The Golden Apples* all reveal how women react to these men and their inevitable departures. Acquiescence is expected as defined by myth; when women rebel they must suffer. In "As-phodel" Sabina pits her strength and passion against that of her heroic husband Don McInnis, which shows her to be, according to Alfred Appel, Jr., an "anti-heroine," when compared to the "beautiful, desirable heroine of Southern romance."[29] Although she has three children by this "god," each dies a violent death before reaching maturity. When she is told by the community of her husband's infidelity, she calls down Medea-like "the curse of heaven on everybody's head—his, and the woman's, and ours." Her community does not condemn him: "But he was a McInnis. He had the wildness we all worshipped that first night, since he was not to be ours to love. He was unfaithful—maybe always—maybe once."

Miss Sabina condemns him—and is condemned for it. "How can I hate him enough?" she asks. "How can I show him the hate I have for him?" But the myths teach women that the unfaithful male is heroic and irresistible, so the community judges that whatever she may say Sabina is suffering as if "life with the beast was the one thing in the world she pined after." Appel argues that "just as Mr. Don represents the pagan, life-giving force, . . . Sabina is a manifestation of the opposing and ultimately destructive urge to control and suppress others."[30] The battle lines have been drawn, and despite his obvious betrayal the male is seen as the hero, the female as the "destructive" villain.

In "At the Landing," Jenny worships and is violated by the sex symbol Billy Floyd. She too reacts wrongly; she goes in search of him because she mistakenly believes they could settle down together (reminiscent, perhaps, of Lena Grove's pursuit of Lucas Burch in Faulkner's *Light in August*). Instead, she is put inside a grounded houseboat and "one by one the men came in to her." One old woman asks, "Is she asleep? Is she in a spell? Or is she dead?" and is told that "She's waiting for Billy Floyd." Jenny has become the town prostitute, because she has sacrificed any hope of self-identity by her pursuit: "She herself did not know what might lie ahead, she had never seen herself. She looked outward with the sense of rightful space and time within her, which must be traversed before she could be known at all. And what she would reveal in the end was not herself, but the way of the traveler." In another time she would have been a priestess, having known the god and now serving in his temple as his bride, dedicated to the sexual fulfillment, the fructifying force, he represents. In herself, she is nothing.

Both Jenny and Sabina make the same mistake: they try to hold their man. The patriarchal myths which underlie Western society show us their error; the role of woman is to be passive and accepting—and satisfied with what she is given. The proper attitude is demonstrated by Mattie Will in "Sir Rabbit," who not only offers herself gladly to the wanderer King MacLain (whose name of course indicates his rank) but has earlier offered herself as well to his twin sons. As with Snowdie, King's patient wife, she has accepted and momentarily shared his glory in echoes of Yeats' poem:

But he put on her, with the affront of his body, the affront of his sense too. No pleasure in that! She had to put on what he knew with what he did—maybe because he was so grand it was a thorn to him. . . . And no matter what happened to her, she had to remember, disappointments are not to be borne by Mr. MacLain, or he'll go away again.

Are we doomed to relive even that ancient past with which Welty identifies the patterns of our lives; do these myths reflect reality or has reality grown to reflect the myths with which we have been taught to define our lives?

That question can perhaps be answered by seeing what happens with the woman who chooses herself to wander. Virgie Rainey cannot be understood by her community, cannot even enter her own kitchen during her mother's funeral because "the women stopped what they were doing and looked at her as though something—not only today—should prevent her from knowing at all how to cook—the thing they knew." Virgie is an artist, as we learn in "June Recital," and as such she seeks a sense of identity separate from the stereotypical female. Welty, as Eisinger has observed, recognizes the paradox of the human needs for love and separateness.[31] Love is the resolution of separateness, and identity is the urge for separateness. Must one be sacrificed to achieve the other? Seeking the self at all may be equivalent to cutting off the Medusa's head, Welty suggests: "the heroic act, perhaps, that made visible a horror in life, that was at once the horror in love, Virgie thought—the separateness." Identity conflicts with love as love conflicts with identity: "Endless the Medusa, and Perseus endless."

Virgie is recognized as different, not only because of her talent but also because of her "vitality" and "airs of wildness": "Virgie's air of abandon that was so strangely endearing made even the Sunday School class think of her in terms of the future—she would go somewhere, somewhere away off, they said then, talking with their chins sunk in their hands—she'd be a missionary." But her difference is encouraged and developed only by an outsider, by the "Yankee" music teacher Miss Eckhart who was herself isolated and could see that the society would discourage any growth in Virgie:

Virgie would be heard from in the world, playing that, Miss Eckhart said, revealing to the children with one ardent cry her lack of knowledge of the world. How could Virgie be heard from, in the world? And "the world"! Where did Miss Eckhart think she was now? Virgie Rainey, she repeated over and over, had a gift, and she must go away from Morgana. From them all.

Miss Eckhart recognizes how the attitudes and demands of the family and community would block Virgie's development in any individual direction. The limiting force is internalized by Virgie as long as she remains a part of Morgana. Miss Eckhart knows and suffers because she too is a "true artist." She lives within the paradox of love and separateness and bears her burden of family love—an invalid mother: "Should daughters *forgive* mothers (with mothers under their heel)?" And although Virgie struggles against her, the awareness she represents and the burden of self she offers, still the chance for growth is held up like a temptation. Yet, loyal to her ties, Virgie resists and represses until she has fulfilled *her* daughterly duties. Only her mother's death frees her to leave Morgana and seek her own identity. She faces with courage a new female alternative—the quest of self which had been reserved for men—and she must face the realization of the suffering implicit in the perhaps endless search as well. She has yet another burden as a woman: she has had to wait until she fulfilled all obligations and must forsake all loves before she can leave. Her first duty, of course, has been to her family; only men can put self first and still be humored and even admired by the community.

If Virgie demonstrates that women can rise above the pedestal, that they can free themselves from traditional limitations and seek the self, she also reflects the tremendous cost of such a choice—a cost far beyond what a man would be asked to pay. Welty will present another woman twenty years later—Miss Julia Mortimer in *Losing Battles* (1970)—who breaks the stereotypes, but she too must sacrifice all else to pursue her career as a teacher. She is a spinster, out of choice and love rather than rejection and loneliness. As Judge Moody tells his wife, "Why, every young blade in Ludlow was wild about Miss Julia Mortimer at one time." Choosing to love her students instead—a humanistic love—Miss Julia must become an outsider. "She read in the daytime," Mr. Renfro comments. "And that was a thing surpassing strange for a well woman to do."

Miss Julia cannot have both a home and a career, because when she departs from her "role" she is barred from the kitchen as was Virgie at her mother's funeral. Male searchers may marry; the women, however, would lose all sense of self in marriage, as is revealed by Aunt Birdie's comment: "She ought to have married somebody, . . . then what she wanted wouldn't mean a thing. She would be buried with him, no questions asked." Marriage still seems to imply the immersion of the woman in the man, as it does in the British Common Law which remained in effect in America until the Civil War:

Man and wife are one person, but understand in what manner? When a small brooke or little river incorporateth with the Rhodanus or the Thames, the poor rivulet loseth its name, it is carried and recarried with the new associate, it beareth no sway, it possetheth nothing during coverture. . . . To a married woman, her new self is her superior, her companion, her master.[32]

Miss Julia must keep her identity, even by resisting love, as long as she is alive. When her friend Miss Lexie tries to help her, she fights even that aid because she has learned, as she tells Miss Lexie, that fighting "kind hands" is the "only way to keep myself alive!"

Admittedly, preservation and development of the individual is difficult for either sex, but the cost for women is higher because they are seen as betraying their "nature" when they deviate from stereotypes, while men are seen as fulfilling theirs when they strive for the self. The ideal of womanhood, whether the fragile Southern lady or the Victorian and Romantic angels, whether the Penelopes or the Virgin Marys, encourages self-sacrifice rather than self-development. To move "up from the pedestal,"[33] women have been forced to pay the highest of prices—they have been isolated from family and community. If such demands have survived, as Welty's fiction would suggest, small wonder women like Gloria Renfro in *Losing Battles* choose the acceptable role even at the cost of self. "She's my wife!" asserts Gloria's husband. "How could Gloria be sitting here at my feet and not be for whatever I do!" In fact, as Gordon's fiction shows, most women condemn themselves when they fail to reflect the stereotypes perfectly.

Finally, if these women feel trapped by stereotypes, unable to measure up to the ideal set for them, how much greater a problem the black woman faces is apparent in Ann Petry's naturalistic novel *The Street* (1946). Lutie Johnson can scarcely be said to be attracted to the stereotypes which are applied to her. Her tension grows out of the seeming inevitability of her conforming to these despite all efforts she may make to break free, because she is trapped in a life that gives her new goals but fails to give her any way to attain these goals. Born and raised in Harlem, she has little family heritage beyond the values of her wise and understanding grandmother. Her mother is dead, her father a drunken bootlegger. Separated from her husband, she is trying to support herself and her son Bub. Loneliness, poverty, the apathy and violence of ghetto life, and prejudice oppose every step she tries to take to improve herself.

Dependency is no alternative for Lutie, because divorce is nearly impossible in New York in the 40's: "The only way of getting out was to find a man who had a good job and who wanted to marry her. The chances of that were pretty slim, for once they found out she didn't have a divorce they lost interest in marriage and offered to share their apartments with her." She must make her own way, and she is handicapped by her ideals. She will not live with a man without the sanction of marriage, despite the fact that most of the women around her do so freely and thus escape the necessity of supporting themselves. She refuses to prostitute herself, although again such behavior is expected of her *kind*: "Sure, Lutie thought, as she walked on, if you live on this damn street you're supposed to want to earn a little extra money sleeping around nights. With nice white gentlemen." She has been enticed by the commercial pictures of white suburban housewives and tempted by the material advantages she observed as a maid for the rich white Chandler family, and she tries to better herself in every way she can. She is attractive and hardworking, has struggled through high school and business school to be eligible for a better paying job—only to find that the next civil service rating that she wants to earn still will not pay her enough to move. The society around her promises much but delivers very little.

Consequently, this strong, moral young woman—attractive and trying to conform to the stereotypes of the white world in which she is caught but from which she is simultaneously excluded— instead conforms to the worst stereotypes associated with the black woman. She lives in a dark, garishly painted apartment (she had requested white walls) and leaves her son alone while she goes to a bar, because "No matter what it cost them, people . . . had to replace the haunting silences of rented rooms and little apartments with the murmur of voices, the sound of laughter . . . so they could believe in themselves again." As much as she tries to be a good mother, Lutie strikes Bub on the street, when she comes home to find him shining shoes with a box he had made himself in an effort to help: "It's also that you're afraid that if he's shining shoes at eight, he will be washing windows at sixteen and running an elevator at twenty-one, and go on doing that for the rest of his life." Finally, she even commits a murder, when the man she has hoped to borrow money from locks her in his apartment and intends to rape her, then pass her on to his white boss Junto. Ironically, she needs money to pay a lawyer to save her son from reform school, and even the lawyer knows that Bub would be freed with no assistance. Lutie does not know this, however. When she rejects Boots and is threatened by him, she grabs a heavy iron candlestick and

a lifetime of pent-up resentment went into the blows. . . . First she was venting her rage against the dirty, crowded street. Finally, and the blows were heavier, faster now, she was striking at the white world which thrust black people into a walled enclosure from which there was no escape.

Lutie becomes exactly what her society has defined her to be through its prejudiced stereotypes. In a similar way, Betty Friedan asserts, the society of the 50's created a feminine mystique and real women filled its roles: "When a mystique is strong, it makes its own fiction of fact. It feeds on the very facts which might contradict it, and seeps into every corner of the culture, bemusing even the social critics."[34] But if the stereotype of the ideal woman had to come back full strength as a mystique in the 50's, its roots grew very deep, wrapped around the very bedrock of Western culture—the myths themselves. And the woman descended from these myths is Snow White (only her hair can be black as ebony) or Cinderella, in all the blonde, blue-eyed glory Walt Disney so accurately chose for her. Neither is black—at least not in the 40's. Lutie Johnson, alone in Chicago, running from the law, has abandoned her child, the person she loves most in the world. Her problem is compound: she is black and a woman. But the integrity she shows; the strength, love, compassion and understanding she displays despite her failure to escape either the negative stereotypes projected on her by a prejudiced society or the idealistic stereotypes which tempt her into unrealistic—even impossible—demands upon herself; suggest what could come from a woman allowed to grow. Her destruction by a society which prefers to foster the survival of passive, "used" women argues strongly for a needed change in that society. "The protest is," Eisinger asserts, "that decent human beings are ruined by social forces they cannot come to terms with."[35]

The idealization of women, which set unattainable and ultimately undesirable goals for women and demanded complete sacrifice of self, was to exert an even greater influence in the 50's, but already writers were demonstrating its destructiveness. Yet women could not easily turn their backs on a stereotype sanctioned by history and religion, especially the latter. Only in the 70's did women begin seriously questioning the tradition which belittled women and presented them as property, which encouraged passivity in women yet praised men for their freedom and independence, and which demanded propriety and dependence from a "lady." In such studies as Merlin Stone's *When God was a Woman* (1976), women would soon reveal the goddess predecessors to these male gods and values and even challenge the Bible itself. While ideas and goals are indeed valuable and encourage growth, impossible goals and prejudicial ideals can only retard such growth. While God becomes human through Christ, Mary becomes divine, the perfect unattainable woman.

LILITH AND UNDINE

If myths had controlled women, it was because men had controlled the myths. As patriarchal society began to be reevaluated by its war-worn citizenry, the patriarchal myths began to be reinterpreted as well. Those women dismissed as demons, witches, or simply bad models were often discovered to possess the very qualities of the heroic males: independence, individuality, sexual freedom, for instance. Even the women admired in myth were often admired for the wrong reasons, while their real strengths were neglected. American women poets early started this reexamination: in "An Ancient Gesture," Edna St. Vincent Millay praises Penelope for her emotion—for the tears she earned the right to shed while waiting years for her husband's return—rather than for her faithfulness. More recently, Susan Sutheim and Jean Tepperman have both composed poems about witches, identifying them as women who choose to be themselves despite social disapproval. Queen of Hell, Lilith has only recently come into her own, but she will be considered here as representing these women who are admired and yet feared because of their strength, beauty and independence. Another legend, that of Undine, provides us with an archetype for the woman who refuses definition, social or personal. Undine is the stream that loved and married a mortal, representing the unpredictability and deep emotions of women. These characteristics have been devalued in favor of stability and rationality in patriarchal society, devalued at least partly because they have been arbitrarily identified as female.

Even in the 40's women writers as traditional as Gordon began to wonder about those women rejected by society—the women labeled insane—and to find mythical precedent for them, women who held a new attraction as they were seen from this new point of view. Their attractiveness was duly noted by Gordon, and their seeming faults often appeared to be virtues in such works as Eudora Welty's *The Robber Bridegroom* (1942). That these myths presented women rejected by the society as well led to serious questioning of the nature of sanity—and of its detriments and benefits for women—which is perhaps best explored in the fiction of Shirley Jackson.

After publishing *The Women on the Porch* in 1944 and a collection of short stories the following year, Gordon was not heard from again until 1951, when *The Strange Children* appeared. In this novel, the upheaval of society resulting from the war clearly underlies the destructiveness and insecurity of the characters. As Eisinger argues, "the strange children of the title are the adults of the book. Insecure and misled, they wander like befuddled children in the maze of life."[36] Their immaturity is the more striking because we see it through the eyes of the child Lucy, much as Henry James had shown the adults in *What Maisie Knew* through the young Maisie's eyes. In both novels, the children learn how *not* to live by watching their parents; as Lucy told herself, "when she grew up she would be a very different person from her father or her mother." Only one adult is free of game-playing, and she is insane. Isabel Reardon is identified with Undine by Gordon. A brilliant student, a poet at seventeen, a survivor of two unhappy marriages (one in which her husband is killed and the other in which he goes insane), Isabel's life reflects her uniqueness. Before she arrives, Lucy's mother Sarah muses:

Do you suppose it's Isabel's humble origins that give her that fairy tale quality? I always feel that the ordinary canons don't apply to her. . . . I mean—well, life's pretty darn complicated, when you get down to it, and Isabel—I never could understand how she just sailed through man after man. Oh, hell, I suppose all I'm saying is that I can't understand being so beautiful that every other man you meet falls for you. I must say, though, that Isabel's always been ethical about that. I never heard of her so much as laying a finger on another woman's man.

Lucy even comments directly on the story of Undine when talking of Isabel and points out that "the gentlemen all seemed to be afraid of these strange ladies, but they were always going around where they were." This ambivalence fits the Lilith legend as well; these independent mythical women are seen as beautiful temptresses. Lucy ponders this ambivalence in terms of the Undine legend: "She wondered what it would be like to be a knight in love with a woman who was not really a woman but a stream. . . . The Knight Huldbrand had remained always himself. How had he felt when the cool arms that encircled his neck changed into foam and spray? And did it happen all at once or little by little?" Undine is undefined, free of stereotypes and apparently even free of the men she loves, but the only role in Lucy's society in which her counterpart Isabel can fit is that of a madwoman. Yet she can also symbolize for Kevin Reardon his faith—his acceptance of responsibility and grace through Catholicism. Kevin is Isabel's "knight," and as she flows away into the arms of Tubby or into her fits of insanity he is able to steady himself through faith. For him the unequivocable Catholic attitude toward marriage provides a secure framework within which the unpredictability of life—and of Isabel—can dissolve and reshape itself.

Gordon does not try to penetrate the mystery of Isabel any more than her structured society has attempted to penetrate the mystery of femaleness: such femaleness is dismissed as magical, mystical, enticing yet threatening because it is beyond social definitions. The same magical quality lends mythical depths to the fiction of Eudora Welty. We have already seen Virgie Rainey in *The Golden Apples* resolve to pursue the heroic quest for her own identity and dare to face the Medusa's head. Symbolically, then, she has faced the madness that could turn all life into stone; a female Perseus, she dares nonconformity (when her familial duties have been fulfilled) and chooses individual growth. Of course, the cost to Virgie, as to other "virgin" goddesses of strength and independence, is great.

Although few women in Welty's fiction so clearly reject social in favor of individual values, many of them do defy society through actions or words. Thus Miss Sabina in "Asphodel" is Medea-like in her refusal to accept passively the infidelity of her husband as Snowdie accepts the wanderings of hers in *The Golden Apples*. Furthermore, Welty seems to admire these rebelling women, as she admires the lovely, lying Rosamund in *The Robber Bridegroom* (1942). Lying may be a necessary attribute for a woman in a society in which her role is so far removed from her own personality. Welty notes the value of Rosamund's talent by the folktale analogue she draws: "As for Rosamund, she did not mean to tell anything but the truth, but when she opened her mouth in answer to a question, the lies would simply fall out like diamonds and pearls."

Yet most of Welty's women are defined by their social roles, and even Virgie Rainey and Miss Julia Mortimer choose areas in which a few exceptional women have always been acknowledged. Most women would think that these two were "crazy" to choose paths which, as Welty shows, demand superior abilities and excessive sacrifices. Welty has not yet presented the "career woman" also being a wife and mother. Each must either complete or sacrifice all hope of personal love and familial relationships and venture alone into the world. Even Miss Julia is left outside, having died of "Neglect, neglect! *Of course* you can die of it!" These "madwomen" reject only the stereotypes directed exclusively toward women (i.e., that they should be passive, dependent, self-effacing) or emotions (that they should be controlled or even suppressed). Particularly discriminatory toward women, these stereotypes are destructive to both sexes, encouraging an imbalance in the total personality. Gordon accepts the label of insanity; Welty reminds us of the cost of rebellion.

Shirley Jackson, however, challenges the label and the cost. Though many critics dismiss her work as gothic horror tales— finding it magical, bizarre, even mad—they miss the real significance: Jackson succeeds in revealing the "divinest sense" in much of women's madness, and she helps to identify the madness as the social disease it is—inherited through patriarchal traditions or transmitted from unhealthy social relationships and expectations.

A woman is mad, Chesler has told us, when she is "too" female or when she appropriates those traits allotted by her society to men: in either case, this generally means whenever she allows her inner self to come to the surface and obscure her roles—whenever the independence of Lilith or the unpredictability of Undine emerges. Neither patriarchal myth nor psychology, which so often justifies itself through myth, encourages female maturation. Yet Jung himself has directed us to learn about life and ourselves by first turning inward: "proceed from the dream outward." Jackson does precisely this in her fiction, considering the dream much as it is defined by Anaïs Nin in *The Novel of the Future* (1968):

The definition of a dream is: ideas and images in the mind *not under the command of reason*. It is not necessarily an image or an idea that we have during sleep. It is merely an idea or image which escapes the control of reasoning or rational mind. . . . The writer can learn to walk easily between one realm and the other without fear, interrelate them, and ultimately fuse them.[37]

Society encourages us to be rational; irrationality is often equated with insanity. Furthermore, the irrational is identified in our society with women; they are stereotyped as weak at reasoning and lacking in emotional control. What does this really mean? The rational mind is that part of us most influenced by social values, by stereotyping. We must exist simultaneously in our inner and outer worlds; fusion of these two worlds provides the basis for a healthy, unified self. The mental illness of our time, schizophrenia, is the total separation of inner and outer worlds, a condition exacerbated by these social attitudes.

Jackson succeeds in her fiction in showing both worlds to the reader and in suggesting their interrelationships without fear (although the reactions of critics indicate they are unable to read her so courageously). To dismiss her insights is like dismissing *Oedipus Rex* as gothic without learning from Freud its underlying psychological meanings. Jackson dares not only to explore the irrational but also to accept its reality, a reality which provides identity and often fulfillment for women who find that the rejection of society is their only way to avoid rejection of self.

Jackson published her first novel after the war, later than any of the writers we have discussed thus far, and the violence and disintegration of the world she pictures clearly reflect that war. The effect of such disintegration, as Gordon has shown, can be seen best through the children's eyes. Jackson's fiction and nonfiction concentrate on youth, children living and dying by the violence of their world, as the suicide of a young boy and the gruesome death of two other children can testify in her first novel, *The Road Through the Wall* (1948).

However, more important than the violence itself is its source; the disintegration of the community allows the wall to be torn down, the wall which had shut out life in all its violence and irrationality. As the wars demonstrated, society merely finds new forms for old violence. At best its forms offer temporary protection from the violence of life; at best logic offers a framework within which we can shape the irrational flow of life. As society weakens and logic fails, we are forced to face the violence and irrationality. Accepting this reality with only occasional nostalgia for the loss of an artificial security, Jackson uses the opportunity to examine society and the self as part of all life. Although she acknowledges a need for social approval and rituals, she affirms the individual perception. If her women seem sick or insane, we may be perceiving the "insanity" of seeking the self at all in an inadequate society and a violent world.

Such a woman is Natalie Waite in Jackson's next novel, *Hangsaman* (1951). Living in the "borderland country of the emotionally disturbed,"[38] according to one reviewer, Natalie must choose to remain her father's daughter or to face the violent world she has found on her own. This is not a simple decision because Natalie is in the process of discovering her own multiplicity. Jackson makes her aware of all the Natalies she can become, as this intelligent young woman realizes the dangers and attractions of maturity—the sexual possibilities in and out of her control from lesbianism to rape, the social options of "belonging" to what she quickly understands as the superficiality of sororities, and the internal potentialities she has inherited from her mother as well as her father and those she is discovering beyond either of them. More than a "subtle and unusual revolt against a father,"[39] Natalie's attempt to break the pattern of females "growing down" through sacrifice of self by accepting and integrating all the aspects of her self and of her experiences ends on a note of optimism rare in these novels of women coming of age in America: "As she had never been before, she was now alone, and grown-up, and powerful, and not at all afraid."

Natalie's successful beginning, which is won with knowledge of and participation in the violence of life rather than in avoidance of responsibility for the self, leaves her exposed to life rather than protected from it. Jackson does not offer her women easy answers. This has led Alfred Kazin to argue that in many of Jackson's stories "a woman as victim is the main figure and . . . her defenselessness *is* the story."[40] Yet women who face that victimization of the individual in our world are not defenseless. Natalie is not the last woman Jackson will describe as "powerful"; hers is the power of the self to make choices. Contemporary reality makes victims (objects) of us all, she would show, men no less than women. We are simply more used to seeing the woman as vulnerable and thus fail to recognize her as embodying our victimization as well. Once Natalie accepts the reality of the world around her and of her place in it, she becomes a subject rather than an object. Carolyn G.

Heilbrun argues that woman as hero can serve "as metaphor for modern man striving to express himself, to *be* himself within a mechanical society"[41]; to be heroic, she must face the same violent realities that he is expected to face. And she must face them alone. Jackson's remarkable assertion in the face of this violence is that her heroes are "not at all afraid." The willingness of her women to face the violence of maturity and their ability to find a source of power within themselves promises alternatives for survival. Jackson will offer in Elizabeth in *The Bird's Nest* (1954) yet another victorious morning as she earns her new name of Victoria Morgan, but then we must wait until Jackson's final unfinished novel, *Come Along With Me* (1965) for another such hero. The woman hero acts in each of her own experiences, choosing her own reality; finding the self is learning to be a subject rather than an object.

Elizabeth begins, however, by avoiding her inner experiences, allowing her personality to shatter. Each of the fragments is a part of her, but as long as they remain unconnected each dismisses responsibility for the other's actions. The surface person rejects those parts as socially unacceptable, but she cannot destroy or punish them without destroying or punishing herself. She must face the loss and rejection she has suffered from her mother and Robin, her mother's lover, including her own guilt for desiring Robin, to grow again. Becoming a woman begins with sexual awareness, but as long as Elizabeth denies that awareness she is in danger of being destroyed by it. After both Robin and her mother are unexpectedly killed, Elizabeth is trapped in the unresolved emotional confusion of adolescence:

I wish I had a diamond ring, she thought, as Lizzie quieted; if I had a diamond ring I could tell them I was engaged to be married. If I was engaged to be married, they couldn't take me back because my husband wouldn't let them. If I had a husband then my mother could marry him and we could all hide together and be happy. My name is Betsy Richmond. My mother's name is Elizabeth Richmond, Elizabeth Jones before I was married. Call me Lisbeth like you do my mother, because Betsy is my darling Robin. . . .

Once she faces her experience and her involvement in it, Elizabeth's personality slowly starts to connect, until she approaches the sense of self that Natalie attains: "It was the first time she had looked at anything with her own true eyes; I am—and it was her first privately phrased thought—all alone; I am all alone." She accepts responsibility for all her formerly fragmented selves: "She could, moreover, answer freely all their questions: 'Who put the mud in the refrigerator?' Aunt Morgan asked her, and she answered with the simple truth, 'I did.' " Then, as Victoria Morgan, Elizabeth can grow and face the morning.

Tearing down the framework of logic within which our society has sought protection from the irrational and traveling the road through the wall is Jackson's way of exposing us to the violence of maturation, of personal responsibility, and of identity. The life she exposes was there all the time; she only makes us face it, knowing that growth demands the death of innocence. Since the irrational is within each of us, the real madness lies in our attempts to ignore it. However, only the strongest women in Jackson's fiction are able to integrate their personalities, to face the terrors of insanity (of nonconformity) and exorcise some of the social stereotypes so deeply ingrained as to be part of their very selves. That the road to individuality for women may be through madness is suggested by Chesler when she argues that "the female social role encourages help-seeking, self-blaming, and distress-reporting behavior" and that when women do this they are judged as "annoying, inconvenient, stubborn, childish, and tyrannical." If, as she has also observed, "what we consider 'madness,' whether it appears in women or in men, is either the acting out of the devalued female role or the total or partial rejection of one's sex-role stereotype," then women *must* face such insanity to mature at all. The more aware women become, the more they feel with Sylvia Plath that they are encased by social stereotypes in "the bell jar as a glass cage of 'femininity' and powerlessness in which many women sit, in and out of asylums, and from which many are trying to escape."[42]

In much of Jackson's fiction, however, when women face the irrational, they seem to find it more appealing than the supposedly sane world—the vulnerable, violent society in which human relationships have been undermined by an inhumane war. These women reject marriage and "normalcy" either because they are not offered or because women have no power in them. As Natalie's mother had told her in *Hangsaman*,

First they tell you lies, . . . and they make you believe them. Then they give you just a little of what they promised, just a little, enough to keep you thinking you've got your hands on it. Then you find out that you're tricked just like everyone else, just like *everyone.* . . .

Since the search for identity puts greater pressures on women than it does on men, these women choose to create their own alternatives and escape into brave new worlds like that projected by Aunt Fanny in *The Sundial* (1958). Aunt Fanny's world, promised by her father, is a product of her faith in the irrational. Faith is always irrational, and her dream provides her with the protection and happiness that the world cannot give her. She tries to preserve the wall that Jackson sees being torn down in the first novel, to recreate the protectivity of childhood and a stable community, as is implicit in the description of "her father's house":

It stood upon a small rise in ground, and all the land it surveyed belonged to the Halloran family. The Halloran land was distinguished from the rest of the world by a stone wall, which went completely around the estate, so that all inside the wall was Halloran, and all outside was not.

The safety of her imaginary world is desired by everyone who remains there with her awaiting the disaster from which they alone were to be saved—everyone except the young Fanny, who cries, "Who wants to be *safe*, for heaven's sake?" In Jackson's fiction, it is almost always the youngsters alone who are willing to face the violence of the contemporary world; and, as the teenager Eileen tells her father's drunken friend in "The Intoxicated," facing the violence is the first step to growth: "If people had been really, honestly scared when you were young we wouldn't be so badly off today."

Aunt Fanny must choose instead the protection of "her father's house," a dreamworld which provides the protection and love seemingly unavailable to her elsewhere. She chooses her private insanity over an insane society which discourages her independence yet fails to provide a secure structure upon which she can depend. As the inscription on the sundial measuring the time of her life reminds her, "What is this world: what asketh man to have? Now with his love, now in his cold grave. Allone, with-outen any companye."

To live in a dreamworld demands faith. Sometimes when a person accepts the concreteness of a world in the mind and rejects the concreteness of this world we call it religion, sometimes philosophy, sometimes insanity; but, as Jackson notes in *The Sundial*, "Being impossible, an abstract belief can only be trusted through its manifestations." She accepts the irrational and recognizes the concrete forms it must take on for human consumption, and the simple, direct style of her seemingly bizarre stories reflects that acceptance. Often, as in this novel, the abstractions of safety, protectivity, and acceptance are concretized in a house; this is true as well of the next two novels, *The Haunting of Hill House* (1959) and *We Have Always Lived in the Castle* (1962). As these houses provide protection for the young women who live in them, they produce fear in others, perhaps thereby both increasing the protection and attesting to their own reality.

Despite its attractions, choosing such private insanity is indeed choosing death over life, stagnation over growth, as is made explicit in the novels. For Eleanor, Hill House offers a haven, an acceptance she has never known. After having fulfilled her familial obligations of caring for an invalid mother for eleven years, she "could not remember ever being truly happy in her adult life." As did Virgie, Eleanor has sacrificed life to duty, put herself last as women have been taught to do. Unlike Virgie, Eleanor has no great talent to turn to. Therefore, she seeks the love of childhood and "Home," as is indicated by the responses Mrs. Montague gets from her unconscious—from "Nell"—in her planchette game:

"What do you want?" Arthur read.
"Mother," Mrs. Montague read back.
"Why?"
"Child."
"Where is your mother?"
"Home."
"Where is your home?"
"Lost. Lost. Lost."

Eleanor's needs become the voice of Hill House, and her suicide returns her to home and mother, but she would have preferred a chance to grow. Her last plea may be the plea of many women who have chosen protection over life: "In the unending, crashing second before the car hurled into the tree she thought clearly, *Why am I doing this? Why am I doing this? Why don't they stop me?*"

Merricat—Mary Katherine Blackwood—commits murder rather than suicide to insure her safety in the Blackwoods house in *We Have Always Lived in the Castle.* The house is reminiscent of that in *The Sundial:*

Blackwoods had always lived in our house, and kept their things in order; as soon as a new Blackwood wife moved in, a place was found for her belongings, and so our house was built with layers of Blackwood property weighting it, and keeping it steady against the world.

Here Merricat and Constance are protected from life; after the hatred of the town has done its worst in attacking and partially burning the house, the two young women live "safely" and to the village become fairy-tale witches, fantasy characters choosing the dreamworld over the terrors of the world outside.

In *Come Along with Me*, on the other hand, Mrs. Angela Motorman accepts and even revels in her irrational power: " 'I dabble in the supernatural,' I told Mrs. Faun; she thought I was making some kind of joke. I quit when I married Hughie; you'd have to. . . . it disappeared entirely when I married Hughie; I have reason to believe now that it is coming back." Marriage and men seem to negate a woman's innate power. Free of these restraints, Angela is now allowed to be her own, powerful self. Women must be free of familial and social definitions to claim their individuality.

To begin her new life as a new person, Angela has found it necessary, as did Elizabeth, to choose a new name. This parallel might also suggest her return from insanity, a social rather than a personal insanity this time. Her former name really belongs to her husband and marriage:

I didn't want any more of Hughie and his names, and Bertha was my grandmother and who wants to be named Bertha, particularly after her grandmother? I thought of Muriel but that sounds like someone who gets raped and robbed in an alley. . . . You have to be terribly careful with names; one too many and you lose.

The significance of a person's name is obviously irrational, yet is it? We recognize the name as a symbol of our identity; primitive cultures have long revered the power of names. Odysseus recognizes that when he gives his name he is giving a weapon to his opponent; still, he is unwilling to leave the island of the Cyclops without proper recognition. Yet women usually sacrifice their names when they marry. How deeply this loss affects self-concept is worth asking. At the same time she rejects "Hughie and his names," however, Angela keeps the *Mrs.* that marriage awarded her; she keeps the social advantage but rejects the personal sacrifice.

When Angela begins her new life with her new name, she regains her irrational power to create the world:

I have always been quite successful at making things up as I went along, and very often surprised at where I led myself. . . . I am not above the law, but somehow I make the law, which so many other people do not. This is not arrogance; I first became aware of this when I was a child and always got everything I wanted. Before God, I thought I wanted Hughie.

Angela creates her own reality, but unlike Jackson's earlier women, she is able to impose that world over ours rather than isolating herself in a protective but stagnant environment. Nor does she allow society to impose anything on her; by accepting and believing in her own power and reality she can share with Natalie and Elizabeth a sense of control.

With her rich humor and her realistic horror, Jackson dares to travel the road through the wall into the violence and irrationality of life. Although many of her women try to build their own walls or to hide behind the walls of a fantasy childhood world (a pattern of insanity they have learned from their society), others choose instead to trust themselves, the sanity of their choice proved for them by the insane alternatives their society would offer. They face madness, but in doing so they learn to "proceed from the dream outward" rather than to retreat inward, recreating their world through the power of their faith in the self. In presenting these women, Jackson not only makes us reexamine the nature of sanity; she also shows us the benefit of women gaining self-awareness. As they begin to see themselves as subjects rather than objects, they cease being victims; as they learn to accept the rational and the irrational, they help free the world they live in from the patriarchal straitjacket in which women especially have felt powerless. The magic and creative power of the self can alone enable the individual to transform the world.

BITCHES AND BURDENS

If the women writers of the 40's had duly registered a protest against the debilitating effect of stereotypes, many of the men writers of the period were protesting the women who failed to meet those stereotypes. The women in their fiction seem destined to be seen as man's enemy whatever they might do. They take on mythic dimensions, in fact, as oppressors of the men. In the fiction of Saul Bellow, the women are constant reminders of the responsibilities that men are either unwilling or unable to assume, or they represent the threat of sexual guilt. Burdens or bitches, they can be blamed for man's failure in true Jewish style, just as Eve was blamed for Adam's fall. For Norman Mailer, women pose a more contemporary threat: they are undermining the personal and social "masculinity" of Americans, calling forth that treacherous "feminine" part of the self known as emotion. As in Stafford, women often represent a block to "the full expression of maleness." Whether burden or bitch—or angel or whore, as the previous century would refer to her—woman must ultimately be left behind as man seeks real identity only in the company of other men or alone. Finally, J. F. Powers, with a Catholic framework to support his contentions, presents a gallery of priests who, in their efforts to preserve sanctity, power, and chastity, look upon competent, assertive women as archenemies while accepting only the vulnerable, often even pitiful, women.

To each of these writers, women seem to have little if any individual reality. Burdens, bitches, even mothers (as Philip Wylie had agreed in *Generation of Vipers*) force man to a consciousness of values and responsibilities that he would much rather avoid. If he is spiritual, as are the men in Powers's fiction, she is worldly and materialistic. If she fits the feminine stereotypes, as do the burdens and victims, then she threatens to drain him by guilt or to destroy his masculinity. If she is a bitch, then she threatens to seduce or otherwise to overpower him and again to destroy his masculinity.

Even in the war years, there seems to have been no temporary amnesty in the war between the sexes—a war impossible to end in the context of patriarchy. Man tries to reject even those parts of *himself* identified as "feminine"; small wonder that attitudes in the men around them discourage these women from any growth.

Even among themselves, men writers fail to agree upon which traits they like in women. What Cozzens admires as practical Powers sees as materialistic or hypocritical. The efficiency and competence are seen as challenges for power which force Powers's priests to oppose these pushy women. Only on one point do the two men seem to agree—the fear of sex. Whether young Hank is being seduced by Mrs. Van den Arend in Cozzens's *Morning Noon and Night* or the worldly Father Urban is resisting seduction by Sally Hopwood in *Morte d'Urban* (1962) by Powers, the same female aggressiveness, male passivity, and mood of terror and revulsion are present.

On the other hand, Powers also presents the suffering female. The vulnerable Irish Catholic Katie is exploited by Mrs. Thwaite in *Morte d'Urban*; the patient Teresa is companion to an eccentric invalid in "The Poor Thing" in *The Presence of Grace* (1956); Old Gramma cares for Mama who is "all broken to pieces on the bed" in "The Trouble" from *Prince of Darkness* (1947). These women, the only type positively portrayed in Powers's fiction, have accepted the female role of sacrifice and suffering. Even though Powers hasn't precisely followed the nineteenth-century pattern of angel or whore, he merely shifts the emphasis of the whore counterpart from sex (so he could even suggest that the seductive Mrs. Hopwood was the "best of a bad lot") to aggressiveness and worldliness, and of the angel counterpart from purity to acceptance of suffering.

The various housekeepers are invariably identified as bitches in these stories; they run the rectories with a competence which makes most priests cower. Father Urban provides the formula for controlling them, however: one must assert proper authority, kindly but firmly. He succeeds so well with Mrs. Burns that soon she "had no reservations about Father Urban. If he in any way fell short of the ideal (and of course he did), Mrs. Burns didn't know it. His word was law." Only in their proper role of dependence are women acceptable. If they are not kept in line, they become as powerful as Mrs. Stoner of "The Valiant Woman" in *Prince of*

Darkness, toward whom Father Firman (an ironic name) is able to express his hostility only in feeble gestures, such as swatting mosquitoes: "Damn it! And only the female bites!"

Powers's women are committed to a male world—in this case, the world of the priesthood. They are frightening or pitiful inasmuch as they make the men feel weak or strong by comparison, and they are to be dominated or comforted—or avoided if possible. The structure of this world predefines the women within it, so that the men merely react to immediate actions as they threaten to affect themselves. Powers has perpetuated the past patterns for women, and the subtle changes only allow the supposedly sexually emancipated writers of his time to follow his lead. The whores can now be condemned for betraying their proverbial "hearts of gold" by being aggressive and materialistic; even the angels can be disliked because of the burden they are for the male. The woman loses by definition either way.

Perhaps the most completely negative view of woman emerges from the fiction of Saul Bellow. Unless she is a motherly, asexual figure like Augie's mother in *The Adventures of Augie March* (1953) or like Queen Willatale in *Henderson the Rain King* (1959), she may demand the very commitment that Bellow's men are unwilling to make. Marcus Klein has traced a pattern in Bellow's fiction in which "the sensible hero journeyed from a position of alienation to accommodation."[43] His heroes are all "dangling men," as the title of his Kafka-esque first novel about a man awaiting induction indicates (*Dangling Man*, 1944). They are willing but unable to make convincing commitments, for in all of Bellow's conscious efforts to affirm life he does not seem to be able to find any life worth affirming. While this pessimism may seem inevitable in the war years, it reveals itself as characteristic of Bellow by the time he writes *Mr. Sammler's Planet* (1969): Sammler sees a world so totally depraved and worthless that Elya Gruner's effort to "do what was required of him" seems heroic. Elya has apparently earned the release of death because "he did meet the terms of his contract."

To heroes who seek accommodation, not commitment, from Joseph in *Dangling Man* (who finally looks forward to Army life) to Sammler (who runs to the uninterested police when he sees a pickpocket but tries to discourage a friend from direct, personal action) a woman might very well be seen as a threat. Woman suggests family suggests responsibilities. Earl Rovit has noted that "the 'family' comes into actual existence only when the protagonist desires contact or aid" in Bellow's fiction with the exception of *The Victim*.[44] For both Bellow and Powers, the male protagonist is everything; women and even children are only irritants in his world. Rovit's allusion to *The Victim* (1947) concerns Asa and his sister-in-law Elena, who seeks his help and advice concerning her sick son. The son dies, and Asa—perhaps justly—blames Elena, but his excessively bad opinion of her and her mother arises out of his own guilt. He thinks that they blame him, projecting his self-hatred on them. The same process underlies other novels by Bellow as well. Since in most of these novels the hero controls point of view, there is little to alleviate a very negative portrayal of women.

Furthermore, as John J. Clayton demonstrates, women symbolize an even greater threat for the Bellow hero: "A terror of the death which he feels he deserves because of sexual guilt."[45] In *Dangling Man*, Joseph goes to visit his ex-mistress Kitty on a wet, dirty night which makes him imagine himself in a "swamp where death waited in the thickened water," only to find her in bed with another man. When he leaves her, the swamp dissolves into "a clean path of street and thrashing trees." Clayton points out the "somber ugliness of nearly everything" in the passage and posits that Joseph has been saved from sexual guilt by Kitty's defection, so he projects his guilt onto a woman on the bus with him: "*He* is clean, *she* is like Kitty, degenerate and decaying, something to be pitied."[46] Later, Joseph will project his guilt on Dolly, whom he imagines to be "farther on the hellward side than ever" after she catches him spanking her daughter Eta. Joseph feels she is accusing him of sexual advances toward Eta.

Obviously, Bellow is not writing about women at all. What we see are projections, usually negative, of the hero's guilt or needs. The women seem "stylized or unreal," as Irving Malin points out;[47] as Rovit claims, "Bellow's gallery of female characters tends to be composed of almost identical stereotypes, differing somewhat in ethnic background, erotic inventiveness, and the capacity for bitchiness."[48]

The wives are the burdens; they are also hardworking, loving, and noncomplaining sufferers. The only indication that they are contemporary is the affair they have had before marriage. Except for Iva in *Dangling Man*, they are weights on their husbands, and even Iva's material support of Joseph only serves to increase his guilt and self-hatred. Although he cannot attack her directly, she remains a shadowy figure. Other women who are or become wives threaten or fail their husbands as well. Mary is gone, visiting her mother, when Asa needs her most in *The Victim*; Augie March is "freed from the threat imposed by continued intimacy: that it will force him to betray himself" when his engagement to Lucy is broken.[49] When he finally does marry Stella she has a lover and, even worse, an inner life which makes Augie feel that "she refuses me—for the time being, anyway—the most important things I ask of her." When Henderson leaves for Africa in *Henderson the Rain King* (1959), he looks back on his wives Frances and Lily, as Leonard Lutwack observes, as "Circe and Calypso, keeping the hero 'captive' for eight years before he can depart on his trip."[50] Margaret in *Seize the Day* (1956) is seen by her estranged husband as draining him (although Daniel Weiss has noted that this too is a projection of "Wilhelm's own insistent need on to the woman"[51]): "Well, Dad, she hates me. I feel she's strangling me. I can't catch my breath. She just has fixed herself on me to kill me. She can do it at long distance. One of these days I'll be struck down by suffocation or apoplexy because of her. I just can't catch my breath." Even Herzog's wife Daisy in *Herzog* (1964) is described as a source of guilt, a "conventional Jewish woman" whom "he had treated miserably."

If wives are burdens who inspire guilt, mistresses are bitches, experts at lovemaking and dedicated to pleasure. Kitty in *Dangling Man* is described by Joseph as "a lively, plump, high-colored, scented, gross girl" who is sloppy about her apartment and "careless about herself." She instigates the affair; Joseph merely " 'saw it her way' for two months, or until she began hinting at my leaving Iva." Herzog commands his own gallery of bitches: Wanda is "*sincere*, loyal, devout toward the body, the flesh. She has the religion of civilized people, which is pleasure, creative and polymorphous pleasure." Such irony is Bellow's chief tool for describing women, as Herzog sees the geisha-like Sono as one who "knew where to invest her sensuality and how to increase it." He is oppressed with the uncleanliness and odors of her apartment as well until "he violently desired Sono, and just as violently did not want to go.

Even now he felt the fever, remembered the smells, experienced the difficulty."

Bellow's wives are all daughters of Eve, subservient to man yet the cause of his suffering and alienation from God. His mistresses are all daughters of Lilith, desirable demons in league with the devil. Most Lilith-like is Ramona, seen by Robert Alter as "that tender aging goddess of the Sexual Revolution"[52] and by Keith M. Opdahl as investing sex with "religious significance," as "a symbol of the personalism Herzog is struggling to reject."[53] In her spike-heeled shoes and black lace panties, Ramona is the perfect whore—until she opens her mouth. "Please, Ramona, Mose wanted to say—you're lovely, fragrant, sexual, good to touch—everything. But those lectures! For the love of God, Ramona, shut it up! But she went on." "Everything" in a woman apparently does not include any sense of self; that should be given up "for the love of God." Again, in Bellow's play, *Orange Soufflé* the hero's mistress offends him by trying to bake him a soufflé, thus betraying her assigned stereotype. A whore must avoid either acting like a man (talking and thinking) or like a wife (who alone deserves admittance to the kitchen). Herzog is always careful to separate his wives and mistresses. While Ramona should not talk like a man, she cannot look like a wife either: "But, speaking of ordinary Americans, what sort of mother would Ramona make: Would she be able to take a little girl to Macy's parade? Moses tried to imagine Ramona, a priestess of Isis, in a tweed suit, watching the procession of floats." If he should marry her, however, she must transform herself immediately from the exotic sex object (somewhat smelly and sloppy) to the wife (neat and diligent). In fact, she must become the sacrificing, suffering angel who will save her man (reminiscent of Warren's women): "Of course a wife's duty was to stand by this often puzzling and often disagreeable Herzog." To Daisy, Herzog had "exclaimed mentally, Marry me! Be my wife! End my troubles!" Similarly, Augie March refuses to see Stella realistically once he decides to marry her, as Opdahl shows: "Having admitted that he fled to love from the world, Augie now sees no truth in Stella's warning that 'you want all your troubles to be over all of a sudden and you're so anxious for it you may be making a mistake' (474)."[54]

The consistently negative portrayal of women in Bellow's fiction obscures the efforts they make to fit the stereotype which each is assigned. They fail because lurking behind the stereotype is a real, if self-negating, human being. If this is detected, as when Stella takes a lover or Ramona delivers a lecture, the hero is justly disappointed. Yet even in Bellow's fiction, as Rovit observes, two women emerge "who force the Bellow hero to rise to a qualitatively different kind of challenge than that of mere bed-fellowship. And, inevitably, he fails both challenges."[55] Both Thea Fenchel in *The Adventures of Augie March* and Madeleine Pontritter in *Herzog* are presented negatively from the hero's point of view. However, after painting these negative portraits, each hero admits that another view might be held. "Was it true, as she said," Augie wonders, "that love would appear strange to me no matter what form it took, even if there were no eagles and snakes?" Even Herzog admits that "everyone close to Madeleine, everyone drawn into the drama of life became exceptional, deeply gifted, brilliant," which for all his sarcasm might still indicate her own gifts. Intense, intelligent, loving individuals, these women suggest that the failure was on the side of the men involved. Thea tells Augie after his one-night stand with Stella that "I thought if I could get through to one person I would get through to more.... Well, I believed it must be you who could do this for me. And you could. I was so happy to find you.... I'm sorry you're here now. You're not special. You're just like everyone else. You get tired easily." Although we don't get Madeleine's direct remarks in *Herzog*, we can piece together Herzog's admissions to sense her disappointment as well:

"She feels I'm a Pharisee. She says so."... "Madeleine wanted a savior, and for her I'm no savior."... "If I say the house is dirty, it stinks, she thinks I'm criticizing her mind and forcing her back to housework. Disrespectful of her rights as a person."... She complained that he never really listened to her. *He* wanted to shine all the time. But that wasn't it. He had heard her lecture on this subject many times.

Thea and Madeleine, struggling for self, are put down—hard. No wonder Clayton asserts that beneath Moses Herzog is Stephen Rojack of Mailer's *American Dream* who murders his wife.[56] Leslie Fiedler has reason to wonder whether "killing one's wife is not the essential American Dream"![57] Bellow's men hate women who depart from their roles, but they are not very supportive of other women either. Women are threatening, personifying the sensuality men try to deny in themselves or the responsibility they fear. The stronger the woman, the greater the threat. By projecting their own guilts and fears of inadequacy on the women, these men ignore them as people. If Bellow's fiction does reflect male attitudes, then even the men are encouraged to accommodate, not assert.

At least Norman Mailer seems to see the possibility of self-assertion, through a philosophy of Hip which he defines in "The White Negro." Mailer's single novel in the 40's, *The Naked and the Dead*, had looked at women only indirectly through the men at war. "To the men as a group," Barry Leeds points out, "sex and women are viewed cynically almost without exception, and a chorus is devoted to their mutterings on the topic."[58] But none of the characters in this naturalistic war novel develop as individuals; war does not lend itself to personal definition. Only in later novels does Mailer have the opportunity to assert life and the self.

Sex is so important to the men in Mailer's fiction that almost every woman is seen first in these terms: is she a taker or a giver; will she accept or demand? Eisinger has commented that "the entire range of questions dealing with sex-fulfillment as life-fulfillment will possess Mailer in later books. Here [in his first novel] he shows how easy it is to fail in the sexual aspects of marriage relationship in America and how the sense of such failure eats away at the manhood of his characters."[59] In fact, most things seem to "eat away at the manhood" of these men, mainly because of the masculine mystique Mailer establishes. To be an individual involves accepting all parts of yourself and achieving your unique human potential, but for Mailer this human potential for either sex is straitjacketed by sexual roles. His men fare as badly as his women: their role has been defined by Ernest Hemingway. "Let any of you decide for yourselves how silly would be *A Farewell to Arms* or better, *Death in the Afternoon*, if it had been written by a man who was five-four, had acne, wore glasses, spoke in a shrill voice, and was a physical coward," Mailer asserts in *Advertisements for Myself* (1959). Associating physical attributes with moral values, Mailer presents an effeminate (I choose the word purposely) male as necessarily cowardly. But at least he is partly male; it only follows that women are below consideration.

To be effeminate, either in action or appearance, is one of the greatest faults a man can have in the gospel according to Mailer. In "The White Negro" he warns us that

If you goof (the ugliest word in Hip), if you lapse back into being a frightened stupid child, or if you flip, if you lose control, *reveal the buried weaker more feminine part of your nature* [my italics], then it is more difficult to swing the next time.

Such a negative view of the "weaker more feminine part" of the self confirms Simone de Beauvoir's assertion that "in actuality the relation of the two sexes is not quite like that of two electric poles, for man represents both the positive and the neutral, as is indicated by the common use of *man* to designate human beings in general; whereas woman represents only the negative, defined by limiting criteria, without reciprocity."[60] This constant emphasis on sex makes Mailer's fiction a favorite target for such feminist critics as Kate Millet[61] and Mary Ellman, the latter of whom argues that "when Norman Mailer talks about feisty men and languid women, one touches the past—hardly in the form in which it persists in bourgeois enclaves, but as it drags at a mind attempting to reconcile an acute appreciation of the present with a passionate attachment to a masculine ideal."[62] It is precisely his "acute appreciation of the present" which makes Mailer important; however, the "masculine ideal" drags at more minds than just his as it reflects that present for some men.

Mailer meant to follow his war novel, William Hoffa tells us, with "a study of the effects of the war on the American woman."[63] What finally materialized was *Barbary Shore* (1951), a novel which led Aldridge to complain that "there was a loin-wrung, post-masturbatory quality about the style"[64] and led Mailer himself to admit in *Advertisements for Myself* that "I was obviously trying for something which was at the very end of my reach, and then beyond it, and toward the end of the novel collapsed into a chapter of political speech and never quite recovered." *Barbary Shore* has only two women, the nymphomaniac Guenivere and the masochist lesbian Lannie. If we care to stretch a few points, both women could be seen as war debris. Guenivere, who is defined as a nympho only by Willy Lovett (who is himself stood up when he invites her to his room), does have ample opportunity for adultery, perhaps because the men have all come home as starved for sex as are the soldiers of *The Naked and the Dead*. "Honestly, every time I've turned around there's been another man propositioning me," she complains to Lovett. When he suggests that she might have invited such advantages (typically asserting the guilt of the sexual victim) she disagrees: "You don't mean to tell me you characters need any help. You run after us like a bunch of hound dogs." Lannie too has been affected by the war, even more violently. As Richard Foster says, her "derangement is a consequence and expression of history."[65] She is shattered by the violence—especially the moral violence—wrought by the war on her world. "Her illusions destroyed, Lannie is devoid of hope for the world, and rejects any possibility for the individual to change it," Leeds tells us.[66]

Yet even Lannie's rejection of self comes from her devotion to the individual. This bisexual young woman with the ambiguous name (which causes Leeds to compare her to Launcelot as well as Elaine, the Fair Maid of Astolat, as the complement of Guenivere) represents the feminine nature of man, which understands through emotion and illusion.[67] Lannie is a Trotskyite because of Trotsky: "He was the man I loved, the only man I ever truly loved with heart and not with body." When Trotsky is murdered, all he stands for goes with him, and she must suffer personally rather than politically. Thus, she turns to members of the opposite ideology—to Hollingsworth and Guenivere—and demands debasement. As Leeds argues, "Lannie intentionally assumes the role of a passively adoring object of exploitation to each of these, thus fulfilling her belief that the will of the individual has no place in this world."[68]

Such passivity, masochism, and emotionalism have been common to female stereotypes. If Lannie did represent the effect that allowing women to express themselves and allowing men to develop rather than repress their "feminine part" would have on the self, then Mailer might have some justification for fearing what he has called in *Cannibals and Christians* (1966) the "Womanization of America." In that work Mailer contends that homosexuality is on the rise because of "a general loss of faith in the country, faith in the meaning of one's work, faith in the notion of oneself as a man." We have seen Lannie lose faith and thus lose her notion of self; this "feminine" tendency is what Mailer sees as pervading post–World War II America. "Masculinity is not something given to you, something you're born with, but something you gain," he continues. "Unless everyone in America gets a great deal braver," he warns us, "everything is going to get worse—including the womanization of America."

Women need not see themselves in Mailer's "everyone" here, since neither Lannie nor Guenivere should be considered women at all. Guenivere is literally a sex object—man's need to fulfill himself through sex, Mailer's basic proof of masculinity, a need which has been blocked and intensified during the war. Lannie is man's "feminine part" isolated and uncontrolled rather than integrated into a total personality. Such schizophrenia is indeed insane, and would be unhealthy in the society. Lannie represents man's emotional weakness in the face of the postwar collapse of faith. Each "woman" is one facet of the shattered personality; to deny either is to postpone the healthy integration of the self even longer.

The women in *The Deer Park* (1955), while less symbolic, are equally stereotypical. Lulu Meyers, the "movie sex goddess," is nothing more than that. Elena Esposito (used by Ellman to exemplify the whore stereotype because she "carries her talent around like an inoperable tumor, sinking helplessly under its weight into anyone's bed"[69]) is a pitiable burden on each man. Even Sergius briefly considers taking her on, a burden he should assume because he had misjudged her. No one really wants her for long. When Eitel finally agrees to marry her, after she asks him to, "he nodded, his heart numb, his will sick, thinking there must be some escape, and knowing there was nothing."

Sergius does meet one woman who is striving to be herself, but she never darkens the pages of *The Deer Park*. In "Time of her Time" Mailer mates Sergius with an intelligent, aggressive Jewish woman who is in psychoanalysis. Their lovemaking resembles nothing so much as mortal combat, and Sergius, it seems, must win in order for either of them to be happy. When she is assertive, he calls her "direct and unfeminine"; when he is aggressive, hitting her "mean and openhanded across the face," she melts and "her body sweetened into some feminine embrace." She loses by her resistance: "She had fled the domination which was liberty for her." If women break the stereotypes, they are supposed to be miserable. Mailer agrees with Powers that men must dominate, force women to accept their role, and that this will bring happiness to all.

If Mailer's idea of happiness is hard to buy, his picture of ideal womanhood is even more repellent. Elena Esposito is an early version of this ideal, but perfection really awaits the creation of Cherry in *An American Dream* (1965). This novel also offers Ruta, a German maid symbolic of Nazism and the disillusionment of the war, and Deborah Caughlin Mangaravidi Kelly Rojack, Mailer's bitch-goddess and Cherry's opposite. Deborah is held responsible, even more than Lannie, for the "Womanization of America."

The ideal Cherry does not willingly fail her hero, although unfortunately (for her only, it seems) she does die on him. Cherry fits snugly into the stereotype of the whore with a heart of gold. She is, as Foster claims, a "plucky victim of the forces of which Deborah is the emblematic goddess and proprietress."[70] Her vulnerability proves her true femininity to Rojack; yet she is still only a burden to him despite his admiration for her. His real aim, as Noble has identified, is "to re-establish the American Adam. . . . Purged of the dirty ape within by his acts of courage, he has achieved freedom from the jungle of the American establishment. A clean ape once more, he heads toward a new frontier."[71] Actually, it is a very old frontier, a reunion with Hemingway in a world of nature without women: "There was a jungle somewhere in Guatemala which had a friend, an old friend. I thought to go there. And on to Yucatan." *An American Dream* is one more cry to leave womenfolk and civilization behind, as Fiedler would say; and in *Why are We in Vietnam?* (1968), Fiedler argues, Mailer does "turn away from the metropolitan world that had long concerned him to the last frontier of Alaska."[72] Coming full circle from war to war, Mailer is once more safe in a world without women.

Mailer identifies America's ills with woman—the bitch goddess represented by Deborah. Larger than life, she embodies Mailer's fears of the independent woman. If Rojack is the American Adam, then Deborah can also be traced back to Eden as it is described in Milton's *Paradise Lost*. She mates with her father (the Devil), which identifies her as Sin and their incestuous offspring as Death. This triumvirate working through her tempts Rojack through his emotions—his feminine part—to his fall from grace—from the paradise of his natural self. The way back to paradise, however, is no longer through Christian love: "God was not love but courage," Mailer tells us. Rojack, the new (or anti-) Christ, must face and attack the materialism of America, of a "womanized" American dream. Even with Cherry, Rojack must assert his authority: "Women must murder us unless we possess them altogether." He must actually murder Deborah to succeed.

In his own way, Mailer has painted as negative a picture of women as did Bellow. Each woman is Eve (or Lilith) reborn, bringing evil into the world, producing weakness in men by bringing out their "feminine" characteristics. Even Cherry, who keeps "her own ills to herself, rather than pass them on," is dependent and therefore a burden. The powerful, demonic bitch goddess must be destroyed—cannot serve as a role model. No wonder women adopted the feminine mystique!

These male writers spawned by the war years were particularly vehement in their unyielding condemnation of women. Women are bitches whenever they disagree or try to assert themselves; they are burdens whenever they are passive and subservient. Either way, they are embodiments of whatever stands in opposition to man from within or outside the self. For Powers, they represent the hypocrisy and worldliness which would smother the spirit; for Bellow, they carry the smell and soil of the beast from which man has striven to rise, the animal nature inimical to society, or the demands of that society on the individual; for Mailer, they *are* that society forcing or burdening the man who would be free to return to paradise. Whatever his goal may be, woman stands between man and that goal in these novels. The stereotypes seem necessary to suppress these evil possibilities of the feminine—in women, in men, and even in American society. Deviation from the stereotypes or lapse of control is destructive to all. If these writers embody the attitudes of American men in the 40's, one cannot blame women for retreating to the feminine mystique of the 50's.

BITTER FRUIT

The 40's were indeed "a time of ripening" for women, but the fruits of war are bitter. Shaken from the Eden of America's innocence before they were fully ripened, bruised by the shattering inhumanity of war, these "strange children" were often condemned to perpetual adolescence or unfulfilled adulthood. With Mick Kelly they felt "cheated"; with Mrs. Waite they knew they had been "tricked." The women writers reveal the contradictions presented women by their society, which offered but couldn't deliver protection. Taught that perfection is embodied in the male image, they were still expected to preserve the spiritual purity of the female image. If a woman failed to satisfy society's stereotypes, she was dismissed as insane.

By the end of the decade, women writers had shown how unsatisfactory and debilitating such stereotyping could be, but few would suggest alternatives for women. Self-definition meant loneliness, isolation, even madness. Only the strongest could venture forth on their own, and the cost of the opportunity to do so was high. Besides, the violence of the world they now knew and the vulnerability of the self discouraged many from pursuing anything beyond the numbing stereotype. Nor did the attitude of their men encourage them to self-development, judging from the male writers; too many things were changing, seemed to be the message, for women to try to change as well. When they returned from the war, men expected the attention and devotion they had missed.

In reaction to the violence and disintegration of the war, the writers of the 50's would retreat even further from the insights of the 40's. While their men were at war, women began to realize the inadequacy of the stereotypes which had defined them. In the midst of world war, however, they also recognized the dangers implicit in the quest for identity, dangers increased for women. The dismal picture that emerges in the literature of the 50's of a world of inevitable compromise and accommodation is only relieved by occasional individual assertions, and even these often either lead nowhere or end in violence. Yet under the surface of these circumscribed lives seethes the equally inevitable violence of life itself, waiting to burst through in the 60's.

NOTES

1. John Stuart Mill and Harriet Taylor Mill, *Essays on Sex Equality*, ed. Alice S. Rossi (Chicago: University of Chicago Press, 1970), 47.

2. Margaret Mead and Frances Balgley Kaplan (eds.), *American Women* (New York: Charles Scribner's Sons, 1965), 47.

3. David W. Noble, *The Eternal Adam and the New World Garden* (New York: Grosset & Dunlap, 1968), 197.

4. An excellent study of Lilith is available in Raphael Patai, *The Hebrew Goddess* (New York: KTAV Publishing, 1967).

5. Phyllis Chesler, *Women and Madness* (New York: Avon, 1972).

6. Karl Stern, *The Flight from Woman* (New York: Farrar, Straus & Giroux, 1965), 5.

7. Annis Pratt, *Archetypal Patterns in Women's Fiction* (Bloomington: Indiana University Press, 1964), 72.

8. Ihab H. Hassan, "The Character of Post-War Fiction in America," in *Recent American Fiction: Some Critical Views,* ed. by Joseph J. Waldmeir (Boston: Houghton Mifflin Co., 1963), 31.

9. Sandra M. Gilbert and Susan Gubar, *The Madwoman in the Attic: The Woman Writer and the Nineteenth-Century Imagination* (New Haven: Yale University Press, 1979), xi.

10. W. Tasker Witham, *The Adolescent in the American Novel, 1920–1960* (New York: Frederick Ungar, 1964), 72.

11. Hassan, "The Character," 31.

12. John W. Aldridge, *After the Lost Generation* (New York: Noonday Press, 1951), 196.

13. Chester E. Eisinger, *Fiction of the Forties* (Chicago: University of Chicago Press, 1963), 4.

14. Ibid., 300.

15. Quoted by Betty Friedan in *The Feminine Mystique* (New York: Dell, 1963), 100.

16. Louis Auchincloss, *Pioneers and Caretakers* (Minneapolis: University of Minnesota Press, 1961), 157.

17. Kate Millet, *Sexual Politics* (Garden City, NY: Doubleday, 1970), 233.

18. Eisinger, *Fiction*, 301.

19. Ibid., 244.

20. Pratt, *Archetypal Patterns*, 32–3.

21. Witham, *The Adolescent*, 60.

22. Louise Y. Gossett, *Violence in Recent Southern Fiction* (Durham, NC: Duke University Press, 1965), 167.

23. Millet, *Sexual Politics*, 211.

24. Dorothy Yost Deegan, *The Stereotype of the Single Woman in American Novels* (New York: Octagon Books, 1969), 172.

25. Ferdinand Lundberg and Marynia F. Farnham, *Modern Woman: The Lost Sex* (New York: Harper & Brothers, 1947), 202.

26. Ibid.

27. Noble, *The Eternal Adam*, 185.

28. John M. Bradbury, *Renaissance in the South* (Chapel Hill: University of North Carolina Press, 1963), 70.

29. Alfred Appel, Jr., *A Season of Dreams: The Fiction of Eudora Welty* (Baton Rouge: Louisiana State University Press, 1965), 86.

30. Ibid.

31. Eisinger, *Fiction*, 274–5.

32. Quoted by Connie Brown and Jane Seitz, "You've Come a Long Way, Baby: Historical Perspectives," in *Sisterhood is Powerful*, ed. by Robin Morgan (New York: Vintage, 1970), 4.

33. I am borrowing this phrase from the title of Aileen S. Kraditor's *Up From the Pedestal* (Chicago: Quadrangle Books, 1968).

34. Friedan, *Feminine Mystique*, 53.

35. Eisinger, *Fiction*, 70.

36. Ibid., 191–2.

37. Anais Nin, *The Novel of the Future* (New York: Macmillan, 1968), 5.

38. "Hangsaman," *Saturday Review of Literature*, 34 (May 5, 1951), 11.

39. Witham, *The Adolescent*, 72.

40. Alfred Kazin, "Heroines," *The New York Review of Books* (February 11, 1971), 31–2.

41. Carolyn G. Heilbrun, *Toward A Recognition of Androgyny* (New York: Harper & Row, 1973), 23.

42. Phyllis Chesler, "Women & Madness," *MS.*, 1 (July 1972), 110–11.

43. Marcus Klein, "A Discipline of Nobility: Saul Bellow's Fiction," in *Saul Bellow and the Critics*, ed. Irving Malin (New York: New York University Press, 1967), 92.

44. Earl Rovit, *Saul Bellow* (Minneapolis: University of Minnesota Press, 1967), 10.

45. John J. Clayton, *Saul Bellow: In Defense of Man* (Bloomington: Indiana University Press, 1968), 105.

46. Ibid., 103–4.

47. Irving Malin, Introduction to *Saul Bellow and the Critics* (New York: New York University Press, 1967), ix.

48. Rovit, *Saul Bellow*, 31.

49. Eisinger, *Fiction*, 356.

50. Leonard Lutwack, *Heroic Fiction* (Carbondale: Southern Illinois University Press, 1971), 104.

51. Daniel Weiss, "Caliban on Prospero," in Malin, *Saul Bellow*, 129.

52. Robert Alter, *After the Tradition* (New York: E. P. Dutton, 1969), 109.

53. Keith M. Opdahl, *The Novels of Saul Bellow* (University Park, PA: Southern University Press, 1967), 91–2.

54. Ibid.

55. Rovit, *Saul Bellow*, 31.

56. Clayton, *In Defense,* 195.

57. Quoted by Clayton, *In Defense,* 195.

58. Barry H. Leeds, *The Structured Vision of Norman Mailer* (New York: New York University Press, 1969), 25.

59. Eisinger, *Fiction,* 34.

60. Simone de Beauvoir, *The Second Sex* (New York: Bantam Books, 1952), xv.

61. Millet, *Sexual Politics,* 321–30.

62. Mary Ellman, *Thinking About Women* (New York: Harcourt Brace Jovanovich, 1968), 73.

63. William Hoffa, "Norman Mailer: *Advertisements for Myself,*" in *The Fifties: Fiction, Poetry, Drama,* ed. by Warren French (Deland, FL: Everett/Edwards, Inc., 1970), 76.

64. John W. Aldridge, *The Devil in the Fire* (New York: Harper & Row, 1972), 176–7.

65. Richard Foster, *Norman Mailer* (Minneapolis: University of Minnesota Press, 1968), 13.

66. Leeds, *The Structured Vision,* 84.

67. Ibid., 85.

68. Ibid., 84–5.

69. Ellman, *Thinking,* 124–5.

70. Foster, *Norman Mailer,* 19.

71. Noble, *The Eternal Adam,* 208–9.

72. Leslie Fiedler, *The Return of the Vanishing American* (New York: Stein & Day, 1968), 14.

2

A Strategic Retreat: Fiction of the 50's

If the war-torn 40's had forced women out of the house and inadvertently into questioning their earlier lives, the peace-plagued 50's would lock them in again with a vengeance. With its fingers burnt to the quick from touching the cremating fires of Europe and setting the fires of Japan, young America was ready to retreat into conformity and traditionalism. Women were not alone in repressing the violent knowledge they had gained; nor were they alone in rebelling against such repression in the next decade.

But the 50's were not completely a lost decade; exposure to the knowledge necessary for growth must necessarily be followed by a period of latency or even retreat during which that knowledge can be internalized and alternatives to old patterns can be discovered. Although the external life of women in the 50's revealed little, the internal turmoil and explorations are evident in the fiction of these years.

This retreat inward can be seen in the writers we have already encountered. Even Shirley Jackson and Eudora Welty, who had already offered the explorers Natalie Waite and Virgie Rainey on the verge of self-discovery, would wait for Mrs. Angela Motorman and Miss Julia Mortimer to assert that self in society in 1968 and 1970 respectively. In the intervening years, Jackson would join the "new breed of women writers" Betty Friedan discusses who wrote "as if they were 'just housewives,' reveling in a comic world of children's pranks and eccentric washing machines and Parents' Night at the PTA."[1] Jackson's family chronicles at least maintained her violent awareness with the humor, as the titles show: *Life Among the Savages* (1953) and *Raising Demons* (1957). Meanwhile, in her fiction women shattered into fragmented personalities like Elizabeth in *The Bird's Nest* (1954) or escaped into the dreamworlds of *The Sundial* (1958), *The Haunting of Hill House* (1959), and *We Have Always Lived in the Castle* (1962). Within each work, even those about her children, the awareness of violence is omnipresent; but, while the women externalize it and try to remain in perpetual childhood within protective houses, only the children can acknowledge the savagery and argue with little Fanny of *The Sundial*, "Who wants to be *safe*, for heaven's sake?"—and nobody listens to Fanny. Children, Jackson realizes, have no social power. Interestingly, Jackson had planned to publish a children's version of *Come Along With Me* (the novel, left unfinished after her death in 1965, which offered the social magic of Mrs. Motorman),[2] suggesting that her retreat in the 50's might have enabled her to bring together the hopes of the child and the realities of the woman just as Mrs. Motorman brings together the rational and the irrational, the world of the imagination and the "real" world.

Welty retreated even more completely, publishing only one short, comic novel, *The Ponder Heart* (1954), and a collection of short stories, *The Bride of the Innisfallen* (1955), in the 50's and nothing in the 60's. Humor has often been a vehicle of acceptance of what appears to be inevitable—the bitter acknowledgment of black humor no less than the gentle satire of comedy of manners. *The Ponder Heart* humorously accepts the protection of childhood and family as the self-sacrificing niece Edna Earle forgoes her one chance to marry to fulfill her familial duty to care for Uncle Daniel. "Suppose I'd even attempted, over the years, to step off—I dread to think of the lengths Grandpa would have gone to stop it," she explains. Providing Uncle Daniel with a childlike protectivity, Edna Earle feels little remorse when his fiancée leaves: "There's something I think's better to have than love, and if you want me to, I'll tell you what it is—that's company."

Family and community again dominate in the short stories, even when their setting shifts to Europe and Ireland. Two stories worth noting, however, are "The Burning" and "Circe." Set in the Civil War South, "The Burning" bitterly condemns a conflict between the social code and a higher moral code. The former demands that Miss Myra and Miss Theo leave their half-Negro nephew in the house to die rather than carry him out in front of Northern soldiers; the latter demands that they hang themselves in retribution. Here Welty affirms the primary claim of human over social values. "Circe" retreats into the past even further to make explicit the archetypal relationship of Welty's wanderers to Odysseus. Circe personifies communal values—she is a domestic, almost motherly figure who admires but cannot understand the passion of the searcher, thus reminding us that the roles identified as female in our society (raising, nurturing, and protecting) are basically communal—are the roles for which society was organized and as such are not sex-defined. That women fill them in our society is another way of saying women have been given social functions rather than individual lives. Continuing to explore myth, Welty is challenging it as well.

America in the 50's offered the face of accommodation and compromise to its writers of fiction. McCarthyism and other conservative backlashes led Americans to repress, at least publicly, any nonconformity; the constant threat of the Bomb and later the Korean "conflict" oppressed them and remained periodic reminders of the violence they were not able to leave behind them. In Dwight D. Eisenhower they found a father who seemed to promise a return to the isolation of national childhood, but that was as illusory as the childhood dreams haunting the fiction. The women who retreated from their insights of the 40's into roles of baby-producing, home-loving wives who felt guilty that they had ever been attracted to a "man's world" were merely following society's lead. The change was reflected in women's magazines (although, as Friedan points out, it was instigated by men[3]) as well as in the novels, as the writers faithfully recorded their social realities. Beneath the facade, however, seethed the violence, and these writers would choose soon the creative violence necessary for growth over the stagnation and repression.

THE AMERICAN ELECTRA

As women's roles were once more prescribed for them by the desires of their men and their society, the exploration which had begun in the 40's was necessarily turned inward. One of the first steps to understanding the self is examining our roots. Welty began our discussion of mythic roots, but even closer are familial roots. In Western society, women are defined in relation to men, beginning with their fathers. A look at the fiction reveals that the father/daughter theme, which William Wasserstrom had traced through earlier American fiction in *Heiress of All the Ages*, received a great deal of attention—perhaps for the same reason that the nation turned to Eisenhower, that Aunt Fanny sought protection in "her father's house" in *The Sundial*. As women characters reflected on their relationships to their own fathers, they frequently discovered that this strong dependency had shaped the rest of their lives and often blocked them from self-development.

Facing their personal versions of Freud's Electra complex are the women in Jackson's *Hangsaman* (1951), in Jean Stafford's *The Catherine Wheel* (1952), in Styron's *Lie Down in Darkness* (1951), and in a number of novels and short stories by Hortense Calisher. We will begin with Styron's novel, which provides the only male perspective in the group.

Lie Down in Darkness presents a gallery of women. In the Loftis household are the mother Helen, the daughters Maudie and Peyton, and the Negro servants Ella and LaRuth. Closely related is Dolly, Milton Loftis's mistress. All these women focus their lives around fathers. Through their religion and "Daddy Faith," the blacks gain the security which the whites never seem to find: "You, Daddy! Daddy Faith! You loves us! You, Daddy!" Their religion is a vital, dependable source of strength in their lives, an unending repository of values and love. "De grass witherith, de flower fadeth," Daddy Faith assures them, "but de word of your God shall stand forever." Similarly, religion will become a refuge for many of Gordon's characters, particularly for the women in *The Malefactors* (1956), and again in the fiction of Flannery O'Connor.

The whites in Styron's novel have no such faith to support them, and they are too weak on their own. So each woman turns to Daddy, Milton Loftis. Dolly's is the smallest share, only the temporary love of a married man who, when he decides to "do the right thing" and abandon her, feels little more than "a certain tenderness for her small deficiencies." Yet she tries to cling to this tenuous little, sending Milton "wistful, pleading notes in lavender ink, scented, and stuffed with humiliating souvenirs," until she finally pays him a drunken visit and then "troubled him no more."

Maudie has been eliminated even earlier; burdened with mental and physical deficiencies, she dies of tuberculosis. Like the idiot Benjy in William Faulkner's *The Sound and the Fury* (the book on which, Malcolm Cowley argues, this novel is based[4]), Maudie is protected from the tragedy around her by her handicap; unlike Benjy, however, she does not become a catalyst for others. Rather, she becomes an escape and a weapon for her mother. Helen turns the emotions misunderstood by her adulterous husband and rejected by Peyton toward the gentle Maudie to make her own life more bearable: "If it weren't for Maudie." When Maudie dies, Helen's emotions turn to hatred, as she weights Peyton with guilt: "Remember when you let her fall? You don't care. About anything. ... You with your whoring around and your drinking."

Helen is another of that lost and dying breed haunting the pages of Southern writers, the ideal Southern lady: "She remembered a time when she was young. She had wanted the future to be like a nice, long, congenial tea party, where everyone talked a little, danced a little, and had polite manners." Her uppermost care at Peyton's wedding was "that people should know: it was Helen Loftis, that suffering woman, who had brought together the broken family." Propriety wins over honesty: "Oh, what was honesty, anyway? After so much suffering, did a woman really have to be honest to fulfill herself?" Peyton's dying thoughts echo her mother's teaching: "I am dying Bunny, dying. BUT YOU MUST BE PROPER. I say, oh pooh. Oh pooh. Must be proper. Oh most proper. Powerful."

Milton's failure to provide her with the protection of a dead Southern aristocracy causes Helen's madness. Peyton's madness, reflected in those last thoughts, comes through her father as well, she realizes: "Those people back in the Lost Generation. Daddy, I guess. ... They weren't lost. What they were doing was losing us." Neither her mother nor her father, as Louise Gossett notes, "wants to be an adult, morally or emotionally";[5] they remain "strange children."

Yet Peyton is bound to her father through his very failure. He promises her protection and denies her growth, while he is inadequate to provide either. We find, as does W. Tasker Witham, this Electra complex possessing Peyton and driving her to suicide: "Peyton Loftis has no use for her mother, and openly rebels against her

during adolescence; her father she loves with an abiding passion
that makes impossible for her any satisfactory adjustment to lover
or husband."[6]

Peyton's complex is really a desire for the dependency of childhood. She too is afraid to face maturation, especially when growing
up seems to mean joining a valueless world. Maxwell Geismar
acutely argues that "the real point of *Lie Down in Darkness* is that,
dealing with the Electra complex itself, it has not only made it
human and domestic but has returned it, so to speak, to its natural
home of childhood feeling itself."[7] Peyton cannot grow away from
her father, nor can she go home to him, except in a coffin. Her
"madness" has once again been the rebellion of the searcher; as she
tries to explain to her husband, "something has always been close
to dying in my soul, and I've sinned only in order to lie down in
darkness and find, somewhere in a net of dreams, a new father, a
new home." For Peyton, as for Eleanor in *The Haunting of Hill
House*, only death promises such a home.

One might excuse men for failing women when so much is asked
of them, but a society which encourages its women to remain
dependent children is responsible. Still, women, the victims, reap
the punishment for both. Similarly, William Van O'Connor complains that Caroline Gordon "seems to ask a lot of the male, more
understanding, courage, and tenacity than most mortals, male or
female, possess."[8] Gordon's women also search for an ideal father
from their Southern heritage, usually in Aleck Maury, who weaves
his way through the background of this fiction, directly or indirectly
judging the daughters who depart from their traditional roles. As
Sarah Lewis protests in *The Strange Children* (1951), "I'm Professor
Maury's daughter, fallen among thieves." However, since Gordon
fails to provide her women with men strong enough to step into
their fathers' shoes, she compensates by bringing in a heavenly
Father. In her two novels of the 50's, Catholicism offers its
protection.

Another father's daughter whose growth is definitely limited is
Katherine Congreve in *The Catherine Wheel*. Katherine describes
herself as "like her father, note-maker, student for study's sake,"
and knows that "she would never participate, . . . she would read
astutely and never write, observe whole-heartedly and never paint,
not teach, not marry God. Untalented and uncompromising, she

would not commit herself." As with Stafford's other women, Katherine tries to suppress the potential violence of the emotions within her; even when her father dies she must watch her cousin Maeve's spontaneous reaction in order to imitate it. Only when John Shipley, Maeve's husband and the man Katherine has always loved, claims that he shares her love and would divorce Maeve, do her passions threaten to break through the surface of her spinster's life to burn as brightly as the Catherine wheel fireworks lighting the sky.

Before John's admission, Katherine had created a world almost as imaginary as those of Jackson's women. Preserving her childhood by arresting her own growth, she "had never healed, had never changed, and but for her white hair, she was the same as she had been at nineteen when her lover married someone else, at seventeen when she had sworn to marry him." Such stagnation did protect her from her violent world:

She did not choose to recognize political alterations in the countries she was fond of: Mussolini and Hitler she looked on as demented eccentrics whose day would soon be over, and she would not be persuaded that their power, moral and philosophical, was more than superficial. . . . There was no progression in time because there was no perspective and therefore no shrouding of the past; the present was exactly the same importance and except in the most minor and mechanical of ways, the future did not seem to exist.

Once this structured existence is endangered, however, her very survival is threatened, and the Catherine wheel of her released emotions burns her beyond recovery.

If Katherine and Peyton are trapped in childhood by the unintentional power of fathers, Mr. Waite's control in *Hangsaman* is blatantly conscious. "It has been *my* plan, Natalie, all of it," he assures her: "without you I could not exist; there can be no father without a daughter. You have thus a double responsibility, for my existence and for your own. If you abandon me, you lose yourself." His godlike stance recalls Strindberg's title character in *The Father* who tells his daughter that "you must have only one soul or you'll have no peace—neither shall I. You must have only one mind, fruit of my mind. You must have only one will—mine!"

Brought up under this iron domination, Natalie has always accepted and echoed her father's attitudes, telling him that her mother "makes the kitchen like a room with a sign saying 'Ladies' over the door." Mr. Waite encourages this by belittling Mrs. Waite's gifts to Natalie. Yet Natalie does accept and appreciate Mrs. Waite's attempts to communicate through "some sort of mother/daughter relationship that might, by means of small female catchwords and feminine innuendoes, separate, at least for a time, the family of women against men." While she doesn't admit it, she "admired her mother at these times, and, although she would go to any length to avoid even the slightest conversation with her mother in the living room, she enjoyed and profited by the kitchen conversations more than even Mrs. Waite suspected."

After she leaves home, Natalie is even more able to weigh her family heritage. Maturation demands the understanding and incorporation of our heritage from each parent utilized through what we learn ourselves. Natalie's forced awareness of her father's influence leads her to pay more attention to that of her mother. Remembering when her father had laughed at Natalie for wishing on a wishing stone for a bike and at her mother for wanting to fulfill the wish, Natalie comes to feel that "her mother had been right. It was less important, Natalie thought, to allow her father's humor to be transmitted to his children than to keep alive her mother's faith in magic." Again the dismissal implicit in humor is rejected.

As Natalie moves away from the dependency on her father, she discovers from her mother the heritage which enables her to grow as a woman and as an individual. The same process can be discerned in the fiction of Hortense Calisher, but in her single collection of stories published in the 50's, *In the Absence of Angels* (1951), Calisher's women reject mothers. As we will learn in her autobiographically based stories in *Tale for the Mirror* (1962), these women are fathers' daughters first. Calisher's counterpart, Hester, appears with her parents, Joseph and Hedwig (bearing the names and backgrounds of Calisher's own parents), in this latter collection. Hester's preference for her father is obvious. While she praises the "Conscientious Practicality" of the mother in "Time, Gentlemen!" who is striving to "get Imaginative Indolence, my father, out of the house somewhat nearer nine than noon," at the same time she revels that "Imaginative always won, partly by refusing to notice the strategic lines of force sent out constantly, all morning, by Conscientious, and partly, as I came to believe, because Time itself, elsewhere being made to skip so violently, was coming to lean more and more sympathetically on my father's side."

Hester's father is not only imaginative and indolent; he is also generous and protective. He retains a Southern attitude of guardianship over his black maid, May-ry, in the story of that name: "He loved taking care of people." Fathers are there to take care of you, whether you are an ex-slave or a daughter. Gordon expresses a similar view in her short story "Tom Rivers" from the collection *Old Red and Other Stories* (1963). "You think you'd hate to be a woman," Rivers observes, "but if you were a woman you wouldn't think anything of it. Or a nigger. Now, a nigger wouldn't want to change with white folks—I mean a nigger that had any sense— because the way he is he don't have to make any effort. He knows somebody's going to take care of him."

In the fiction of both women, husbands are there to try to continue a father's care. As Garner watches his wife Amelia in Calisher's title story of *Tale for the Mirror*, he realizes that "this was really what Amelia and the other mothers were after. They were trying to recast the fathers of their children in the image of their fathers. They wanted this authority for their husbands, they wanted them to exude this importance to the children." While Aleck Maury hangs over Gordon's fiction, Joseph Elkin dominates that of Calisher.

Consequently, Calisher is cautious of the narrator of the title story of *In the Absence of Angels*, who describes herself as one "of those women who were to refuse to stay in their traditional places either as wives, whom we identified with our mothers, or as teachers, whom we identified with lemon-faced aunts, lonely gas rings, and sexual despair." Yet this woman pictures mothers who echo those described by Friedan's exposé of *The Feminine Mystique*:

Mostly, they are pleasantly favored women who had never worked before marriage, or tended to conceal it if they had, whose minds were not so much stupid as unaroused—women at whom the menopause or the defection of growing children struck suddenly in the soft depths of their inarticulateness. . . . And on us, their intransigent daughters, who wished to be poets, actresses, dancers, doctors—anything but merely teachers and wives—they looked with antagonism, secret pride, or dubious assent.

More than ten years later Friedan offered her description of the mothers she and her generation loved but rejected as models. "Did we understand, or only resent, the sadness, the emptiness, that made them hold too fast to us, try to live our lives, run our fathers' lives, spend their days shopping or yearning for things that never seemed to satisfy them, no matter how much money they cost?" Friedan asked. Yet she also recognized the love and the "secret pride" Calisher mentions for the rebellious daughter.[9] Still, most daughters, Friedan further observed, were "so terrified of becoming like their mothers that they could not see themselves at all. They were afraid to grow up." From this fear comes the conformity Friedan attests to as young women adopted "the composite image of the popular girl."[10] Similarly, Calisher's narrator speaks of "a quality in our homes, all of which subscribed to exactly the same ideals of comfort," and of the mothers who were "nursing the sly prescience that marriage would almost certainly do for us, before we had quite done for ourselves." No wonder she describes growing up as learning "to stumble along somehow between truth and compromise, . . . never too sure of what we were or what we believed."

Yet individual growth is still a value worth dying for, as this middle-class narrator who has sacrificed her young hopes still dreams of "old integrities." But individuality is deformity in the 50's, as is evident in "The Woman who was Everybody." This title character sees "each one of them, of US, locked up alone with the felony of his private difference." To expose that difference is to be condemned to life as an outsider, as is Selena in "The Watchers," who is "always watching tentatively, thirstily, on the fringe of other people's happenings." Hester had privately admired this "secretive spinster" aunt who wore corals from Capri, but she learns when Selena is forgotten during the preparations that this lonely outsider is pitied and pitiful. Better for Hester to learn to be like her mother, although she is depressed by the prospect: "Chilled, Hester, watched her [mother] go wondering, as she dressed herself haphazardly, if the hard little correctnesses—the properness that seemed so difficult to acquire—crept in gradually as one grew, or whether, on some unspecified day, one came of age, stepped into the finished, hypocritical shell, and was suddenly grown."

The destructiveness of the Electra complex for women does not rest exclusively in the perpetual dependence on fathers, however. Equally destructive is the corollary, the rejection of mothers. With social and personal attitudes both denigrating maternal heritage, young women saw a surface of conformity and hypocrisy obscuring the individuals who were their mothers. As a result, they dreaded the maturation process which threatened to make them into mothers as well.

SURROGATE FATHERS

Even women who did not cling to their own fathers found other ways of perpetuating dependency. Religion can be more protective than any individual, as Gordon and O'Connor recognize. Gordon may demand perfection from her male characters, as Calisher too tries to recreate the ideal father in the husbands of her women, but only in religion can the ideal be assured. Mary McCarthy too, despite her reputation as a "liberated" woman, reveals her Catholic upbringing as she shifts all responsibility for problems to her males.

Flannery O'Connor shares both the Southern and the Catholic heritage with Gordon. Each has expressed appreciation of the other, and Gordon acknowledges O'Connor as unique among recent writers in her adherence to orthodox theology.[11] There the similarities end. Gordon's traditional view of women dependent on strong fathers is still able to see them as concerned with values and trying to find meaning in life. In O'Connor's fiction, to play on the title of her first collection, a good *woman* is hard to find. O'Connor shares with Calisher the tension toward mothers, but neither in her fiction nor in her life is this tension ever resolved. Her father's death when she was sixteen of the crippling lupus she inherited left her dependent upon her mother, actually in her care for the last thirteen years of her short life. As Theodore Solotaroff comments, "her residence was not a choice but a fate, and judging from the number of well-educated and bitter spinsters and bachelors in her later stories, who for physical and/or psychological reasons live cooped up with their mothers, it was not a fate that she accepted easily."[12]

This tension of unresolved hatred combined with childlike dependency of young people on parents—usually mothers—does govern much of O'Connor's fiction. Gossett, comparing O'Connor with Robert Penn Warren, never finds in her Warren's healthy "accommodation of parent and child"; "the past is alien to Miss O'Connor's young people," she argues. "Because it threatens their being alive in the present, they seek no relationship with it through their elders."[13]

Actually, women of any kind are few and far between in this fiction, except for what Solotaroff calls the "foolish but well-intentioned elderly daughters of the old South"[14] and a few younger, more rebellious daughters. In her two novels, *Wise Blood* (1952) and *The Violent Bear It Away* (1960), only the memory of a preaching child in the latter and the shallow Sabbath Lily in the former have any importance. *Wise Blood* does, however, open with a look at one of the complacent, conservative mothers—Mrs. Wally Bee Hitchcock, who looks at Hazel Motes and notes that "the suit had cost him $11.98. She felt that that placed him and looked at his face again as if she were fortified against it now." Materialism and hypocrisy identify the mother of the 50's (as well as the women negatively portrayed by Catholic writer J. F. Powers).

As far as O'Connor is concerned, the only female heritage seems to be physical survival. As *Wise Blood* teaches, today's values come from Mary Brittle rather than the Virgin Mary:

Light necking is acceptable, but I think your real problem is one of adjustment to the modern world. Perhaps you ought to re-examine your religious values to see if they meet your needs in life. A religious experience can be a beautiful addition to living if you put it in the proper perspective and do not let it warp you.

O'Connor's men are "warped" by their values; her women are either incapable of such faith or, like Sabbath Lily (whose name again recalls Lilith), they have "counted the cost of the Christian choice and [found] it too high."[15] She wants to enjoy the world; as she tells Haze, "I seen you wouldn't never have no fun or let anybody else because you didn't want nothing but Jesus." She leaves him because "she hadn't counted on no honest-to-Jesus blind man." As Stanley Edgar Hyman argues, "if the male characters are all God-intoxicated, the female characters in Flannery O'Connor's fiction are mainly self-intoxicated. Smugness and self-satisfaction, often represented by women, is another important theme."[16]

Only one woman in *A Good Man is Hard to Find* (1955) gains at least momentary stature. This is when the grandmotherly, Southern lady recognizes her murderer, the Misfit, as one of her own children—when she, as O'Connor tells us in "On her Own Work," "does the right thing, she makes the right gesture."[17] She needs the pressure of imminent death to bring out her good qualities: "She would of been a good woman," we are told, "if it had been somebody there to shoot her every minute of her life." Unfortunately, most of these women have no one except their dependent children. That they still manage to survive rather well casts them as O'Connor's villains, which Robert Drake attributes to her "spiritual double standard." These widows and divorcées, he argues, "are apparently as independent of God as they are of sex and marital involvement; it is almost as though they regard *men* as an imperfection or a scandal (like Christ?) that the universe would be better off without."[18]

The parallels between these single Southern ladies usually on Georgia farms with their adolescent or older children and O'Connor's own life are obvious. That she should so violently reject these women seems, Electra-like, a way of reaffirming her acceptance of the male salvation she seeks. It perhaps even justifies her dependence; to grow up is, at least in one sense, to become one's mother, and for O'Connor that seems to be a fate literally worse than death. Death promises eternal life in "her father's house"; life in the hopelessness of the 50's with no chance of independence couldn't compete.

O'Connor's young people identify with the mother only when they perform what in the worst sense might be considered an "adult" act—one devoid of innocence. Sex, for instance, is often seen in these terms. Hyman has mentioned that "when Leora Watts first goes to bed with Hazel Motes, she tickles his chin 'in a motherly way,' calls him 'son,' and calls herself 'Momma.' "[19] Even more importantly, when Joy is in the barn loft with the Bible salesman in "Good Country People," their lovemaking is described as follows:

His breath was clear and sweet like a child's. He mumbled about loving her and about knowing when he first seen her that he loved her, but the mumbling was like the sleepy fretting of a child being put to sleep by his mother. Her mind, throughout this, never stopped or lost itself for a second to her feelings.

Not only is the salesman childlike in Joy's eyes, but her rational control throughout robs the act of innocence. Yet, while sex seems thus identified as a mother's role, the mothers themselves lead sexless lives. In most cases, their men are gone by the time we meet them; as Josephine Hendin observes, the ineffectual male is "a stock personage" while the husband and father, "those potent men," are "as hard to find as Christ."[20] When sex does enter the picture, in fact, it usually brings violence with it. In "Greenleaf," from O'Connor's later collection, *Everything That Rises Must Converge* (1965), Mrs. May has run her farm with "an iron hand" to keep the men under control, including Mr. Greenleaf and his two sons and her own two dependent sons who hate the farm. "I am the only *adult* on this place," she tells them, but she is finally destroyed by the masculinity and violence she thought she could control when she is gored to death by a bull who "buried his head in her lap, like a wild tormented lover."

"Greenleaf" suggests that these Southern ladies survive by denying the violent physical forces in the world and themselves or by keeping them under control. Yet neither denial nor more than temporary control is possible, especially in the modern world, so these ladies must come to recognize their own *hubris*. Mrs. Hopewell cannot protect her daughter from the Bible salesman because she does not suspect the danger; to her he is only a dull, simple boy. Her naive attitude blinds her to the reality of corruption. Thomas's mother in "The Comforts of Home" from the later collection is also a "hope well" as she invites the corrupted Sarah Ham alias Star Drake right into her home, over the protests of her dependent adult son Thomas, who notes "an observable tendency in all her actions. This was, with the best intentions in the world, to make a mockery of virtue, to pursue it with such a mindless intensity that everyone involved was made a fool of and virtue itself became ridiculous." Thomas knows that in today's world the ways of the Southern lady, "being 'nice to everyone,' " no longer work. To invite the "little slut" into their home is to let in corruption and to deprive Thomas of the protection of childhood. Star's presence brings out the father in him—forces him to deal with his masculinity and sexual nature as he should never have to do under his electric blanket and among all the "comforts of home." He is determined to get rid of Star, and when circumstances finally lead him to shoot his father's gun (the Freudian symbolism is clear), he believes that he has succeeded: "Thomas fired. The blast was like a sound meant to bring an end to evil in the world. Thomas heard it as a sound that would shatter the laughter of sluts until all shrieks were stilled and nothing was left to disturb the peace of perfect order."

Instead, Thomas shot his mother, who had "thrown herself forward to protect" Star. She tries to protect Star as she would protect Thomas, identifying the killer and the victim as did the grandmother in "A Good Man is Hard to Find" as her children. Earlier she had even suggested this insight to him: "Thomas, . . . it might be." He had denied it vehemently: "It is not me!" At the end, we see that his mother was right, as "over her body, the killer and the slut were about to collapse into each other's arms."

The mother, wrongly perhaps, has tried to protect them both—to bring Star back to innocence so that Thomas could remain innocent. But the world is too violent for such a reversal; with her death, instead, Thomas must enter the "world of guilt and sorrow." O'Connor gives her most understanding portrait of a mother in this story; the facts don't change, but the mother is seen with new compassion. Because of this, O'Connor's anger toward women is clarified. The mother is attempting a hopeless task when she tries to obliterate the corruption of the world through graciousness and the comforts of home; only through the grace of God can O'Connor posit any hope for today's society.

Perhaps, then, the daughters and sons in this fiction are not so much angry toward women as toward their ineffectuality. Mothers are there to protect them from the world, yet they cannot. To break away completely demands more strength than these young people can muster, because the world outside seems hopelessly corrupt. But to remain dependent demands, as Joy/Hulga tries for in "Good Country People," "someone who has achieved blindness by an act of will and means to keep it." These young women seek the protection others have found; unfortunately, they have been deprived of fathers. A heavenly Father is the only known alternative. In contrast, the women, especially the ineffectual mothers, seem grossly materialistic. They represent, therefore, the "secular grotesques" whose involvement in life robs them of a more significant involvement with the spirit.[21]

O'Connor's presentation of women is very pessimistic, even hostile. The only women who offer any values are the Southern ladies, and their truths have become empty clichés. Deprived of a maternal heritage, the daughters haven't the strength to face the modern corruption; deprived of fathers, they turn to religion, which offers them an eternal purity. While they cannot grow, their dependency offends them so much that they make vicarious and ineffectual attacks on the mothers, as does Mary Grace against Mrs. Turpin in "Revelation," and then retreat back into the world of childhood: "The girl's fingers were gripped like a baby's around her [mother's] thumb." O'Connor, whose "themes are so traditional as to make her fiction seem unique within the context of the 50's,"[22] paints (as does Calisher) a world that is irrevocably corrupt, in which growing up means sharing its corruption. If her metaphors are timeless, her observations are very timely. The alternatives to growth for her women are a hated dependency on mothers or a perpetual but socially sanctioned dependency on a heavenly Father.

McCarthy's women, on the other hand, seek a protective god in the men around them. Few critics have failed to notice the paradox in her writing between the modern woman she seems to represent and the traditions she is unable to discard. Louis Auchincloss even argues that her "female characters enjoy only in the bleakest fashion the liberties of their emancipated era under the gimlet eye of their own hyperactive consciences."[23] Considering the autobiographical nature of much of her writing, John Chamberlain finds it "conservative in the best sense" with "all the traditional virtues" and "fundamentally conservative ideas." While she has denied this conservatism, Chamberlain argues that "she doesn't see herself as clearly as she sees Jane Austen."[24]

McCarthy's conservatism is similar to that of O'Connor in that she, too, is searching for an external framework for her women, a form of dependency which can help them understand themselves and which will take responsibility from them. If her writing suffers, as Norman Podhoretz suggests, from her "fear of appearing ridiculous,"[25] her women suffer from the same fear. Perhaps an understanding of her need for dependency can be found, as it is for O'Connor, in her personal life. Orphaned at six and placed with her grandparents, she had neither a father to keep her a protected child nor a mother to show her what it means to be a woman. "An orphan," she writes in *A Charmed Life* (1955), "was just a figment who was sentimentalized by the whole world, like the heroine of a story book." As her critics have recognized, [26] many of McCarthy's characters take on a similar fairy-tale quality. Margaret Sargent in *The Company She Keeps* (1942) sees herself as "a sound and normal woman who had been spending her life in self-imposed exile, a princess among the trolls," for example. Since there is an unreality about orphans, the McCarthy woman finds it frequently necessary to assert her own existence. That she often does this as an object reveals her insecurity.

Margaret Sargent, McCarthy's earliest heroine, sets the pattern of dependency which will be followed by later women as well. McCarthy describes the book as Margaret's vain search "amid her many identities, for some real identity underlying them all,"[27] but Irvin Stock is more accurate in seeing it as "a development of which the ultimate goal is not to know what she is but to behave as an adult should."[28] There is a definition somewhere; Margaret need only recognize it and accept it. She makes little attempt to do so, however; she is too busy remembering the "right" things to do. She is caught even then between two sets of values—between the modern standards of her intellectual, Bohemian world and the traditional values of feminine stereotypes and Catholic dogma in which she was raised. Margaret seems to identify the former with the flesh and the latter with the spirit, as can be seen in her final prayer: "Do not let them take this away from me. If the flesh must be blind, let the spirit see."

The freedom of modern woman is justifiable in McCarthy's world only if it is accompanied by dislike or guilt. In "The Man in the Brooks Brothers Shirt," when Margaret gives herself to the traveling salesman Breen the second time, she is sacrificing her self, knowing that she does not want him and that her suffering will purify the act: "this was no simple abstention like a meatless Friday or a chaste Sunday; it was the mortification of the flesh achieved through the performance of the act of pleasure." While we might hope to credit this to McCarthy's gift for satire, similar situations throughout her fiction assert her seriousness. Martha Sinnott's decision in *A Charmed Life* to have an abortion because "all her inclinations were the other way" is one such parallel.

Repeatedly, when a McCarthy heroine is faced with making a

decision, she can recognize the moral choice because she doesn't enjoy it. Furthermore, since she has chosen only what she does not want to do, she can blame her decision and its consequences on that external standard to which she is bound. Margaret works very hard to make her choice the one she least likes. When she decides to leave her husband in "Cruel and Barbarous Treatment," for instance, she not only convinces herself of her husband's goodness and of her love for him, but she must also admit her lover's inadequacies and her failing affection for him. More often, however, Margaret avoids making any decisions. In relentless dedication to female passivity, she abdicates all responsibility. She is either merely playing the part that society assigns to her, as she does in moving from being "The Woman with a Secret" to being the potential divorcée and *femme fatale*; or she is the object acted upon, destined to be whatever the other party wants or expects. When Breen invites her to his compartment, for instance, "she did not know (she had never known) how to refuse."

Margaret is passive because she can neither face nor resolve her own feelings; she is too afraid of how others will interpret her actions. Seeming to be an adult, she still wants the freedom from responsibility of a child. Thus, when Breen assures her of the propriety of an open door "in a kind, almost fatherly voice," she can accept his protection, then blame him when he fails to protect her. Most of the men in McCarthy's fiction fail their women this way. Even the boys Margaret had dated as a teenager would "misinterpret" her friendliness: "she had merely been trying to be a good fellow, to show that she was sophisticated and grown up. . . . It had not been *fair*." As an adult, she is still "misunderstood."

Yet Margaret should not be judged too harshly; to be an adult, one needs some idea of the self. Margaret has only other people's ideas; she must see herself through someone else's eyes—usually male eyes—to feel any sense of identity: "What she got from his view of her was a feeling of uniqueness and identity," she finds. "She could feel the power running in her, like a medium on a particularly good night." As a medium, she takes on identities not her own in trying to be all the female stereotypes, because she has no real idea of what it means to be a woman. When men respond to her sexual stereotype by "leaping at her," she is frightened: "art is to be admired, not acted on." The closest Margaret comes to womanhood is a portrait composed of all she has been told about women. Truly a literary creation, like a fairy princess, she can scarcely define womanhood for others. Devoid of inner reality, Margaret dreams of herself as the perpetual victim, giving herself to the Nazi she detests, her only spiritual victory in her knowledge that she does not enjoy the evil she is committing. Such a rationalization would not even satisfy Martha Sinnott in *A Charmed Life*, whose theory is that "people, whatever they said, did in the end what they wanted."

That Margaret is seeking a god—in the right man—to take responsibilities off her shoulders is obvious. "She would never have left one man unless she had had another to take his place," she admits when the threat of spinsterhood momentarily terrifies her. She must respond to every man who notices her in case he may be her savior; thus, when she first sees Breen, although "full of contempt for the man, . . . she nevertheless allowed her voice to rise a little in response to him." She always follows through with the "game" even when she knows from the beginning that nothing will come of it, as she does in "The Genial Host": "You would go to bed with him finally, but it would not last long, because you had both been compromised at this dinner party, and you had both understood this and understood each other."

Margaret shows in "Ghostly Father, I Confess," that she is herself aware how little realism she had used in her selections (rather, her inevitable capitulations for which she is scarcely responsible): "this one was too selfish, that one too lazy, the other too pliant to permit her being herself, though actually it was these very qualities that she had relied upon for protection." Protection is the key word; Margaret wants to be protected from herself. As long as men "fail" her, she can blame them for any inadequacies. The man to "save" her will be a father, offering her the permanent protection she seeks. Until then, as Stock observes, "all will *not* be well, that unable to love herself except through the love of men, she will again seek a new love to rescue her from past failures and will again snatch at it blindly and perhaps unscrupulously."[29]

Cast A Cold Eye (1950) reintroduces the McCarthy heroine as she burrows her way through "The Weeds." The wife in this story is still married to her Nazi-like husband, who dares to tell her that "you use your wonderful scruples as an excuse for acting like a

bitch" and allows her complete abdication of responsibility because
"the dictator is also the scapegoat; in assuming absolute authority,
he assumes absolute guilt." When the wife does leave, she learns
quickly why she had endured his authoritarianism as she discovers
that "she had exchanged the prison of the oppressed for the prison
of the self, and from this prison there was not even the hope of
escape." By the sixth day, she knows that "if he were to summon,
she would obey. With the dissolution of her belief in herself, her
case against him had collapsed." With no new man lined up to save
her as Margaret had, the wife in "The Weeds" is ready to be "forced"
home. Small wonder that when her husband does so he treats her
like "a truant child."

Stock kindly interprets this story as a view of "the marriage that
destroys the individual's integrity, his troublesome loyalty to the
truth of his own nature,"[30] and Barbara McKenzie feels that it is a
"bleak story precisely because in it honesty and hypocrisy triumph
over sincerity and truth."[31] Both ignore the actions underlying the
interpretations put forth by the wife. Actually the husband repeatedly tries to communicate with his wife—to interest her in her
garden, to bring her flowers, even to profess love for her flowers
with "tears in his voice." She seems indifferent to everything as
she pouts, then throws a tantrum when he suggests hiring help to
restore her garden. Her one kind action, to tighten her clasp on his
hand and agree to his remark, is seen by her as an abdication of
integrity. Believing her own "authorized version" of his actions
and emotions, she feels that she has failed her "flowers, facts, truth"
and has "let him put them into his authorized version." The details
convince this reader, however, that the happily dependent, dominated little girl has once again done what she did not like—has
martyred herself—so that she does not have to decide what she
really wants to do or to be.

The saga of the frustrated female is continued in *A Charmed Life*
without a break, as Martha Sinnott tells Dolly that "he claims to
know what I am, to interpret me according to his authorized version" when speaking of her ex-husband, Miles Murphy. Having
found a savior in John Sinnott, Martha has left the boorish Miles,
but now chooses to return to New Leeds where she had lived with
Miles. Our first picture of her is once more reminiscent of the fairy-
tale princess: "Martha [was] sewing tranquilly, like some Protestant

pastor's wife in an old tale, her mother's gold thimble on her finger. And like the wife sewing in the fairy tale, Martha was wishing for a child." Later, after Martha visits Miles and as a result suspects she is pregnant, she slips right back into the fairy tale—this time moving from Snow White to Beauty and the Beast. She and John had considered Miles as "the Other; that was how they had construed him together, studying his traits with wonder, as if in some old Book of Monsters. And for her to have lain with him, breeding, was a sort of hideous perversion, like sleeping with your wicked uncle."

Martha's comments on her first marriage present the passive girl, a victim of the power of the male. She tells us that "with Miles she had steadily done what she hated, starting from the moment she married him, violently against her will." Just out of college, not yet twenty-one (although the veteran of an engagement and "a rather squalid abortion" already), Martha portrays herself as an easy victim, sleeping with Miles the night they met "against her natural inclinations." When she is freed of this tyrannical monster and remarried to a man who loves her, however, she is bothered that this lovable savior has "deprived her of an opportunity, an opportunity of loving against the grain."

Apparently, Martha can only assert herself by returning to a man who represses her and by destroying the child she carries. In both cases, Martha is literally acting like a child. Her abortion is not a moral choice, although she presents it as one. Her desire to have a baby had been a childish rebellion against Miles's new marriage: "They have a baby. I want a better one. I never thought seriously of having one till we came up here." She describes herself in relation to Miles as "an open-minded child who listens unsuspiciously to what is told him and expects no evil." She had left him for a childish reason as well: "If he had ever taken seriously her passionate desire to leave him, she might not (she now believed) have been driven to show him in practice how little he knew." Even her submission to his current seduction seems childish: "his hunger for her now, when he was so well fixed at home, was a compliment, which she ought to accept lightly."

Miles has again enabled Martha to feel evil so that she can feel good about herself when she makes the grand sacrifice. Deciding to punish herself by having the abortion (one wonders what reasons she gave herself for the first "squalid" abortion), she admires her internal "lawgiver" and is in awe of her own "integrity. In the midst of her squirming and anguish, there was a sensation of pleased surprise."

McCarthy's women do not grow as individuals because they do not accept responsibility for their own actions. In a perverse, even masochistic way, they seek dictatorial men and submit to a vague standard of values which seem to be measured by the pain or unattractiveness of the moral act. Jackson has already shown us the need for integrating the personality in order to grow; McCarthy shows us how to survive with the divided self. Martha can admire her "lawgiver"; she can pose as a fairy princess; she can submit as a victim; she can punish her pliant self. Yet she cannot integrate the parts nor accept responsibility for her own actions.

Conveniently, Martha does not survive; she dies in an automobile accident at the end of the novel. Her fragmented self is resurrected, however, as the cast of *The Group* (1963). If Margaret Sargent had been looking through her many identities for the real one, *The Group* suggests that they were all real and that she should just choose one. The winner, not surprisingly, will be the fairy princess.

The Group, John Chamberlain argues, says "that it is better for a woman to be a woman, but having a good man might help."[32] Yet John W. Aldridge feels that "all of these women are either destroyed by, or forced to give up their identities to, the men with whom they become involved" and that they desire "a return to the lost Eden of Vassar virginity."[33] The only "really happy and successful women in *The Group* are unmarried women," he contends, especially "Lakey, the most beautiful, most intelligent, most intact of them all, and Lakey is a lesbian."[34]

Although Lakey, as Aldridge suggests, may share with Polly Andrews the distinction of being another fairy princess, McCarthy doesn't see her lesbian lover Maria as a suitable Prince Charming: "On the one hand, there was Lakey-and-Maria, as you might say Polly-and-Jim, a contented married pair; on the other, there was an exquisite captive of a fierce robber woman, locked up in a Castle Perilous, and woe to the knight who came to release her from the enchantment." The beautiful Rapunzel is incarcerated with a witch and must still be saved. Polly is the true heroine, the Cinderella of

our time. Stock has commented on her relation to McCarthy's own
history:

> Polly seems, in fact, to be an audacious embodiment of a McCarthy day-
> dream, the author's "ideal," the sort of person the little daughter of her
> gay invalid father and beautiful mother might have become if her hair
> were long and golden, if her parents had lived, and if her happy childhood
> had fulfilled itself, after the inevitable fairy tale trials, in a properly happy
> ending.[35]

Polly is immediately set off from the others as the "girl [who]
had to accept a scholarship to finish college, and nobody thought
the worse of her for it." Her father is a manic depressive; yet "they
were the *gayest* family to visit." Polly is trustworthy: she refuses a
date and goes home to keep "a silly promise she made." She is
domestic, making "pomander balls for Christmas presents" (Martha Sinnott too had a drawerful of pomander balls which she had
made and the insensitive Miles had failed to appreciate). Finally,
Polly is compassionate: "her heart hastened to the losers of any
battle, and she loved small sects with quaint doctrines."
    Polly's affair with Gus, a separated husband, seems to have oc-
curred because of her female passivity: "The die was cast, for,
having let him love her, she loved him." In reality, however, she
is "waiting for the right man": "If she made it difficult for him to
find her, that was part of the test he had to pass." Even her first
lover had seen her as "a girl in a story book—a fairy tale. A girl
with long fair hair who lives in a special room surrounded by kindly
dwarfs."[36] When she finally meets her Prince Charming, Dr. Jim
Ridgely, he announces his love for her after he learns that she has
sold her blood to have Christmas money for her invalid father,
who is now living with her. "Maybe I feel strongly because I'm
falling in love with you," he says, and with most of her readers,
Polly "wished he could have said something different; he sounded
like the hero of a woman's magazine story." It must have been one
of those typical 50's magazines that Friedan had mentioned; the
dreamworld which McCarthy offers Polly could scarcely exist outside of their pages.
    When Polly decides to accept Jim, she gains the godlike protector

and even retains the lost, invalid father. Jim suggests that her father live with them: "To tell the truth, Polly, I think most of our patients would be better off at home. The Victorian system was better, with mad Auntie upstairs. More human." Polly Andrews (or Pollyanna) will live happily ever after, no doubt.

Most of McCarthy's women, however, never succeed in overcoming the tensions which keep them from self-knowledge. Deprived of family tradition (as McCarthy herself was deprived of her parents), they are torn between their desires for the security and dependence they had never known and the independence and freedom promised by the modern world. When they discover the demands and loneliness of freedom, they retreat. Fairy tales, stereotypes, and dogmatic morality seem to promise protection and clarity—but not growth. Finally, they can blame men for their unhappiness, because tradition assures them that the "right" man— Prince Charming, the gentleman hero, or a god with an "authorized version"—would make their dreamworld real and offer them eternal happiness.

DAYLIGHT DREAMERS

If women had no father, heavenly or otherwise, to protect them from the bleak realities of post–World War II America, they turned to other forms of withdrawal and escape. We have already discussed the dreamworlds of Jackson's women; others worth examining are found in the fiction of J. D. Salinger, of Carson McCullers, and of Ann Petry.

For Salinger, neither women nor men have much chance to develop as individuals in a world in which the "nice" people are misfits and "phoniness" is the necessary path to survival. Unlike Bellow and Mailer, Salinger does not blame women for society's ills; he merely presents no hope for anyone in the modern world. The result of such pessimism, as James E. Miller, Jr. points out, is still accommodation, if not alienation.[37] Salinger illustrates both why women chose to escape into the feminine mystique and why so many of them suffered from what Friedan has called "the problem that has no name."[38]

Many of Salinger's women conform, as has been pointed out by his critics. Muriel Glass, Seymour's wife in "A Perfect Day for

Bananafish" in *Nine Stories* (1953), as Mary Ellman argues, is an indifferent idiot wife who "does her nails and talks to her mother on the telephone from Florida, while Seymour is out on the beach talking to a child (but of course) and advancing through deep, sad, secret thoughts to his suicide."[39] Again, the narrator of "For Esme—With Love and Squalor," as Donald Barr contends, lives "in the humorous world of the American Matriarchy, the world of Dagwood and Jiggs, the world of generous impractical husbands with strong sensible wives and grim mothers-in-law."[40] Yet just as many of his males are blatantly stereotyped as well, such as the husband in *Raise High the Roof Beam, Carpenters* (1963), a first lieutenant in the signal corps who wears "a very interesting Air Corps pilot's cap—a visored hat with the metal frame removed from inside the crown, which usually conferred on the wearer a certain, presumably desired, intrepid look." And no one is more stereotyped than Lane Coutell, Franny's boyfriend in *Franny and Zooey* (first published separately in *The New Yorker* in 1955 and 1957). To fit into society, these characters lose individuality, male or female. Some people might fit the mold more easily than others is all.

Salinger is more concerned with those who struggle against such conformity, however. These are the misfits, as Zooey tells Franny: "We're the Tattooed Lady, and we're never going to have a minute's peace, the rest of our lives, till everybody else is tattooed, too." This individual struggle, however, ends as Seymour Glass ends—in suicide and sainthood. The inevitable disillusioning truth of Salinger's world is that to survive one must accommodate oneself to a squalid world. Franny must pass through the same soul-sickness as does Holden Caulfield in *The Catcher in the Rye* (1951). But the spiritual rather than the physical determines the self; as Buddy tells Zooey about meeting a little girl who had two boyfriends, Bobby and Dorothy: "all legitimate religious study *must* lead to unlearning the differences, the illusory differences, between boys and girls, animals and stones, night and day, heat and cold."

Salinger's pessimism encourages his characters to hold fast to the remnants of childhood, with its possible innocence and honesty; indirectly this begins to break down the sexual barriers which had entrapped women for so long. Many young people identified with Salinger's adolescents, especially with Holden Caulfield, because the "adult" world is not always attractive, is never innocent, and always alters us to some degree. Similarly, Eloise in "Uncle Wiggly in Connecticut" has become a bitch through her compromises with life and remembers nostalgically when she was a "nice" girl. Salinger tells us that one cannot live in the world without being compromised. He recognizes that we must either mature or die, but he does not approve, and many young people shared that disapproval.

Consequently, Salinger's characters, like those of Jackson's fiction of the 50's, withdraw into illusory alternatives whenever possible. Holden withdraws in *The Catcher in the Rye*, although he recognizes a need to return and to compromise. Other characters try to hold onto the world of the imagination as long as possible. That this "nice" world of the imagination and of spiritual, or irrational, values is preferable to the "phony" world around us is evident, which echoes Natalie Waite's insight in Jackson's *Hangsaman* that her maternal heritage was worth preserving. Particularly in "Elaine," an early story, Salinger illustrates how much better an illusory world often provides the needs of women. The "extremely beautiful moron" Elaine somehow manages to marry a young usher named Teddy. Before the marriage can be consummated, however, Elaine's mother intervenes and takes her instead to a "nice" movie starring Henry Fonda. As Warren French observes, "the girl's mother does not whisk her 'home,' but out of the arms of her flesh-and-blood husband into the temple of a two-dimensional god who will never violate her."[41]

In fact, such a strong preference for the illusory over the real world as is shown in this fiction goes far beyond Jackson's loyalty to the imagination. Her women choose illusions only because they cannot achieve or have not been offered a chance at real life; even then their choice, unless temporary for a break from the constant pressure of identity, is shown to be destructive, leading to isolation or even death. Salinger, on the other hand, commits himself to the illusions of childhood out of fear and a pessimistic attitude toward the cost of growing up. That he admits to the same fears the women discover is one more attack on the artificial boundaries between the sexes. If he is any indication of a shift in male attitudes, the 50's are indeed a period of strategic retreat. As his men find themselves facing the same problems as do their sisters (as Zooey and Franny realize), they find themselves "unlearning the differences." Neither sex is satisfied with the transparently hypocritical society of their decade. Although both seek an escape from the seeming inevitability of compromise, that escape route leads them into the world of the irrational, of illusion, of death.

Ann Petry recognizes the same attraction of illusion in her second novel, *Country Place* (1947). However, she does not credit the illusion with being "nice," as does Salinger. Rather, she sees it as seducing women from life. Set in a small Connecticut town in which, as David Littlejohn mentions, "the cast . . . is almost entirely white,"[42] *Country Place* explores the illusions into which women escape—illusions which prove as harmful to small-town whites as the impossible promises of middle-class America did to Lutie in Harlem.

Not only does Petry choose a white cast but she also appoints a male narrator, perhaps to penetrate the bias of male and female as well as black and white in the reader. The narrator doesn't even like women; he considers his female cat "more primitive than a male cat": "Like most females, she makes no effort to control her emotions." Yet the animal nature of the men does not escape him, either—especially when they are around women: "Ed at that moment was like a tomcat walking stiff-legged toward a female— ready, waiting, hungry."

Still, the novel is about two women, a mother and a daughter. Glory is married to Johnnie Roane, who is just coming home from the war, and she has been living with his mother while he was gone. Her mother Lil is married to Mearns Gramby, the richest man in town, who married her when he was nearly fifty and took her to live with his mother. Both mother and daughter are unfaithful with the same man—Ed Barrell, the town rake. In *Barbary Shore*, Mailer had intended to write a novel about the effects of the war on the women back home; in *Country Place*, Petry achieves that purpose. She not only demonstrates the collapse of tradition but also shows what society had become; Lil and Glory are the products of their narrow-minded small town just as much as Lutie is a product of Harlem. However, they lack Lutie's underlying integrity.

Johnnie comes home eager to see his young wife Glory and through her to forget what he has been through. Glory plays the part in her flimsy "Victory" nightgown, "designed by someone who had never been to war, but who knew that wars were won and lost in the bedrooms." But Glory is not ready to resume her wifely role. "Women aren't made the same as men," she tells Johnnie. "They don't enjoy sexual intercourse."

The stereotype is only an excuse, of course. Freedom from the structure of a marriage has brought out the worst in the unstructured Glory: "Instead of a sharp demarcation between right and wrong, Gloria and her generation had found only the vague blur made by erasures—it was all that remained of a moral code after the impact of two world wars." Glory's beauty is a further handicap, as was Lutie's, who was seen as "too good-looking to be decent." Her mother Lil (another echo of Lilith which is also the name Petry gave the mistress of Lutie's father in *The Street*) offers her no protection; rather she dismisses Glory as soon as she marries, eager to "put my mind on myself."

Lacking external supports and remembering the popularity her beauty had brought her in high school, Glory would quarrel with Johnnie "just to break the monotony of their existence." While he is overseas, she feels "free for the first time in her life" and decides that she will not resume "a life of cooking and cleaning in that small frame house of theirs. . . . She was the prettiest girl for miles around and all the men who came in the store paid homage to her." Never would she become a dowdy wife like the customers she serves, she further decides, imagining herself forced to economize to support several children while Johnnie comes to ignore her, sitting "sprawled in a chair half-asleep until time to go to bed." This dismal picture is hauntingly accurate, as the narrator confirms when he imagines a similar fate for her, even realizing that the children would be accidents rather than blessings—"born of a moment of careless, lazy passion."

Glory is ready to jump at any escape from her life. In fact, she has been brought up to believe in illusions, for which Johnnie's mother blames the movies: "They make it easy for a girl to believe that somewhere there's a beautiful carefree life if they could just find it." Just so does Glory see the glamour of having an affair with Ed, even up to the time she watches Johnnie fight him after finding Ed and her in a cabin. Watching her, Johnnie recognizes that "he had seen that same expression on her face when they used to go to the movies" and knew that "she had transformed herself into the glossy heroine on the screen." Following the dictates of her experience, Glory makes herself an illusion—a heroine in a life she has transformed into a Grade C movie.

Glory lives in illusions today because she cannot face the realities of tomorrow. Her mother Lil lives the tomorrow of the illusory choice. Having supported Glory and herself by working long hours as a seamstress and knowing that her only alternative would be a "good" marriage, Lil manipulates and plots to win the rich Mearns Gramby and live happily ever after. The marriage comes off; the sequel, however, is disappointing, as they move into his mother's house and he gives Lil money only when she "humbly" requests it, for which he expects "a proper show of gratitude." She does have a mink coat but nowhere to wear it. Soon she too turns for comfort to Ed to offer herself "the undivided attention of a lover" which she "needed and wanted . . . to use as a bulwark against the indifference and the hostility she had found in this house." Of course, Lil has simply found another illusion, as Ed's attention is scarcely undivided. She loses again when Mrs. Gramby dies, because the will—which Mearns had influenced—gives her anticipated inheritance to the servants.

Yet even Mrs. Gramby can admit that, if Lil were "someone else's daughter-in-law," she could understand her need for an affair because "she must have been desperately disillusioned . . . with no place of her own in another woman's house." Revealing the sordidness of postwar America, the inequities and false illusions of society, and particularly the inadequate choices for women which robbed strong and weak alike of a chance for personal development and integrity, Petry empathizes with the very women others would condemn.

Nor will the picture brighten in *The Narrows* (1953). In this novel Petry brings together whites and blacks in another small New England town to show that the rebel—the black man who dates a white woman—fares even worse than those who give in to the inadequate stereotypes. In this portrayal of a young black man of integrity and stature who is driven to violence and eventually destroyed, Petry continues her empathic portrayal of young Americans, black or white, male or female, to reveal a world in which the people with the most integrity are either destroyed or forced to become an expression of the very society against which they have rebelled.

She shows the weak, regardless of race, misled by illusions and stifled by poverty and other social pressures. Her first concern is for the acceptance and realization of individuality, and her novels protest against the society which would contrive to treat any individual as less than human.[43]

So too has Carson McCullers asserted her dissatisfaction with the loneliness and isolation of our society, as well as with the compromises it demands. In the 50's, McCullers published only one novel, *The Ballad of the Sad Café* (1951); in it she explores the illusions of love and identity. The love/hate triangle of Miss Amelia, Cousin Lymon, and Marvin Macy is also a triangle of the shattered personality.

The novel has received widely differing evaluations by critics, ranging from French's charge that it is a "thin follow-up" to her earlier work[44] to Oliver Evans's claim that "had she written nothing except *The Ballad of the Sad Café* her position among the half dozen or so who comprise the highest echelon of living American authors would still be unassailable."[45] McCullers offers her own view in "The Flowering Dream: Notes on Writing":

The passionate individual love—the old Tristan-Isolde love, the Eros love— is inferior to the love of God, to fellowship, to the love of Agape—the Greek god of the feast, the God of brotherly love—and of man. This is what I tried to show in *The Ballad of the Sad Café* and in the strange love of Miss Amelia for the little hunchback, Cousin Lymon.[46]

To accomplish this, McCullers frames the frustrations of the love triangle with the warm fellowship of the café and even of a chain gang. Without the café, the town is "lonesome, sad, and like a place that is far off and estranged from all other places in the world," much like the isolated dreamworlds of Jackson's women. While it is open and flourishing under the overflow of Miss Amelia's love for Cousin Lymon, however, the café brings "fellowship, the satisfactions of the belly, and a certain gaiety and grace of behavior." After it closes with the departure of that love, the only fellowship to be found is the chain gang, where music rises from "just twelve mortal men who are together," while Miss Amelia is once more boarded up within her isolation, as is the town itself.

Although McCullers provides us with a key to the surface of her story, more insight can be gained by placing it among contemporary novels. With Edna Earle in Welty's *The Ponder Heart*, McCullers too seems to have experienced a "failure of nerve" and to have chosen "company" as the one thing "better to have than love." Even the enforced communal acceptance of prison life seems preferable to the isolation and vulnerability of the alternatives she envisions.

Yet even the love of Agape seems to be dependent on Eros. If the individual love is often illusory, as it is for this mismatched trio, it still stimulates the growth of the self as John Singer had stimulated growth in those who sought his support in *The Heart is a Lonely Hunter*. Marvin Macy reforms himself completely during the two years he loves Miss Amelia secretly. Miss Amelia herself not only blossoms personally but also opens the café, creating an atmosphere of love in which the brotherly fellowship inherent in others could thrive and express itself, while she is in love with Cousin Lymon. Although McCullers's conclusion may idealize even inadvertent fellowship within society's prisons, the story has shown the need for individual commitment to provide the environment in which true brotherhood can thrive.

Choosing the semblance of brotherly love over the frustrations and contradictions inherent in the passionate commitment of personal love, however, McCullers echoes Salinger's insight into "unlearning the differences, the illusory differences," between people and things. An even closer parallel to Salinger can be found in her short story, "A Tree, A Rock, A Cloud." The old narrator in this story tries to convince others that human love should not be faced before one has first learned to love "a tree, a rock, a cloud." The old man has learned through experience that loving a woman, the love of self-realization and maturation, is starting "at the wrong end of love. They begin at the climax. Can you wonder it is so miserable?" Yet, as Mark Schorer has noted, "that the lesson is not communicated is of the essence. That the old man wanders out alone into the dawn of a loveless world is no less so."[47]

Although she chooses to retreat to whatever artificial protection society can offer in *The Ballad of the Sad Café*, McCullers does examine the struggle between love and identity within her three misfits. In each pair, the incomplete individual seeks its complement. In Miss Amelia, Marvin finds the family heritage and privacy he has missed as "one of seven unwanted children whose parents could hardly be called parents at all; these parents were wild young-uns who liked to fish and roam around the swamp." Miss Amelia is an only child who has inherited everything from her father. That she and Marvin together could make one person might be symbolized in their descriptions. They are only an inch different in height and "in weight they were about even—both of them weighing close to a hundred and sixty pounds." Like Molly in Stafford's *The Mountain Lion*, Miss Amelia is rugged; the same features earn Marvin the title of "the handsomest man in this region." Miss Amelia also likes men's clothing, which accentuates her masculine appearance. So it is that she falls in love with the weakling hunchback Cousin Lymon, who embodies her lost and deformed femininity. Grotesquely, he fits the stereotypes by being small, dependent, and emotional. He even elicits her "feminine" side by letting her care for him as if he were a child ("she spoiled him to a point beyond reason") and by bringing out her nurturing talents at the café.

Finally, in the handsome, adventurous Marvin Macy, Cousin Lymon finds the ideal masculine appearance which has been denied him. Trapped in his dwarfed, weak hunchbacked body, he could not help loving this handsome, tall, curly-haired man. The love each has for the other in this triangle is a reflection of self-hate, a failure to accept those deforming private differences that, as Calisher has suggested, appear in some form in each of us and constitute our individuality. That these differences should be seen as grotesque is another indication of McCullers's retreat; that love should be the attempt to gain for one's self the beloved characteristics of another underlies her definition of the lover and the beloved:

Almost everyone wants to be the lover. And the curt truth is that, in a deep secret way, the state of being beloved is intolerable to many. The beloved fears and hates the lover, and with the best of reasons. *For the lover is forever trying to strip bare his beloved.* The lover craves any possible relation with the beloved, even if this experience can cause him only pain. [my italics]

McCullers recognizes the destructiveness of such love, love which seeks to complete the self by "strip[ping] bare his beloved." In rejecting such self-negating and demanding love, she clears the way for a different view, which she feels can only be Agape. Other writers, however, will suggest other alternatives, finding love as an affirmation of life and the self from which both society and the individual can benefit as does McCullers's society from the atmosphere of the café before it becomes sad. Their answer will lie in the acceptance rather than in the attempted resolution of our differences. Only death resolves all differences, and the denial of self is a death-in-life, even when our chains keep us upright.

To be capable of such love, to "unlearn the differences," we might do well to start with appreciation of "a tree, a rock, a cloud." We must also learn to accept our private differences within the self as good. For Salinger, the "phony" accommodations we make to survive eliminate even the potential for individual development, however. For Petry, the individual is misled by illusions: ambitious blacks like Lutie are seduced by unattainable promises and are destroyed by inescapable realities, while dreamers like Lil and Glory turn their backs on the dismal realities of their lives to seek temporary escapes in affairs or at the movies. Even their highest goals seem to be those fed them by their society.

For McCullers, neither society nor the self is intact. *The Ballad of the Sad Café* is much more pessimistic than were her studies of the external limitations placed on Mick and Frankie as they grew up female in America. These three seekers—Miss Amelia, Marvin Macy, and Cousin Lymon—are incomplete within themselves. Rather than giving up what they have, they seek in others what they feel they lack and call it love. No wonder McCullers presents such love as a victimization of the beloved. Still, it is only through love—through the external support systems that Mick finds temporarily in John Singer and that Frankie envisions as a member of her brother's wedding—that the individual learns to recognize internal potential. Miss Amelia really is a more complete person when she loves Cousin Lymon, for instance, and the "feminine" traits she reveals are hers, not his. Not only is she more alive in the relationship but also she gives life to the community as her café offers the opportunity for brotherly love relegated only to the chain gang later.

Although McCullers seems to be praising Agape, the heroic act in her novel is to love on an individual basis. This facilitates the full realization of one's own potential which then overflows into the community as well. The enforced brotherhood of the chain gang by comparison is simply a naturalistic attempt at survival, comparable to the response of the four survivors of a shipwreck in Stephen Crane's nineteenth-century tale "The Open Boat." Pitted against the overpowering forces of nature and/or society, individuals find they have only each other to give value to life.

Accepting differences within the self is difficult at best in the literature of this decade when the prevailing attitude is one of conformity and the individual who resists is "maladjusted," a "misfit," even "grotesque." Social values and illusory escapes only distract these individuals from self-realization. Only love offers support—and, as McCullers fears, love also leaves us vulnerable. Yet such vulnerability is a commitment to life, while the final escape is death.

THE BRICK THROWERS

A few writers of the 50's, while equally aware of the repercussions of two world wars on America, yet present women who are ready to meet the challenges of identity and the violence of maturation. That these women seldom succeed seems almost inevitable in the social context; that they sometimes do succeed, even temporarily, indicates the direction of the next decade. Furthermore, that some of these women are the creations of male writers shows a breakdown of sexual stereotyping that promises growth as well. Therefore, the women in the fiction of Bernard Malamud, James Baldwin, Shirley Ann Grau and Gwendolyn Brooks may provide the transition necessary to understand the extensive changes which are about to occur in American life and literature.

Norman Mailer asserts that the 50's were a time of "that national conformity which smothered creativity, for it delayed the self-creation of the race,"[48] and many of the writers we have discussed reflect this suppression. A world of conformity which demands accommodation rather than growth does not encourage its women to abandon the dependent roles into which they have been tucked away previously; in fact, the men seem to join the women in passivity and rejection of "a world [they] never made." The question which must be asked eventually is who then did make the world what it is? To divorce oneself from the guilts of the past and realities of the present is also to block oneself from changing the possibilities of the future. The women in the fiction of Bernard Malamud demand new values as well as new lives. Although their world is still bleak and compromising, they sometimes provide new directions as well as new burdens for themselves and for their men.

Malamud seems to agree with Bellow and Mailer that a woman is often a burden and a responsibility, but he adds that a good woman can also ennoble her man. His discouraging pictures of the difficulties of human relationships within the context of the economical and social pressures on the individual are reminiscent of some of Calisher's early short stories, such as "In Greenwich There are Many Gravelled Walks," in which the couple seem to get together because "misery loves company." Yet Malamud repeatedly creates women who choose to commit to relationships, not out of dependency but out of an effort to improve the world and themselves. *The Natural* (1952) is a symbolic novel, as critics have noted, with the story of a baseball hero paralleling the medieval Grail legend,[49] but even the presence of that mythic quest underlying the novel emphasizes that Malamud's characters are searchers, are setting forth as do Welty's searchers on quests for identity. While the hero lacks the strengths of his medieval model, he does learn a few lessons along the way—some of these from the "good" woman of the novel, Iris. Iris sets the pattern for Malamud's "good" women in fact: she has earned her goodness through suffering. As a teenager she had been seduced in the park by a stranger and left to raise a daughter alone. The first lesson she tries to pass on to the hero is that, in William Freedman's words, "what we need now are the right goals, 'the right things' which suffering teaches us to want, possible, non-destructive things like love and service and self-sacrifice. The price is discipline, self-control, the capacity for renunciation."[50] Self-sacrifice is not a new role for women; however, Iris is more committed to the quest and to integrity than is the hero himself. She willingly stands up publicly to show her faith in him, "because I hate to see a hero fall. There are so few of them." She gives herself to him willingly, and only his inadequacies leave her, as Theodore Solotaroff points out, "at the end almost exactly where she started—seduced by another stranger in the park, made pregnant, and probably abandoned."[51]

Malamud's men often fail his women. Sometimes they simply

have too many odds to overcome, as does Morris Bober in *The Assistant* (1957), who "had hoped for much in America and got little. And because of him Helen and Ida had less. He had defrauded them, he and the blood-sucking store." Other times they fail because they don't accept their roles of suffering—they don't acknowledge that they too are Jews. The Jew in Malamud's fiction is a symbol; as Ihab Hassan observes, he is merely "a suffering man with a good heart, one who reconciles himself to agony . . . for the sake of the Law—the Hebraic ideal of virtue."[52] To succeed, a hero must willingly take on suffering, as does the shoemaker's assistant in "The First Seven Years" in *The Magic Barrel* (1958) who works for seven years for the right to ask the shoemaker's daughter Mirriam to marry him; as does Frank Alpine in *The Assistant*, who takes over Bober's store and his burdens.

If there must be victims in the world, is it virtuous to *choose* to be one? Malamud's men say yes; his women say no. Sometimes the women become victims, but they never choose to be. They do not want to be Christ, nor do they demand that someone else be Christ for them. In *The Assistant*, Helen Bober accepts Frank's aid, although she is not likely to marry him and nail herself to his cross. Nor is she simply materialistic; Louis, another suitor, is also refused when he offers her better *things*: "But what if she wanted to make herself a better person, have bigger ideas, live a more worthwhile life? We die so quickly, so helplessly. Life *has* to have some meaning," she explains to Louis. "I want a larger and better life. I want the return of my possibilities." Sensitive and compassionate, Helen recognizes Frank's good qualities even after he confesses to his bad ones. She does not approve of her father's self-victimizations either:

He was no saint; he was in a way weak; his only true strength lay in his sweet nature and his understanding. He knew, at least, what was good. . . . People liked him, but who can admire a man passing his life in such a store? He buried himself in it; he didn't have the imagination to know what he was missing. He made himself a victim. He could, with a little more courage, have been more than he was.

Similarly, while *Idiots First* (1963) refers by its title to the old adage "women and children first," in doing so it ironically points out that these "idiots" are willing to take advantage of the chivalry of their male saviors in order to have a better chance at survival. Yet Malamud's women do not victimize the men; the men choose that victimization. Even Sy Levin, who crosses the country to seek a new life in *A New Life* (1961), only chooses to marry Pauline Gilley after he decides that he no longer wants to. Women neither choose to suffer nor to sacrifice their values; with Helen they strive for better lives through action rather than sacrifice. Nobody wins very much in Malamud's fiction, but his women do try.

If we are to believe David Noble, however, James Baldwin does blame women for the frustration of his men. "Baldwin's dream of national redemption by the crusading phalanx of Negro or white Negro saints," he argues, "would seem to be destroyed by the same unredeemable factor which frustrated Mailer's hope of social salvation—women." The problem, Noble continues, is that "women refuse to surrender their separate identities and reach perfect communion with the saints."[53] Actually, however much Baldwin may share with Mailer in other ways, his women are infinitely more real than those in Mailer's fiction. Baldwin presents women, both black and white, as the only humans strong enough to exist in the world of contemporary American corruption and still to maintain some values. None of his men can accept commitments; they escape, they turn to their unthreatening childhood source of love from a brother, or they stay and fail their women and themselves through compromise and despair. The women, on the other hand, suffer but survive; their strength is seldom rewarded with much beyond endurance. Black men, Baldwin concedes, do have some excuse for their failure: American life and white supremacy have combined to rob them of any chance for victory. The narrator of "This Morning, This Evening, So Soon" in *Going to Meet the Man* (1965) acknowledges the differences once he leaves America and is in Paris where, "for the first time in my life I felt that no force jeopardized my right, my power, to possess and to protect a woman, for the first time, the first time, felt that the woman was not, in her own eyes or in the eyes of the world, degraded by my presence." Small wonder that the black hero is tempted to leave America as he does in *Giovanni's Room* (1956); but, as Leo Proudhammer realizes in *Tell Me How Long the Train's Been Gone* (1968), "I was part of these people. No matter how bitterly I judged them, I would never be able to leave this country. I could only leave it briefly, like a drowning man coming up for air. I had the choice of perishing with these doomed people, or of fleeing them, denying them, and in that effort, perishing."

Baldwin's world is like that of Petry in *The Street*, in which black and white alike must sacrifice values and conform, but where blacks must sacrifice hope as well. His men, though they seek the protective love of a brother or a mother, can only return to a childhood devoid of innocence, an innocence of which blacks are deprived from birth. As Ida tells Cass in *Another Country* (1962), as she envisions the arrival of a man worth loving: "And no matter when he arrived would be too late—because too much had happened by the time you were born, let alone by the time you met each other." Yet even in this world Baldwin's women dare to love; with Hella in *Giovanni's Room*, they realize "that I wasn't free, that I couldn't be free until I was attached—no, *committed*—to someone." If Hella asks later "if women are supposed to be led by men and there aren't any men to lead them, what happens then?" she also answers her own question—they learn to walk alone.

Often these women lose their men to death, as do Elizabeth and Aunt Florence in *Go Tell It on the Mountain* (1953). "The menfolk, they die, all right," Florence explains. "And it's us women who walk around, like the Bible says, and mourn. The menfolk, they die, and it's over for them, but we women, we have to keep on living and try to forget what they done to us." The women do keep living, and they pay a heavy price for their survival, as Ida explains in *Another Country*: "you've never decided that the whole world was just one big whorehouse and so the only way for you to make it was to decide to be the biggest, coolest, hardest whore around." Still, Ida does not compromise her values—even for love. "I just want you to know that I wouldn't have been with you so long and wouldn't have given you such a hard time, if . . . I didn't love you," she confesses to Vivaldi. "That's why I had to tell you everything I've told you." She is not satisfied with illusions; she offers Vivaldi her complete self and hopes for the best. He admits the difficulty of such honesty: "He thought to himself that he had at last got what he wanted, the truth out of Ida, or the true Ida; and he did not know how he was ever going to live with it."

Baldwin's women refuse to compromise with love, whatever they might do to survive in a corrupt and vicious world. His men may choose homosexuality to avoid such commitments or to become, in one sense at least, women themselves, because they see women as survivors and men as failures. Still, Baldwin doesn't blame his women. Society must accept that blame, while his women are admirable, unhappy, struggling human beings who have the courage to commit themselves in a violent reality.

If within the bleakness of the decade male writers can admire and accept the integrity of their women, women writers should have even more to offer—and they do. Shirley Ann Grau presents women with the strength and self-confidence to challenge the unchallengeable—to throw bricks even at the "hard blue sky." As Petry's narrator in *Country Place* described his female cat as "much closer to the primitive than a male cat," so too have Grau's strong women been called primitives by Louise Gossett. "In Miss Grau's first fiction the Negro is largely another primitive whose violence expresses uninhibited passions and temper,"[54] Gossett says of *The Black Prince and Other Stories* (1955). Other primitives are the bayou Creoles of Louisiana who people her pages.

In contrast to the primitives are the city-bred Southern women. We meet again the surviving version of the Southern lady here, and Grau shows the conflicts produced by the survival of this anachronism in modern society. The other type might be called the "modern woman," if we are referring again to a lost sex as defined by Lundberg and Farnham.

The first three stories of *The Black Prince* deal with Grau's black primitives, who accept violence as part of life. Violence is often, in fact, honest and constructive, an attempt to deal immediately with the problems which confront them. "White Girl, Fine Girl" shows how one woman protects herself from becoming a victim. Aggie's husband Mannie has been murdered by her lover Jayson, who is now returning from prison. Aggie's son by her marriage died from drinking lye, and since then she has had three daughters, one by Jayson and one by his friend Joe. Joe warns the returning Jayson that "Aggie got plain mad" after that. "So she ain't having nothing to do with no men. She don't let anybody come in her house no more. And she got the kids so they don't let their daddies walk down the street. They got to go round the next block or the kids throw rocks at them. And they big enough to hurt." Jayson, however, risks the rocks to reach the house and wreck all he can.

He is less rough with his daughter, Alice Mary, whom he had never seen before, and purposely doesn't hit her with the rock he throws at her to stop her from following him. If a woman needs to protect herself, perhaps a daughter needs to know her father at least. The story is violent but affirmative and humorous as well; all the cast are survivors.

The legendary Alberta in the title story attracts and then follows the virile but satanic Stanley Albert Thompson into the realm of fantasy. But Alberta is no lost dreamer, nor is she left behind as are Welty's worshipping women. She is "a handsome girl, taller than most people in her part of the country, and light brown. . . . She was not graceful—not as a woman is—but light on her feet and supple as a man." This independent young woman will commit to love only on her own terms: she "shook her head, no, she would walk; no man needed to lead her." She even bargains with Stanley: "I don't see as how I could stay though . . . I don't see as how. You ain't give me none of the things you said." She is willing to fight for what she wants; when Willie attacks Thompson, "quietly, smoothly, in a single action, without interrupting her step, Alberta picked up a bottle . . . and swung it against Willie's head." A fitting model for a strong woman, she leaves to wander with her man, loving but equal. We will meet her psychological descendant Margaret in a later novel.

The blacks in "Miss Yellow Eyes" seem somewhat less isolated and more contemporary than those in the other two stories, but Lena, to whom the title refers, retains the primitive strengths. She is very fair, and she and her husband Chris hope to move to Oregon and pass for white. However, Chris is wounded in the war and dies in a field hospital. When her brother Pete, who lost a hand to avoid the draft, taunts her—and himself—with the wisdom of his choice and the hopelessness of her plans, she breaks out of her depression by hitting him. Lena's violence serves no constructive purpose, perhaps, but we have difficulty not approving. As Gossett says, Grau's primitives are "un-complicated, outgoing people whose actions are made violent more by circumstance than by flawed human nature."[55] Lena is a precursor of women who become so frustrated by social restrictions on constructive outlets that their energies are channeled into destruction.

Grau's bayou primitives appear first in "Joshua." In her first novel, *The Hard Blue Sky* (1958), Grau will trace the maturation of a young woman; in "Joshua," "The Way of a Man," and "One Summer" she concentrates on the maturation of boys. "Joshua" gives us only a brief glimpse of a bayou mother as she tries to protect her son from too early an initiation into manhood. The father has decided to send Joshua to "run my [fishing] lines," but the mother refuses to let him go: "You ain't sending that little old boy out where you scared to go." She loses; mothers in this primitive world cannot stop the inevitable maturation of their children any more than they can stop any other act of nature, such as a hurricane. Their nobility lies in their willingness to try. These women share their husbands' labors and have acquired an equality born of knowing that they are not dependent. They speak their minds and never hesitate to fight for what they want.

Grau's more civilized types do not have the same core of self-respect, although they reveal great strength and determination at times—almost always misdirected. The Southern lady is best seen in Mrs. Ramond and her daughter, "The Girl with the Flaxen Hair." Mrs. Ramond is introduced as a daughter as well; she lives on the legends of her father, Senator Winslow, and her carefully selected memories. Rose is a fragile girl who "had a face like a Botticelli angel" and whose hopes for the future were centered around her mother's plans for a dazzling wedding. Even after they are deserted by Mr. Ramond—apparently because he was made to feel too much beneath his "aristocratic" wife—the two continue to live genteelly with no means of support. Rose sneaks out at night to gather coals at the railroad yard for heat, until one night she is killed by a train which had changed its schedule. The two Ramonds are trapped in the mystique of the Southern lady, and the excessive fragility and ultimate destruction of the daughter echo the death throes of the tradition itself.

A more modern mother and daughter are shown in "Fever Flower," but modernity alone is no improvement over the stereotyping of the past. The divorced Katherine Fleming cannot even convince herself that she is concerned about her daughter Maureen. Katherine is not selfishly pursuing a wild life; her idea of happiness is solitude, preferably lying in a hot tub: "She had a perfect body; she was a superb animal. But she was not quite human. She did not need anyone." She has furnished Maureen's room as if the small girl were a teenager, trying to skip the "awkward growing years, the child years" that demand parental responsibility and to push Maureen into the "four or five years of the girl's first beauty." For Katherine these would be the best years they could share, even though she would probably see very little of Maureen and both would "realize that they did not really like each other very much." Like Lil in Petry's *Country Place*, Katherine is eager to be free to live her own life.

Despite rare moments of affection, for her father (remarried and expecting another child) Maureen is a risky investment: "He was spending quite a bit of money on his daughter and he could not quite convince himself that it was worth it." Maureen will pass through three husbands before she too chooses the advantages of solitude in "a beautiful, very expensive apartment for one." Rose Ramond, the Southern belle, may have been a dying blossom; but Maureen, the "fever flower" of her parents' sicknesses, scarcely improves the garden.

The reader turns with relief to the vibrant, primitive island people of *The Hard Blue Sky*. Grau, Gossett feels, "is likely to oversimplify human relationships" in this novel,[56] but what really emerges is the intensification of those relationships, similar to the mythic impact of John Millington Synge's portraits of the Aran Islanders in *Riders to the Sea*. Both writers capture the awareness rather than the innocence of the people: Synge's characters are aware of the violence of life and they accept it; Grau's characters are equally aware of it, but they rebel when the violence is destructive.

Particularly interesting are Grau's portraits of Annie Landry and Cecile Boudreau. Annie is on the verge of womanhood; Cecile is an adult facing the responsibilities and the glories of her life. Although the older women, especially Annie's stepmother Adele and Cecile's mother Philomene, have known more disappointments and are therefore more subdued, they too share the commitment to life and to the present that defines all of Grau's primitives.

Annie, typical of the adolescent in her innocence, is a slow developer compared with her peers, yet unique in much of her knowledge among her literary contemporaries. She is ready to offer her virginity to the young and handsome Perique (who is too drunk at the time to take it), and her innocence is revealed when we learn that she doesn't know if anything has happened or not because she doesn't know what was *supposed* to happen. Annie had lost her mother and then was sent to a convent; at sixteen she is back on the island to attend her father's wedding. There is, of course, much tension between Annie and her stepmother Adele, which helps Annie to mature. Nor does her father try to protect her: when she stays out all night and Adele is worried that "she was with some man, for sure," he merely replies, "My girl, she is not queer, che."

After her "failure" with Perique, Annie turns to Inky, a stranger on the island, and is successful. She doesn't understand her feelings, but she acts on them, which seems to bring her instinctive knowledge of the future:

She didn't want to go back. But she didn't want to forget. She wanted to have Perique tucked away carefully in a corner of her memory.... And again woman-fashion, she recognized that this memory would be a comfort; when things did not go well with Inky: she could conjure up another image and hide behind it.

While Annie now believes she is in love with Inky, she already suspects that "she loved him because there wasn't anybody else." She accepts life as it happens to her—"Things were the way they were. And she was the way she was"—realizing that each experience is both unique and universal. Annie matures as each girl matures; recognizing that the experience of sexual awakening must be shared, she also sees that the universal merely utilizes the particular who happens to be on hand. She still loves Inky, but she identifies as well with the cycle of life itself.

Identifying with the cycle of life is, paradoxically, the first step toward individuality. Cecile Boudreau takes the next step—rebelling against that cycle. Like Annie, Cecile lives in the present. She is like a big sister, listening to Annie's dreams, talking to her about childbirth and cooking, providing the maternal heritage that Annie might have otherwise lost with the death of her mother. Cecile encourages her to grow. When Annie resists "the way things keep changing . . . I hate that most of all," Cecile reminds her that "sometimes they get better." Cecile accepts Annie's ambivalence; at the same time, she prefers life to stagnation:

"I used to worry with things like that," she told the baby. "Then I got married, me, and there wasn't time anymore." Annie had made her vaguely sad. So she tickled the baby's foot and grinned back down at him. "Seems like there's just time for all the business of living and nothing else." She's not doing anything right now, Cecile thought, not even living. When she starts that business, there won't be any time.

Living keeps us from fearing the future. Annie is afraid to grow older, and Philomene claims she is *too* old: "You get heavy sometimes and tired of living." Cecile merely responds to both of them, "Now I plain know you don't mean that." She has survived the violence of maturation and is immersed in the violence and beauty of life. She is at the age which frightens McCullers's women—the age of commitment, passion, involvement. While McCullers presents this time as painful, Grau presents it as vital and affirming. Cecile is not a blithe, mindless housewife trapped and dependent in her roles; she is strong and independent, living a hard life under a hard blue sky. The violence of life alone traps her, and it traps men as well. "It don't matter that we get caught and die, us," she knows. "It don't even matter that we been alive. . . . Damn, damn." But she can rebel against the human condition; she can throw a half-brick at the sky, then turn and run home, "not waiting to see it fall." Even useless action can express our willingness to fight for life. As Gossett says, "These people preserve rather than destroy themselves through violence."[57]

Nor is Cecile intimidated by her husband Hector. When he orders her to leave the island because of hurricane warnings, she flatly refuses. Hector's father had warned him that "No woman ever goes." She even hides the baby so he won't force her to leave. Hector beats her in his frustration; yet he is proud of his able, determined wife: "She'd be inside, making sure that the covers were tight under the furniture, and that the kids were in bed. And then she'd sit down, rocking and waiting. . . . He was grinning when he turned and closed the cabin door behind him."

Next to these vital islanders, almost anyone would seem less alive. In the next decade Grau will treat with equal empathy the women trapped in the towns and cities of the South and in its image of the Southern lady. But not even Chicago can trap the title character of Gwendolyn Brooks's single novel, *Maud Martha* (1953). Poets often penetrate directly to the truths which must evolve slowly through the social context of fiction. As a poet, and as a writer of fiction this time, Brooks reaffirms faith in life and in the individual.

The "writer is dangerous," Hortense Calisher says in "In the Absence of Angels," "because he cannot help celebrating the uncommonness of people." Both Grau and Brooks reveal that the uncommonness emerges most clearly in common actions. Maud Martha embodies this truth. Coming from a loving family and parents who at least own their own home, she is not the favorite daughter; rather, she seems to be the tomboy and the smartest child. Boys—and her father—prefer her prettier sister Helen, who warns Maud Martha to conceal her "unfemale" traits: "You'll never get a boy friend . . . if you don't stop reading those books." But Maud Martha, unlike the insecure adolescents we have met, is not daunted: while she could describe herself, as does Katherine in Stafford's *The Catherine Wheel*, as "untalented and uncompromising," she knows that she has a unique contribution to offer the world:

To create—a role, a poem, picture, music, a rapture in stone: great. But not for her.
What she wanted was to donate to the world a good Maud Martha.
That was the offering, the bit of art, that could not come from any other. She would polish and hone that.

Maud Martha is true to her goal. Not even pretty by the current standards which call for light skin while she is "the color of cocoa straight," Maud Martha knows she is special. While she teases her boyfriend Paul about her lack of beauty, she knows that "I am what he would call—sweet, and I am good, and he will marry me." And she is good—she cannot even kill a mouse once she thinks of its "fine small dignity" and family: "Go home to your children." Similarly, while plucking a chicken she thinks of it as "a sort of person, a respectable individual. With its own kind of dignity." In the chicken she finds a metaphor for the racial tensions she has experienced: "What was unreal to you, you could deal with violently. If chickens were ever to be safe, people would have to live with them, and know them." While society demanded conformity from its members, Maud Martha could see through "the illusory differences" which Salinger had warned us against to admire even the dignity of the chicken.

As a wife, Maud Martha maintains her independence, comparing herself to pioneer women: "strong women, bold; praiseworthy, faithful, stout-minded; with a stout light beating in the eyes. . . . Women who would toil eminently, to improve the lot of their men. Women who cooked. She thought of herself, dying for her man. It was a beautiful thought." It remains only a thought, however, for Maud Martha is a survivor. Still, her passionate commitment to herself and her loved ones motivates her actions. Nor are those actions confined to the mothering and housewife roles that she so clearly enjoys. She is also a creator of tradition through her ability to act and make choices: "She had wanted to found— tradition. She had wanted to shape, for their use, for him, for little Paulette, a set of falterless customs."

Nor does Maud Martha judge others. Accepting their choices, as when her sister Helen marries a doctor much older than herself, she feels no need to justify or condemn the actions of others. Her faith in the individual helps her maintain faith in humanity in this bleak decade: "It was doubtful whether the ridiculousness of man would ever completely succeed in destroying the world," she prophesies as she considers the horrors of her time, and "while people did love they would be grand, would be glorious and brave, would have humble hearts that would beat and beat." The beautiful poem that is Maud Martha reveals our beauty as well.

PROMISES AND COMPROMISES

America in the 50's seemed to promise peace, prosperity, and protection to its tired veterans from the Eastern, the Western, and the Home Fronts. What it delivered, however, were compromises. This discrepancy between the actions and the assertions of an already-suspect society drove both men and women to resignation and withdrawal. While the fiction of the decade reflects this, it also offers a few characters who reject the social pressures which would recast them or cast them away, choosing—violently if necessary— for themselves.

For those resigned to the inevitability of compromise, relationships amount to little more than the company misery loves. Life offers little and delivers less, tempting some to suicide, others to escape. Some try to escape backward into childhood and the protectivity of familial—often fatherly—love. Some try to escape forward, into the protection of a heavenly Father. Most escape inward, into dreamworlds which do keep the promises—or seem to. Every escape leads outward, however—out of life, involvement with others, even the world.

However, just as the fiery war of the 40's was only superficially disguised as the cold war of the 50's, so too were fires burning beneath the icy facade of the feminine mystique. The daughters especially would intuit the discontent of their mothers and add to it their own disillusionment. Soon the growing tension would burst forth in a flood of protests and assertions, revealing that the period of latency was past.

The 50's were in many ways a period of strategic retreat for women. Their dissociation from the surface which their lives were forced to maintain led them inward, a necessary step on the route to self knowledge. It is not enough to know how others would define us; we must discover ourselves. These women further suggest that the emerging self may redefine its world. Understanding the multiple possibilities of the self leads to understanding a similar truth about society. While the artificial brotherhood even of the chain gang seemed preferable to individual isolation and grotesqueness, such a negation of differences in a common oppression would encourage, for instance, Lutie Johnson to accept the Harlem stereotypes simply to share her fate with others. Her heroic attempts to achieve even distorted and inappropriate goals fed to her by the very society which oppresses her is still preferable to her conformity.

These women are survivors; even beyond that, they demand more than the death-in-life offered by their society. Trapped in the boxes that defined their decade—from the feminine mystique to the Brooks Brothers business suit, from tract homes to bomb shelters—Americans began to see them as coffins closing life out rather than containing it safely.

NOTES

1. Betty Friedan, *The Feminine Mystique* (New York: Dell, 1963), 50.
2. Mentioned by R. L. Phillip in "Shirley Jackson: A Chronology and a Supplementary Checklist," *Bibliographical Society of America Papers*, 60:2 (1966), 209.

3. Friedan, *Feminine Mystique*, 47–8.

4. Quoted by eds. Nona Balakian and Charles Simmons in *The Creative Present* (Garden City, NY: Doubleday, 1963), 130.

5. Louise Y. Gossett, *Violence in Recent Southern Fiction* (Durham, NC: Duke University Press, 1965), 124.

6. W. Tasker Witham, *The Adolescent in the American Novel 1920–1960* (New York: Frederick Ungar, 1964), 69.

7. Quoted by Ihab H. Hassan in *Radical Innocence* (Princeton, NJ: Princeton University Press, 1961), 126.

8. William Van O'Connor, *The Grotesque: An American Genre* (Carbondale: Southern Illinois University Press, 1962), 173.

9. Friedan, *Feminine Mystique,* 65.

10. Ibid.

11. O'Connor praises Gordon in "The Nature and Aim of Fiction" in *Mystery and Manners* (New York: Farrar, Straus & Giroux, 1969), 78; Gordon discusses O'Connor in "With a Glitter of Evil," *New York Times Book Review* (June 12, 1955), 5, and "Flannery O'Connor's *Wise Blood*," *Critique*, 2 (Fall 1958), 9.

12. Theodore Solotaroff, *The Red Hot Vacuum* (New York: Atheneum, 1970), 173.

13. Gossett, *Violence*, 83.

14. Solotaroff, *Red Hot*, 176.

15. Robert Drake, *Flannery O'Connor* (New York: William B. Eerdmans, 1966), 20.

16. Stanley Edgar Hyman, *Flannery O'Connor* (Minneapolis: University of Minnesota Press, 1966), 36.

17. O'Connor, *Mystery and Manners*, 112.

18. Drake, *Flannery O'Connor*, 31.

19. Hyman, *Flannery O'Connor*, 33.

20. Josephine Hendin, *The World of Flannery O'Connor* (Bloomington: Indiana University Press, 1970), 12.

21. Thelma J. Shinn, "Flannery O'Connor and the Violence of Grace," *Contemporary Literature*, 9 (Winter 1968), 62–3.

22. Kenneth Krieling, "Flannery O'Connor's Vision: The Violence of Revelation," in *The Fifties: Fiction, Poetry, Drama*, ed. Warren French (Deland, FL: Everett/Edwards, 1970), 111.

23. Louis Auchincloss, *Pioneers and Caretakers* (Minneapolis: University of Minnesota Press, 1961), 173.

24. John Chamberlain, "Mary McCarthy," in *The Creative Present*, 255.

25. Quoted by John W. Aldridge in *The Devil in the Fire* (New York: Harper & Row, 1972), 223.

26. Cf. Aldridge, *Time to Murder and Create* (New York: David McKay

Company, 1966), 95–132; Irvin Stock, *Mary McCarthy* (Minneapolis: University of Minnesota Press, 1968), 42.

27. Stock, *Mary McCarthy*, 14.

28. Ibid.

29. Ibid., 19.

30. Ibid., 20.

31. Barbara McKenzie, *Mary McCarthy* (New York: Twayne, 1966), 97.

32. Chamberlain, "Mary McCarthy," 254.

33. Aldridge, *Time to Murder*, 129, 132.

34. Ibid.

35. Stock, *Mary McCarthy*, 42.

36. Ibid.

37. James E. Miller, Jr., *J. D. Salinger* (Minneapolis: University of Minnesota Press, 1965), 20.

38. Friedan, *Feminine Mystique*, 11–28.

39. Mary Ellman, *Thinking About Women* (New York: Harcourt Brace Jovanovich, 1968), 110.

40. Donald Barr, "Ah, Buddy: Salinger," in *The Creative Present*, 46.

41. Warren French, *J. D. Salinger* (New York: Twayne, 1963), 51–3.

42. David Littlejohn, *Black on White* (New York: Viking Press, 1966), 154.

43. Cf. Thelma J. Shinn, "Women in the Novels of Ann Petry," *Critique*, 16 (1974), 110–20.

44. French, *The Fifties*, 10.

45. Oliver Evans, *The Ballad of Carson McCullers* (New York: Coward-McCann, 1965), 194.

46. Carson McCullers, "The Flowering Dream: Notes on Writing," in *The Mortgaged Heart*, ed. by Margarita G. Smith (Boston: Houghton Mifflin, 1971), 275–9. Originally published in *Esquire* 52 (December 1959), 162–4.

47. Mark Schorer, "McCullers & Capote: Basic Patterns," in *The Creative Present*, 84.

48. Norman Mailer, *Advertisements for Myself* (New York: G. P. Putnam's Sons, 1959), 264.

49. Cf. the chapter on Malamud in Jonathon Baumbach, *The Landscape of Nightmare* (New York: New York University Press, 1965).

50. William Freedman, "Bernard Malamud," in *The Fifties*, 138.

51. Solotaroff, *Red Hot*, 76.

52. Hassan, *Radical Innocence*, 163.

53. David W. Noble, *The Eternal Adam and the New World Garden* (New York: Grosset & Dunlap, 1968), 215–16.

54. Gossett, *Violence,* 186.
55. Ibid., 179.
56. Ibid., 180.
57. Ibid., 183.

3

Growing, Growing, Grown: Fiction of the 60's

If the bleakness of the 50's had dulled even the most daring of the women writers of the 40's, the 60's would encourage not only Welty and Jackson but also the conservative Hortense Calisher to explore new possibilities for their women. However, the individualists of the 60's are more radical and eccentric than were their sisters, Virgie Rainey and Natalie Waite, in the past. Miss Julia Mortimer in Eudora Welty's *Losing Battles* rejects rather than fulfills familial and marital duties, and the Renfro clan with their hilarious family outing take on an absurdity not found in Virgie's community. Similarly, Mrs. Angela Motorman in Shirley Jackson's unfinished novel, *Come Along with Me*, has left her home and even her name behind to take a single "room of her own" and admits to "dabbl[ing] in magic." Even the narrator of Calisher's *The Railway Police* (1966) adds a new twist, accepting her individuality by revealing her baldness. Each woman asserts the self, but each is aware of the apparent absurdity of such an assertion in the modern world, is aware as well of the absurdity of that world itself. Conformity had become the ideal in America; the fear of the Bomb and the reaction to the inhumanity of the war had suggested to many that the individual was no longer of any significance.

However, the strategic retreat of the 50's as chronicled in the fiction revealed, even in the dismal illusions of a sad café, that only from the individual commitment comes a nonconfining but supportive social structure. Change began in the 60's, as Gail Paradise Kelly argues, "with a few people who were upset at their own oppression":

The sit-ins, the freedom rides, and the anti-Vietnam demonstrations all brought to the Left people who thought that changes would be made which would ameliorate people's lives, that progress could be made in destroying the system by demanding that it modify to meet responsible demands.[1]

With the election of John F. Kennedy as President in 1960, a new belief in heroes surfaced. The establishment of the Peace Corps in 1961 furthered the hope that a new age of action and commitment on an individual basis was dawning, a humanistic "Age of Aquarius." Women began revolutionizing their own lives, Marlene Dixon notes, believing that "if one lived the revolution, the revolution would come":

Liberation has been defined as freedom from traditional roles, from participating in the mainstream of chauvinistic America, or being trapped by the traditional family, or being haunted by the socialization process which we as women have undergone. This kind of definition of liberation implies that individuals can be free in the midst of oppression.[2]

Realizing the truth of this final sentence enabled men and women alike to break out of the dreamworlds of the 50's. Once more they accepted a truth Henry David Thoreau had offered a century earlier in "Civil Disobedience":

There will never be a really free and enlightened State until the State comes to recognize the individual as a higher and independent power, from which all its own power and authority are derived, and treats him accordingly. I please my self with imagining a State at last which can afford to be just to all men, and to treat the individual with respect as a neighbor; which even would not think it inconsistent with its own repose if a few were to live aloof from it, not meddling with it, nor embraced by it, who fulfilled all the duties of neighbors and fellow-men.

"Civil Disobedience" was written in opposition to the enslavement of one part of the human family. In 1848, when it was first published in Elizabeth Peabody's *Aesthetic Papers*, Lucretia Mott and Elizabeth Cady Stanton were organizing another statement in opposition to the enslavement of yet another part of the human family, a statement which echoed the original Declaration of Independence for those who attended the first national women's rights convention in Seneca, New York, that year. Similarly, both blacks and women rose up again in the 1960's to protest their continued oppression, once more accepting the individual responsibility to guide the state. In 1968 the second national gathering of militant women's groups was called—more than a century after their fore-mothers had met. The 60's brought forth heroes of the human family, regardless of color, creed or sex. For the blacks, Martin Luther King dared to dream; Malcolm X dared to speak out.

One by one, each hero met a similar fate. America seemed to be out to prove that such rebels were insane to challenge the status quo, as the new KKK became the Killing of King and Kennedy. Such destructive violence drove many Americans back into the dreamworlds permanently: they turned on, tuned in, and dropped out into the drug culture or another subculture movement. Others, however, met the challenge with ever stronger assertions. King himself had already argued for continued activism in the face of contempt, explaining that if "repressed emotions do not come out in these nonviolent ways, they will come out in ominous expressions of violence."[3]

To be judged absurd by an insane society can be seen as a confirmation of sanity, recalling Emily Dickinson's insight that to "demur" from the consensus of opinion shows that you are "dangerous" and need to be "handled with a chain"—or even eliminated by an assassin's bullet. To be "divinely mad" not only dissociates the individual from the society in which she can no longer believe; it also gives her the power which the insight of writers like Thoreau and Jackson recognize as belonging to the independent, truly *human* being. Philip Roth, another writer of the 60's, sums up the rewards of achieving identity as "the sheer fact of self, the vision of self as inviolable, powerful, and nervy, self as the only real thing in an unreal environment," a reward that "has given to some writers joy, solace, and muscle."[4]

For those writers who, with Roth, enjoy the rewards of self-assertion, the 60's were years of fruition. Women characters walked from the cages of their lives to the pages of history—of *her*story and *our*story, in fact. Although the process of growth brings pain, the realization of identity brings power and sometimes even pleasure. Other women characters, however, still succumbed to the despair which has always threatened the seeker—a despair born of the inequalities of the struggle between self and society. Nora may have slammed the door of her doll house, but she only found herself out in the cold.

Individual identity has never been easy to achieve; for women the way is even rockier and lonelier in our society than it is for men. Those women who do choose to face the absurd world find themselves confronted with more questions and fewer answers than ever. Theirs is now the privilege to share with their brothers the task of bettering the human condition, if only through setting the example of a life well lived. As women, theirs is also the task to preserve that knowledge and example for the future, to pass on at least the heritage of growth so that the next cycle will not have to repeat all of the mistakes of the past.

The fiction of the 60's indicates that the particular cycle of growth we have been examining does achieve such preservation. Even if the fiction itself goes out of print, still the spreading changes made or at least begun concerning social attitudes toward masculinity and femininity, the rational and the irrational, and reality and fantasy have removed some of the artificial barriers of the past. Nor is dependency possible in a world aware of the violence of life; today's life patterns allow little leisure to escape into or even imagine dream worlds. In a world forced to recognize its own diversity, sexual differences seem to matter less and less. Women don't have to become men, nor men women; but each of us is free to discover the unique formula of our individual selves. In the future, perhaps, the insights in this fiction will encourage further growth.

TOO LITTLE OR TOO MUCH

"Nothing can come of nothing," Shakespeare's King Lear assures us. There is no victory without its trail of casualties. The violence of maturation, as Jean Stafford suggests in *The Mountain Lion,* cannot always be survived, especially if male and female maturation are seen as mutually exclusive, competing processes. Women seem little more than abstract obstacles to the growth of men in Stafford's frightening portrayal, and as such they must be destroyed or otherwise negated in order for men to reach their full potential. Such seems to be the view in the fiction of John Updike as well, and two more women writers whose characters are late casualties of the wounds inflicted by World War II are Katherine Anne Porter and Sylvia Plath.

The 1965 report of the President's Commission on the Status of Women, *American Women*, concludes with a section called "Women's Right to Choose their Lives," which supports the rights of women

to remain unmarried, their right to a personal life without children, to a career alone or to a life of devotion to a small circle of others. . . . Women can only be given real opportunity by being offered real choices, each one underwritten by fair laws and fair practice and a social climate that ensures that each life pattern will be considered a feasible and dignified one.[5]

This quotation may seem unrelated to a discussion of Updike's fiction; it is. In his world, women are functions rather than people, and those functions serve men only. The single woman who would choose a career rather than marriage is not disparaged; she is nonexistent. Updike writes about wives and mothers; even most of the affairs in his fiction take place with other men's wives. The few single women have not chosen their disuse; they are often involved in affairs (borrowing the men of others because they have none of their own). Nor do they have careers; as Ruth asserts when Harry Angstrom asks her in *Rabbit, Run* (1960), she does "Nothing." A few exceptions can be found, such as Hester Appleton in *The Centaur* (1963), who is a parallel to the chaste goddess Artemis or Diana in this mythological puzzle. Still, even though critics describe Hester as "the spinster who has accepted without bitterness her restricted life,"[6] she too would have preferred being claimed by some man. We are told that she "has long cherished an unspoken love for George Caldwell." Waiting on the shelf or in the bed, these single women still exist for the use of men.

Updike's men may be involved, as Robert Detweiler argues, in a spiritual crisis, seeking new values or attempting to find new meaning in old values,[7] but they are dismayed when a woman, like Joan Maple in the stories collected in *The Music School* (1966), seeks an identity apart from husband and children. Updike does acknowledge the existence of such women, perhaps even admires the "new woman" that Piet Hanema of *Couples* (1968) recognizes in his ex-wife Angela, but these women must leave his pages as soon as they find themselves, suggesting that either Updike doesn't understand them or he just does not want to discuss them.

Searching for an artificial ideal, Updike's men are as seldom satisfied with their women as are Caroline Gordon's women with their men. As Bech observes in "The Bulgarian Princess" section of *Bech: A Book* (1970), "He had loved, briefly or long, with or without consummation, perhaps a dozen women; yet all of them, he now saw, shared the trait of approximation, of narrowly missing an undisclosed prototype." Even when Bech feels that he has found in the Bulgarian poetess a woman who might fit his ideal, he knows that the only way to keep faith in her is for them to live on "opposite sides of the world." Such idealization is, as we have seen earlier, another way of dismissing women as human beings. In fact, Updike's men idealize only their own reflections in these women. Hook in *The Poorhouse Fair* (1959), Updike's first novel, sets the tone by announcing "a war we can wage without blood. Now Nero murdered his mother as the logical out-come of his philosophy. What surprises me in this day and age is that everyone doesn't do the same. Make no mistake, there is little store of virtue left." The clue to his attitude toward women is in Hook's definition of that vanishing brand of virtue:

An austerity of the hunt, a manliness from which comes all life, so that it can be written that woman takes her life from man . . . men once served invisible goals, and grew hard in such service and pursuit, and lent their society an indispensable temper. Impotent to provide this tempering salt, men would sink lower than women, as indeed they had. Women are the heroes of dead lands.

For a man to renew his faith in himself and to overcome the impotency of which Hook accuses modern man, his woman is supposed to fit a certain stereotype. Her function is to have the "sturdy realism" of Amy Mortis, whose name means "friend to death,"[8] who can "speak plainly of death" and yet admire and preserve the patterns of the past, such as the patchwork quilts she makes: "I like to see young couples have them, but you know how they only care for the new things."

Still, Amy "finds it increasingly difficult to obtain patterned material" in the modern world, as Alice and Kenneth Hamilton have noted, because modern women are presented as preferring the blankness of empty skies.[9] That they prefer a blank page to someone else's formula seems promising to this reader, but for Updike's men no woman could be blank enough. Although they have perversely abandoned the patterns of the past into which the men would happily fit them, the women even more perversely try for personal patterns which obscure the images of their men. Imagine a mirror returning its own image rather than yours; surely breaking such a bewitched object would bring nothing but good luck. Hence even matricide—especially matricide—is heroic to Hook.

Updike's ideal woman would also share the qualities of the blind Elizabeth Heinemann in *The Poorhouse Fair*. Because of her outer blindness, Elizabeth has learned to look inward and to achieve the spiritual insight essential for the angel. She and Amy together offer both the "common sense wisdom" and the "common spiritual insight" that is expected from Updike's good women.[10] This composite woman can both admire the men for their virtues and save them from their faults.

But what of the woman herself? Updike's woman takes her definition from her man, which means that she must be empty to house his spirit and ideals. Harry Angstrom in *Rabbit, Run* is explicit about what attracts him to Ruth, for instance:

Now the noon of another day has burned away the clouds, and the sky in the windshield is blank and cold, and he feels nothing is ahead of him. Ruth's delicious nothing, the nothing she told him she did. Her eyes were that blue. Unflecked. Your heart lifts forever through that blank sky.

Again, Peter Caldwell tries to touch the "nothing" between Penny's legs in *The Centaur*. Once more, in a *New Yorker* story called "Museums and Women," the hero William is attracted to the girl he later marries by what he feels to be "an innocence and blankness [in her] where I must stamp my name."[11] While his men reflect an egotistical selfishness in love which negates the women completely, one can hope that the Hamiltons are right that Updike does not share this view.[12]

Perhaps the impossible idealization of women into nothingness is related to a strong mother/son tie just as the similar idealization of men is related to the father/daughter tie. The mothers in Updike's fiction are strong women devoted to their sons and, like the mother in *Of the Farm* (1965), critical of their sons' wives. Those wives invariably fall short of expectations, from the dumb, dull Janice Angstrom who spends her days drinking and watching television to the assertive Joan Maple who participates in civil rights demonstrations, donates blood for a distant relative, and finally takes lovers in her attempts to express her own identity. Harry Angstrom must run from Janice for fear of becoming as second-rate as she is; later he will run from Ruth as well when she confronts him with her own reality after he has filled her nothingness with his child. Richard in *Of the Farm* has left his first wife Joan, to marry Peggy, which is somehow his mother's fault, as she complains:

> "I can't imagine why you blame me for Joan," she said.
> "What do I blame on you, the marriage or the divorce?"
> "Both. Your father was like that. Women made the rules, women made the babies, women did everything. He used to say he had no recollection of asking me to marry him, it was just something I'd made happen."

The idealized woman, a composite of what the man wants from her, is also the scapegoat for his actions, just as McCarthy's women used their men as scapegoats.

Richard is just as ready to blame his new wife for their marriage and his guilt as he is to blame his mother. After he learns from his stepson that Peggy had slept with her ex-husband after their divorce, he sees himself as the receiver of damaged or even rejected goods: "If she had slept with him after their separation, after their divorce, it could only mean that she had wanted him back, and in the end he had not come." Richard is ready to agree with his mother when she tells him he has "taken a vulgar woman to be [his] wife":

> "She is stupid." I am always a little behind my mother, always arriving at the point from which she has departed. She smiled, seeing me sitting upright, excited like a boy by my discovery of the obvious. "Remarkably stupid."
> "Well, you knew that."
> "No," I said. "I threw myself into her. I gave her credit for everything I thought. I couldn't believe anything so beautiful could be less intelligent than I. I must have thought she had made herself."

Once again Updike's hero has admired his own reflection in the "nothingness" of femininity and is disappointed when the mirror claims its own image. And once again the woman is the scapegoat: "my failure to be able to see both her and the farm at once seemed somehow another failure of hers, a rigidity that I lived with resentfully."

The picture of male/female relationships changes little between *Of the Farm* and *Couples*. Piet Hanema leaves the good angel, appropriately named Angela, for the semiwhore, Foxy. Although he may admit that he "still felt, with Angela, a superior power seeking *through* her to employ him" [my italics], Piet still describes his first courtship in such a way as to blame everyone but himself for the marriage. It was "something instantly forgotten, like an enchantment, or a mistake." His future father-in-law "failed to disapprove. . . . Fertility at all costs. He threw business his son-in-law's way."

Angela seems traditional; in fact, Piet is worried that "without him she would raise their daughters as she had been raised, to live in a world that didn't exist." Yet she grows away from Piet. When she decides that she wants to go back to teaching, he accuses her of being "afraid I can't support you." Her response foreshadows her departure: "Of course you can. But I'm a person too. My children are growing up."

Piet is constantly being "betrayed" by his women. Even his former mistress Georgene objects to his dishonesty. "Let women in," he thinks, "and they never stop lecturing. Pedagogy since the apple. Be as gods." Even Foxy betrays him, as Ruth did Harry in *Rabbit, Run*, by becoming pregnant. She will never show him the road to salvation, he decides, because, as he tells her, "Your God is right there, between your legs, all shapeless and shy and waiting to be touched."

Although Foxy enjoys her pregnancy, she must learn that Nature is a false god. Shades of McCarthy—the moral choice in Piet's definite opinion and Foxy's passive acceptance is, of course, abortion. "You may not have it. May not, may *not*," he orders her.

"Oh, of course. Absolutely. I agree," Foxy whimpers. As in *The Poorhouse Fair*, the man provides the values "so that it can be written that woman takes her life from man." Piet knows that he "lived in a moral world of only men, that only men demanded justice, that like a baby held in a nest of pillows from falling he had fallen asleep amid women." At best, Foxy can only claim a childlike existence: "Yet she suffered, beneath the woman there was an animal, a man like him, an aged child rather, judging, guessing, hoping, itching." As the minister says in the sermon that Richard attends in *Of the Farm*, "Webster defines *woman* as 'an adult female person as distinguished from a man or a child.' The impression lingers that, so distinguished, she lies somewhere between."

Foxy wins Piet by becoming stereotypically female:

I am not, for all my vague intellectual poking (about as vague as Freddy's, and he knew it), good for much—but I knew I could be your woman. As an ambition it is humble but explicit. Even if we never meet again, I am glad to have felt useful, and used. Thank you.

In contrast, Angela has walked away and become "a new woman downtown—that elastic proud gait announcing education, a spirit freed from the peasant shuffle, arms swinging, a sassy ass, trim ankles." Perhaps Updike does women a service by making marriage and success with his men so unattractive.

Updike's male does not want a woman to be a separate person; as Charles Thomas Samuels has pointed out, "faced with woman's irrevocable otherness, he beats against the barrier between them or he pursues his ideal complement by attempting to love many women."[13] Even though Updike mainly presents women already defined in relation to men as wives, lovers, or mothers, not even these women can satisfy the "nothingness" his men seek. Despite Updike's emphasis on "coupling," his men and women are at war: women rob man of his spiritual quest and perhaps of his very identity; men deny that women are capable of either. No growth is possible in such relationships.

It is on the dangerous horns of the male/female relationship that woman's quest for identity is torn apart in the fiction of Sylvia Plath and Katherine Anne Porter as well. Plath, who turns from her poetry to fiction to understand how her personal history evolves from its social context, explores the difficulties of a young woman in the 50's through her autobiographical novel, *The Bell Jar* (published in England in 1963 and in the United States in 1971). Plath stresses in her poetry the victimization and repressed violence of modern woman, violence which is usually self-directed, as it was in Plath's own life, which ended in suicide. The novel presents the circumstances which led to an earlier suicide attempt.

As Harriet Rosenstein suggests, "Plath wanted her heroine, Esther Greenwood, to seem less aberrant than symptomatic. She hoped to imply that for any girl with half a brain, coming of age in the fifties was a brutalizing experience. By making her private horrors funny, Plath also makes them general, exemplary."[14] By comparison with the other comic novels of the period, we might also suggest that the humor makes these "private horrors" seem inescapable as well.

Esther is constantly being torn between opposing parts of herself, a desire to mature being contradicted by internalized social definitions and external social pressures. Often the forces remain unresolved, and Esther is unable to act. Her final retreat, more violent than most, is to the womblike room in the cellar where she hopes to end the frustration as she ends her life. The death wish so prominent throughout Plath's writing is shown in *The Bell Jar* to be a desire for rebirth, for a new beginning. Yet Esther seeks rebirth not through acceptance of the self but by reunion with her dead father. When she is rescued and resurrected through analysis, she feels that "there ought... to be a ritual for being born twice—patched, retreaded, and approved for the road" and hopes that she will "feel sure and knowledgeable about everything that lay ahead." Unfortunately, retreads often throw off the new covering and once more the bare, treadless, vulnerability is exposed to the dangers of the road. Rather than feeling the power of identity awarded Elizabeth and Natalie Waite in the novels of Shirley Jackson, Esther Greenwood knows only that "I wasn't sure at all. How did I know that someday—at college, in Europe, somewhere, anywhere—the bell jar, with its stifling distortions, wouldn't descend again?"

Just what are the contradictions which close Esther within herself? Some become apparent as she discusses her roommates at the Amazon, a hotel for women in which she stays while in New York City. Most of these young women are rich, popular, and bored. "Girls like that make me sick," Esther admits. "I'm so jealous I can't speak." Her ambivalence reveals the attractions of the stereotypical popularity and wealth they enjoy conflicting with the rejection of the artificiality and materialism they represent. Even more telling is the ambivalence Esther feels toward Doreen and

Betsy. Doreen is sophisticated and sexually emancipated; Betsy is wholesome and pure. After accompanying Doreen to the apartment of a disc jockey named Lenny, Esther walks out when the liquor and sex seem to get out of hand. Back in the hotel, she tries to wash away her exposure in a hot bath. On the edge of sexual awareness herself, Esther feels soiled by actual contact. She would rather remain a child with Betsy: "Deep down, I would be loyal to Betsy and her innocent friends." Her fear of and fascination with sex are both apparent as she "still expected to see Doreen's body lying there in the pool of vomit like an ugly, concrete testimony to [her] own dirty nature." As with many girls who were raised to believe that "sex is dirty" and then told to save it for marriage and someone they loved, Esther's training wars against her growth.

Denying part of herself is destructive to Esther; it splits her personality even further until she treats her mind and her body as unrelated entities. Similarly, Margaret Sanger had prayed that "if the flesh must be blind, let the spirit see" in McCarthy's *The Company She Keeps*. When Esther considers possible methods of suicide, the separation is complete, as she imagines her body refusing to carry out the wishes of her mind. Identifying only the body with life, Esther sees the self—the "I"—as choosing death.

Esther's ambivalence toward sexuality has been increased by social attitudes toward virginity. Her mother sends her a *Reader's Digest* article by a woman lawyer that "gave all the reasons a girl shouldn't sleep with anybody but her husband and then only after they were married," but Esther objects to its lack of concern for "how a girl felt." She has had personal experience with the double standard, since her boyfriend Buddy Willard has admitted to a summer affair with a waitress. Her reaction is to think she "ought to go out and sleep with somebody" herself to assert her equal rights.

Esther rejects other stereotypes when she can because she realizes how little they reflect her feelings. When Mrs. Willard tells her that "what a man wants is a mate and what a woman wants in infinite security" and "what a man is is an arrow into the future and what a woman is is the place the arrow shoots off from," Esther feels that "I wanted change and excitement and to shoot off in all directions myself, like the colored arrows from a Fourth of July rocket."

Nor can Esther, having earned all A's in school, imagine herself doing dishes and making meals interminably while her husband goes out. Not even motherhood attracts her, because she has come to associate it with brainwashing, although she feels guilty about being so "unnatural and apart." What she is protesting is the "Motherhood Myth," which, as Betty Rollin has argued, was "based on need, inevitability, and pragmatic fantasy—the Myth *worked*, from society's point of view."[15] When she is fitted for a diaphragm and feels free of that particular bell jar, Esther thinks: "I am climbing to freedom, freedom from fear, freedom from marrying the wrong person just because of sex. . . . I was my own woman. The next step was to find the proper sort of man." Esther wants the right to choose, to choose the right time and the right man.

Rosenstein has noted that the roots of Esther's breakdown can be found in both the "culturally inherited and thus eradicable" victimization of women and in the "unique, self-induced" victimization of Esther herself.[16] Esther's personal problem is the death of her father (which was true as well of Plath). With neither the protectivity nor the male model a father could provide, Esther is too much on her own too soon. Bewildered by "a multiplicity of choices and a multiplicity of fears," as Rosenstein has further observed, "she feels her certainties wither, her sanity slip."[17] To return to childhood for Esther leads to suicide, to the grave of her father. He is her first and greatest ambivalence: she loves him and needs or desires his protection, but she also hates him for his desertion. Before she buries herself in the cellar, she visits his grave in order "to pay my father back for all the years of neglect"—an ambivalent phrase!

Esther feels no sense of power or identity when she is "born again" because she has not chosen life; she has not resolved her relationship with her father nor accepted the contradictions between personal and social definitions of the self. Plath recognizes the same problems in her brilliant poem "Daddy," in which she tells him that he had "died before I had time." The poem not only offers her personal struggle but also transforms her own experience, as was the aim of the novel as well, into one paradigmatic of the modern world. The poem parallels the woman with Jewish victims of the Holocaust and the father with a Nazi "Panzer-man" as well as a Transylvanian vampire. While he becomes a symbol of pa-

triarchal oppression, the woman is equally a symbol of self-victim-
ization as she chooses to be oppressed—even loves her oppressor
and the pain he inflicts. Women may choose to be victims through
their passivity, much as the Jews remained passively in Germany,
continuing to hope that a mad world would come to its senses on
its own until they were destroyed by that madness. Such masochistic passivity is rejected by many in the 60's. The woman in
"Daddy" does not remain passive; she drives a stake through the
vampire's heart. Esther, however, is only saved by external inter-
vention, and Plath's death may be considered evidence of the inadequacy of such a "retreading."

As Plath's young Esther has lost a father and with him the protection of childhood which could prepare her for adulthood, so too
Katherine Anne Porter's women—and men—in *Ship of Fools* (1962)
have lost their holds on the past and the protection of tradition.
Porter has worked through her relation to traditions in what has
been called her "Miranda stories," which reveal the maturation of
a young woman.[18] Her mother having died before she is born,
Miranda, like Jenny Brown in *Ship of Fools*, is raised mainly by her
grandmother. Her father, referred to by the grandmother as "her
son Harry," seems to share childhood with his own children. The
grandmother, on the other hand, is a strong representative of "The
Old Order," as the title of one story suggests. But Miranda, gradually learning both the legend and the reality of the past, finds that
order too oppressive toward women to merit her approval. By the
end of "Old Mortality," Miranda has refused the traditions that
her family would pass on to her, seeing them as "aliens who lectured
and admonished her, who loved her with bitterness and denied her
the right to look at the world with her own eyes, who demanded
that she accept their versions of life and yet could not tell her the
truth, not in the smallest thing."

Divorced from the past, Miranda seeks her own world, and she
finds it to be, in "Pale Horse, Pale Rider," a nightmare of sordidness
from which death would be an awakening into "a deep clear landscape of sea and sand, of soft meadow and sky, freshly washed and
glistening with transparencies of blue" in which she would meet
"all the living she had known. Their faces were transfigured, each
in its own beauty, beyond what she remembered of them, their
eyes were clear and untroubled as good weather, and they cast no

shadows." But the pale rider Death refuses to take her; instead, he robs her of her illusions, of her belief in a salvation through love as embodied in her lover Adam. As Louis Auchincloss asserts,

Adam, her lover, is free like her, but he is in the army and about to be shipped abroad. He has no need for vicarious thrills. The irony of the story is that he, with all the physical and moral strength that she lacks, the symbol of what the world perhaps once was and perhaps could be again, the Adam of the Garden of Eden, succumbs to the flu that he has caught from her.[19]

Woman has once more brought death to Eden, more deadly to the male than the war raging in the world. Thus Miranda, stripped of the "hopefulness" and the "ignorance" with which she had faced her own world at the end of "Old Mortality," is ready to face the world once more at the end of "Pale Horse, Pale Rider," expecting nothing more than bitter survival: "No more war, no more plague, only the dazed silence that follows the ceasing of the heavy guns; noiseless houses with the shades drawn, empty streets, the dead cold light of tomorrow. Now there would be time for everything."

The pessimistic view that Miranda carries away from the first world war is not relieved for Porter's women by the subsequent events of the depression, the second world war or the 50's. "It's astonishing how little I've changed; nothing in my point of view or my way of feeling," Porter told an interviewer in 1963.[20] Nor has the outlook of her characters changed noticeably, as can be seen in the stagnation of Jenny Brown and Mrs. Treadwell. Although both women show strengths and moments of personal integrity, neither offers any hope for the future. Porter's women still survive on their bitterness rather than dying from their idealism. When Mrs. Treadwell notices that the "good-looking, gold-braided young officer" who reminds her momentarily of her childhood illusions of love really has a "goatish gleam" in his eyes and then tries to kiss her, she reveals her disillusionment:

She remembered as in a dream again her despairs, her long weeping, her incurable grief over the failure of love or what she had been told was love, and the ruin of her hopes—what hopes? She could not remember—and what had it been but the childish refusal to admit and accept on some term or other the difference between what one hoped was true and what one discovers to be the mere laws of the human condition?

Not the society but humanity itself has failed Mrs. Treadwell. She rejects human contact when she beats the drunken Denny with the heel of her shoe. As Theodore Solotaroff points out, "Mrs. Treadwell's violence is not directed at Denny so much as at the 'human sexual relationship' which she fears and hates and which he, like most of the other characters, embodies in a particularly hideous manner."[21] Like the severely disturbed Esther Greenwood in Plath's novel, Mrs. Treadwell also equates sex with evil, and her attitude is echoed throughout the novel in sordid and sleazy relationships. True love may be the antidote for the poisonous hopelessness which permeates Porter's vision, but she pictures a loveless world. Her few attempts to offer true love, as William L. Nance argues, are strikingly unreal. Auchincloss has argued that "it may be precisely to demonstrate that requited and happy love *does* exist, even on the VERA, that she introduces the blissful but nameless honeymooners who never speak or have any contact with the other passengers, but are seen occasionally on deck, hand in hand, with eyes only for each other";[22] but Nance has noted that "true to the pattern, every marriage is predominantly unhappy, and only inferior characters are portrayed in stable unions." As for the newlyweds, he has further recognized through their relationship to "similar cases" in Porter's Miranda stories that theirs is "only a temporary romantic euphoria, remote from the surrounding reality and based primarily on the first strong waves of sexual pleasure which will inevitably soon diminish."[23]

Jenny Brown offers no positive alternative in her relationship with David, either. The only good thing about their mutually destructive union is that they haven't locked themselves into it by marriage. The destructiveness rather than the hope of a future can be seen vividly in Jenny's dream memory of an Indian couple she had once seen in Mexico:

They swayed and staggered together in a strange embrace; as if they supported each other; but in the man's raised hand was a long knife, and the woman's breast and stomach were pierced. The blood ran down her body and over her thighs, her skirts were sticking to her legs with her own blood. They were silent, and their faces had taken on a saint-like patience in suffering, abstract, purified of rage and hatred in their one holy dedicated purpose to kill each other. Their flesh swayed together and clung, their left arms were wound about each other's bodies as if in love.

If love is so sadistic and destructive, what hope is there? As Nance asserts, "love is presented in *Ship of Fools* as fundamentally unreal. Thus the only real escape from a world of oppression is firmly closed off."[24]

Porter's only novel, appearing as it does out of its natural context more than twenty years after she had finished most of her other writing, suggests that even the frustrating growth cycle which we have been discussing has advanced beyond the earlier hopelessness of the "Lost Generation." Most of the women have recognized the inadequacies of old stereotypes as does Miranda; most have also experienced the disillusionment of a war-torn world, seemingly left without values. Yet these modern women refuse to give up on the future. Perhaps because they see the love relationship as one important step but not as the "only real escape from a world of oppression"—because they are not waiting for an Adam or a Christ to save them, perhaps also because they accept the sexual as well as the spiritual self, they can walk alone if need be. Those who cannot accept the self may destroy it as does Plath's Esther, but others refuse the passive "nothingness of femininity" that Updike's men search for in them and join their brothers to face the violence of maturity. These Radiant Daughters inherit equally from paternal and maternal values and break the bell jar which would keep them caged from their own possibilities.

BREAKING THE BELL JAR

Although Esther Greenwood was rescued from her first attempt to escape the bell jar, Plath herself was broken by it in the end. Other novels of this decade present women who do break free, even violently, refusing to be defined externally. For Susan Sontag, who uses men as well as women characters almost interchangeably to embody aspects of the self, the individual is defined exclusively through action, and rejection of any part of the self is suicidal. For Shirley Ann Grau, whose primitives could face the violence of life even in the fiction of the 50's, those women still trapped in the bell jar of Southern womanhood or floating in a world of dependency are forced to confront the realities of their own lives. For Ken Kesey, who still uses woman to symbolize the enemy of man in *One Flew Over the Cuckoo's Nest* (1962), a more personal portrayal in *Sometimes A Great Notion* (1965) of Viv Stamper reveals a woman who walks away from two men when the bell jar closes in too tightly around her.

Susan Sontag has argued persuasively against interpreting art because, she feels, "by reducing the work of art to its content and then interpreting *that*, one tames the work of art."[25] Although she is right, taming the art does yield great profit. Sontag has much to offer, as a model herself and as a writer, to the understanding of modern women; even more than most women writers, she embodies the changing attitudes of and toward women. Even her choice of male protagonists in both novels she has written is in no way a repudiation of women; rather, it is her way of reaffirming the individualist approach to fiction. Sontag approaches the world through an individual, letting his actions rather than his society define him. That the individual is male comments on our expectations; in her second novel, where the central characters are aspects of the same person,[26] the single female character seems to symbolize how limited is our acceptance of "female" traits.

Sontag explores the relationship of the individual to life, encompassing both the "real" and the "illusory" worlds that he inhabits, proceeding "from the dream outward." In many ways, hers is the "novel of the future" that Anais Nin has projected, recognizing the dream as any "ideas and images in the mind *not under the command of reason*" and learning "to walk easily between one realm and the other without fear, interrelate them, and ultimately fuse them."[27] Her first novel, *The Benefactor* (1963), through an artificial yet remarkably successful fusion of form and content, obliterates the line between dream and reality for the narrator, who begins by talking about his life and the strange dreams he has and ends by convincing us that his dreams are real. The reader is never quite clear which is the illusory world because, of course, both are real and both are illusions. Actions in dreams are simply those for which we do not admit responsibility, as the quotation from De Quincey which prefaces the novel indicates: "If there be anything amiss—let the Dream be responsible."

The narrator divides his life into those "unwholesome moral alternatives" which fill it and the more conventional pattern he also lives. To be freed from the asylum, he claims that the former were dreams, the latter reality. Once he is freed and begins narrating the story, however, he reverses the identification. In doing so, he reveals himself as another example of the person judged insane simply because he goes against the traditional societal pattern. When this narrator once more identifies with the reality of his own antisocial acts, he asserts "that I made a choice, admittedly an unusual one. I chose myself." He chooses to be defined by "only acts—acts cleansed of thought," a principle he has learned from his friend Jean-Jacques. Having told him the story of two pacifists, one who defines himself as a pacifist and one who "acts like one" until he murders his wife, Jean-Jacques explains that the latter, in not attempting to define his life before he has lived it, is more alive than the former. When we try to make life conform to any pattern, to trap it in a bell jar, we negate it. Life may be violent, it may go against social definitions, but to deny it is to negate the self.

Unfortunately, most of the women in this novel do just that. Frau Anders begins as a "liberated" woman, acting out her sexual emancipation and preaching it to her daughter Lucrezia. But she is merely following another pattern—as an Autogenist—believing "that good and bad are only human opinions" and that refusing such moral judgments will help one "to become weightless, to free the person from being only himself." The Autogenist is free—free of the self. Negation through sexuality or crime, both in which "the end is fixed; in sexuality, the orgasm; in crime, the punishment" is achieved by seeking the act for itself—sex for the sake of sex—not for any personal relationship to it. Even the most important "acts" of life, as Grau has shown, can be impersonal; it is we who invest them with meaning and individual value—or not. The narrator's wife, whom he had chosen for her traditionalism, is a perfect Autogenist, successfully eliminating her self throughout her life, as the Autogenist Professor Bulgaraux recognizes at her funeral:

What was the life of this young woman? She was born—schooled—married. She obeyed her father and her husband. She died.

You must have a vocation for such a life. You cannot choose it with the mind. The secret of life is vocation—which she had. It also takes a vocation to die well, which the criminal and the virgin soul possess.

This chaste wife, who has never lived, does have a vocation for dying. The virgin soul, which may be immersed in the acts of sex but remains untouched by life, and the criminal soul, which seeks the expected end of punishment in its negation of life, both share the art of dying by losing the self in predetermined acts rather than by defining the self through choice. Even the narrator's mistress Monique negates her self by letting society define her completely so that even "the charm of the private person needed the public certificate of fame to affect her."

Frau Anders, however, is able to reverse the Autogenist pattern of her life through a reidentification with nature and natural values, through the basics of survival which had encouraged individuality in Grau's primitive characters as well. The narrator does not even recognize Frau Anders on her return except as "someone who is happy." She had pursued sexual fulfillment until she was abandoned to a water-carrier in a desert village. With many years of abuse behind her, she chose to stay with this "amiable and gentle man" for a decade. There she learned "how it fortifies one's character to have to be concerned only with the problems of survival." Finally forced to define herself by her acts, she even overcomes the beliefs of the village that women must be subservient and is appointed their ruler. After serving successfully in that capacity by creating a "model community," she abdicates—again by choice—because she realizes that "one can't remain a queen forever."

Through *The Benefactor* Sontag suggests an existential view of identity: do not replace outworn traditions with other artificial structures and values. Rather, discover what you are and what you believe through what you do. Define yourself—and perhaps humankind as well—by doing, by facing life and reacting to it. Then dreams and actions, like the form and content of Sontag's novel, are one. What is real is what *is*, and our past, as does the past of the narrator, "dreams and waking life alike, presents itself to me as fantasy." As do Grau's primitives, Sontag's ultrasophisticated moderns live in the present moment to learn to understand themselves.

Sontag's second novel, *Death Kit* (1967), deals with the individual who chooses death, just as the first novel had dealt with the choice of life. Solotaroff argues convincingly that "Diddy's . . . 'business trip' is the business of completing his death, following his successful suicide attempt at the beginning of the novel."[28] If *The Benefactor* concludes that we are defined by our actions, then it necessarily follows that the definition is only complete when we cease acting—when we die. Thus, with his final act of choosing death, Diddy begins to discover the death-in-life which he had chosen to live as well. He is, as Solotaroff describes him, a "decent, well-behaved Madison Avenue type WASP, the typical unsolid citizen of our day who, 'not really alive,' merely, 'inhabited' his life."[29]

Sontag shows us through Diddy that the quest for identity is a choice of responsibility rather than abandonment. We are inevitably defined by our actions; what we choose is whether or not to be aware of this, to accept the responsibility it entails. Diddy has sought to be defined by externals, to avoid the self for what he does not like or cannot accommodate to the patterns of his life. The result is that he chooses to destroy the "animal" in himself by killing Incardona (gift of fire), as Esther Greenwood had chosen to destroy her animal—her body—in Plath's novel. What is apparent, however, is that the destruction of the basic, violent part of the self is still suicide, the destruction of all the possibilities of the self. Diddy's first sexual encounter with Hester (who is defined by Solotaroff as "an aspect of the theme of perception . . . as well as Diddy's life force, feminine nature, and self-idealization"[30]) immediately after he murders Incardona is a desperate last wish to preserve the good in himself, which significantly is a female stranger who sees what he cannot see and is blind to his world. But Diddy has been defined by his actions despite his ideas; his self-negating life inevitably ends in suicide. At the end, walking naked in the dark tunnel of death, he still dreams of Hester, whom he has left "asleep" after a final desperate coupling. Refusing to admit that she is dead, he has propped her against a wall and "dreams that he will find Hester at the end of his tour . . . Her role is a perfectly clear one, and well within her powers. To save him, like the princess in some fairy tale, Love's power sweeping him up from the kingdom of death."

Still choosing death over life, choosing the abdication of responsibilities that dreams seen only as Dreams represent, Diddy contrasts sharply with the narrator of *The Benefactor* who finally chooses himself and can say that "I do not dream now." Incardona could give Diddy the gift of life as his name suggests, but he destroys that gift and hopes for salvation by coupling with the neglected female stranger within him. The fragmented personality destroys itself unless it can recognize and accept its many parts. Diddy doesn't.

Equally trapped in external definitions are the heroines in the two novels published by Shirley Ann Grau during the 60's. However, both women choose to direct their violence of frustration outward instead of inward, thereby preserving the second chance denied Esther and Diddy. Birth is a violent push into life, not a retreat to the safety of the womb; perhaps rebirth demands an equal violence toward the world which would hold us in. That abortion is the subject of the first of these novels, *The House on Coliseum Street* (1961) might suggest the outcome of the rebirth that is attempted as well.

One of several daughters of an ambitious, single mother in their house on Coliseum Street, Joan has always done whatever Aurelie, her mother, "taught her to do." She nearly marries her boyfriend Fred for the same reason. But the roots of rebellion feed on her inability to conform to social stereotypes mentally or physically. She irritates her mother by going to college: "A bookish woman . . . is simply impossible," Aurelie asserts, and the veiled threat is obvious in her reminder to Joan that "a woman alone . . . is so very sad." Joan parries her attack by announcing that "I think I'll go to medical school and never get married." Nor does Joan see herself as the Southern belle: "She looked a great deal like Elizabeth of England; people told her that often." Cast in the wrong role, Joan remains passive, allowing the more talented Aurelie to direct her performance. Only when she is confronted internally with the realities of life does Joan leave the stage of her childhood and write her own scripts.

This confrontation begins when Joan has an affair with Michael Kern, her college instructor, and becomes pregnant. Aurelie arranges an abortion, a decision supported by Michael and passively accepted by Joan. Afterwards, she begins seeing Fred again. Why then, should she start spying on Michael—try to break up his affair with another girl—ruin his career by telling half-truths about the abortion to his superior? Most of all, why should she benefit from this destructive rebellion? Louise Gossett answers the last question: it "frees her from the valueless, empty life" she has known.[31]

Joan's assertion grows out of her reidentification with the "basic survival" which Frau Anders had discovered in Sontag's novel, with the cycle of life which governs Grau's primitives. Joan's attack on Michael affirms the life she has given up—that of their child. Through the pregnancy, the abortion, and her later efforts to have another child, Joan has not only confronted parts of her own body and her own self unknown to her before but she has also touched the impersonal realities of life and made them personal. Almost against her will, the experience changes her, and her new commitment to her own life demands a protest against the destruction of life. Michael is the natural target for that protest, as can be seen when Grau carefully contrasts Joan's natural reaction to the pregnancy with the social considerations which bother Michael. Joan feels "heavy and smug and lazy and full . . . she didn't feel tired, or sick. Just content." Michael, conversely, worries about legalities: "We can get married, you know. Maybe it wouldn't be so bad."

After experiencing the contentment nature offers, Joan must also know the suffering it entails if she is to grow. After the abortion, she "became aware of her body's emptiness. She had always thought of herself as solid. A solid lump. . . . But now she knew she wasn't. That she was just a tissue of skin stretched around a frame of bone." Before the pregnancy, Joan had been willing to act like "a solid lump" because that is how she saw herself. Now she sees herself in all the vulnerability of the human condition and as a hollowness which should be filled with life. Coming home changed to a family still concerned with appearances, she echoes Mick Kelly in *The Heart is a Lonely Hunter* when she had received no reaction from her family after her first sexual encounter. "They were going to pretend it hadn't happened, that nothing had happened," Joan discovered, and she realized that "they had to pretend. Always."

Michael's reaction is no better; he is delighted that Joan had "sense" enough to get the abortion, not expecting such intelligence in a woman. Joan's reactions, on the other hand, are complex. She finds herself waiting, filling time with college courses, although she isn't conscious of what she is waiting for. As her thoughts return to the abortion, they embody the mythic universality of childbearing: she feels herself to be "empty inside and lonesome. Caverns and caves, echoing. The Holy Ghost now. Or the Shower of Gold. . . . Being one is so lonesome. With another heart ticking away inside. A different beat. A ragged pattern. The little ticking heart. The soft floating seaweed bones. . . . " The experience is uniquely female, unique to Joan, yet as impersonal as the universe itself—probably echoing memories shared by Grau herself, a mother of four children.

In this single experience, combining the creation and destruction of life, the personal and the universal, albeit in an exclusively female version, Joan must and does confront herself as a woman and as an individual involved in the violence of life. When she moves on from the abortion, sleeping with Fred in an effort to refill the emptiness within, she sees sex as the medium of nature: "it's a pity you have to have a man for it. It would be so much nicer if it just happened." Joan is not rejecting men; rather, she is merely recognizing that the individual becomes unique by involvement with the universal experience. In fact, "sometimes she was surprised to find how happy she was with [Fred]. Surprised because she knew he wasn't the right man after all."

When neither a baby nor a marriage comes out of Joan's affair with Fred, her frustrations are directed back to Michael. She destroys his facade and "it did not matter to her. She had no control any more. She did not feel vicious. She was not afraid. She did not feel anything at all. Except not a part of herself any more." As Sontag suggests, immersion in the acts of life alone can destroy the self as effectively as can withdrawal from them. One must accept life, then struggle against it to preserve the self as Cecile does in *The Hard Blue Sky*. If one does not shape the violence of life by the power of the individual choice, then that violence will take its own shape. What could create can equally destroy.

Yet choosing to act, even violently and destructively as Joan does, is the beginning of self-definition, as Sontag has shown us. And if her society does not approve of the monster it has created in Joan (and Ellen Moers has revealed that Shelley's *Frankenstein* is also a distorted birth myth[32]), then it is responsible for giving her and other women no healthier alternatives. A parallel violence is produced in Abigail Tolliver in Grau's next novel, but because of a family heritage of integrity from her grandfather, Abigail is able to be reborn as an individual defining her own life, which is conveyed through birth imagery at the end. In *The Keepers of the House* (1964), Grau departs from internal affairs to examine the external tensions of Southern racism.

The Keepers of the House is the story of the Howlands, a wealthy Southern family, particularly of Abigail Tolliver, granddaughter of William Howland. Raised in the protective environment of the Howland house with her mother, her grandfather, the black housekeeper Margaret, and Margaret's three children by Howland, Abigail has been trained even by the silences what knowledge is acceptable to Southern ladies. Regarding the parentage of Margaret's children, for instance, she remembers that "no one told me. I'm sure of that. I don't know what my mother thought, but she never said a word. She always pretended to believe that Margaret's children had just come." Similarly, her grandfather "never talked about himself or his business with me. As for me, . . . I didn't mind at all—after all, there are lots of Southern men who treat their ladies that way."

Her training well prepares Abigail for her role as the wife of ambitious politician John Tolliver. John doesn't tell her even about their phone being tapped, protecting her as did her grandfather. He *does* tell her how to behave, so that she is even successful when following his precise instructions at campaigning, although "I didn't like it. No, I never did, but I was able to do it." She is fearful to raise important issues with him, knowing that "if I got in an argument with him I always lost." When she decides to get pregnant the first time out of loneliness, she offers to "get rid of it" if John doesn't approve. He kindly allows her to keep it: "A child will be company for you." Yet she accepts her circumscribed life, even after she learns that John is having affairs (which of course she never confronts him with, having been taught the value of silence by her mother): "I sat in the quiet familiarity of my house, the house where I had lived as a child, in a country I had known as a child, and I was happy and content. My children were healthy and my husband successful." Unfortunately, as Grau knows, the violence of life will reach Abigail even in her grandfather's house.

As Gossett asserts, "the protection which their men and customs have supplied the Howland women (and the South) has now been ripped away and the exposed person craves revenge."[33] The end

of Abigail's illusions comes from the past, with the startling revelation, not that her grandfather had fathered Margaret's children,
but that he had married her before the eldest was born, making
them his legitimate heirs and descendants. This unforgivable sin of
the fathers is visited on Abigail: John quickly leaves her and the
townspeople try to burn her out. To Abigail, on the other hand,
the news proves only "that my grandfather had been a good man."
Unwilling to see his integrity abused, she has her revenge by pulling
Howland money and goods out of the town and thereby ruining
its economy.

Abigail wants more than vengeance, however. With this new
understanding of her heritage, she can be reborn. That the rebirth
must be violent reflects again the violence of maturation which has
been so long postponed for Abigail, the death of innocence which
she gladly accepts and which the townspeople violently reject (but
might have to learn to accept because of Abigail's growing awareness of power over them). Violence, as Robinson Jeffers reminds
us in his poem "The Bloody Sire," "is not too old to beget new
values." Abigail's rebirth is painful but seemingly successful, as we
see her at the end "huddled fetus-like against the cold unyielding
boards," and promises social change as well.

Finally, with the growing sensitivity to women as individuals
which we began to see in the men writers of the last decade, even
Ken Kesey balances his stereotypical portrait of women in *One Flew
Over the Cuckoo's Nest* with the complex portrayal of Viv Stamper
in *Sometimes A Great Notion*. The former is in the tradition of
Cooper's and Twain's explorations of what Leslie Fiedler has called
the "westering" theme: "westering, in America, means leaving the
domain of the female, since in our classic books fathers are usually
invisible or conveniently dead."[34]

Fiedler sees in McMurphy and Chief Bromden, the half-breed
Indian, "the old, old fable of the White outcast and the noble Red
Man joined together against home and mother, against the female
world of civilization."[35] And Big Nurse is the embodiment of that
civilization, of the Combine as Bromden calls it: "she sees the
purpose of the asylum as being precisely to persuade men like him
to accept and function in the world of rewards and punishments
which he has rejected and fled."[36] In a society geared to machines
rather than human beings, those individuals who cling to their

humanity are judged as insane—at least maladjusted. Bromden conveys the mechanical nature of Big Nurse's efficiency in contrast to
the humanity her body would demand of her, for instance:

> She stops and nods at some of the patients come to stand around and stare
> out of eyes all red and puffy with sleep. She nods once to each. Precise,
> automatic gesture. Her face is smooth, calculated, and precision-made, like
> an expensive baby doll, skin like flesh-colored enamel, blend of white and
> cream and baby-blue eyes, small nose, pink little nostrils—everything
> working together except her bosom. A mistake was made somehow in
> manufacturing, putting those big, womanly breasts on what would of
> otherwise been a perfect work, and you can see how bitter she is about it.

Big Nurse succeeds in conquering McMurphy's body if not his
spirit, but not before he succeeds in once stripping away her defenses and revealing her breasts to the other patients, who then
have a weapon to defend themselves against her:

> Her face was bloated blue and out of shape on one side, closing one eye
> completely, and she had a heavy bandage around her throat. And a new
> white uniform. Some of the guys grinned at the front of it; in spite of its
> being smaller and tighter and more starched than her old uniforms, it could
> no longer conceal the fact that she was a woman.

McMurphy's rebellion, one shared by many of the women we
have discussed, is against the insanities of modern society. It is
unfortunate that he chooses a woman to represent that society, but
not surprising. Fiedler has shown that such stereotyping is an honored tradition in American literature—in the literature which has
been preserved, at least, most of which is written by men. When
men picture the struggle against the dependency of childhood, their
opposition is naturally embodied in the mother just as we have
seen it embodied in the father for women. Equally understandable
is their discovery that women, confused by stereotypes and discouraged from the quest for identity which was traditionally reserved for men, often buried themselves in the roles assigned them
and became vehicles of their society. Seldom have men tried to
penetrate these surface realities to strip bare the woman beneath,
for other than physical reasons at least (noting the fiction of Hawthorne and James as possible exceptions). Kesey will penetrate more

than a woman's clothing or her body in the next novel. Even in *Cuckoo's Nest* McMurphy struggles for an acceptance of life rather than a surface of "adjustment."

From the first time we see her in *Sometimes A Great Notion,* Viv Stamper is breaking rather than conforming to patterns. When Hank Stamper meets her, he is intrigued by her individuality. When he asks her about herself because "from experience he knew that women felt entitled to this type of talk as a kind of payment" she responds unexpectedly: "Now do you really care? I mean, come on, there isn't any need, really; it's fine just being a man and a woman; it's fine." Viv knows exactly what she wants out of life:

I want somebody. . . . I want a lot of other unusual things, too, like a page-boy cut, and a good sewing machine and a German roller singing canary like I remember my mother had—but mostly, I guess, I want to really mean something to somebody, to be something more'n just a jail cook and watermelon weigher.

Before she marries Hank, Viv believes in herself and in her future. When she leaves to marry him, she says good-bye to her old room and her old self and kisses her own reflection in the mirror, promising "allegiance to all the holy old dreams and hopes and ideals that these walls had held." But from the moment she leaves, she begins giving those up. The "page-boy cut" she wanted conflicts with Hank's preference for long hair, so "she never made the second request" for a canary. After reaching Hank's home, she learns "to fit in with the Stamper life. . . . She could be like that if they wanted."

Gradually, Viv becomes more and more one of Hank's possessions, until she hardly recognizes her own face: "What about these stranger's eyes that sometimes look back at her? And did she really once kiss those alien lips? She can't remember." While Viv loves Hank and his brother Lee for what they are, neither pays her the same tribute. Hank owns her, and Lee needs her. Finally she cries out, "Need! Need, is that *all*?" She too has a need—to be herself. "But I won't let her use me any longer," her inner self argues against the person she has become. "I love them but I can't give myself up for them. Not my whole self. I have no right to do that."

Viv's personality is in danger of shattering when she realizes how many of those "holy old dreams" she has abandoned. Deciding she can no longer compromise, she decides to leave. When a child asks her where she is going, she responds, "Who knows? I'm just going. . . . Just me."

THE FAILURE OF FATHERS

While the fiction of the 60's shows women, one by one, walking away—or at least trying to—from the bell jar of feminine stereotypes in which a patriarchal society would confine them, it also shows how much more difficult they find walking away from their personal fathers, even when the failures are apparent and psychologically damaging to the entire family. Plath may have tried to free herself from memories of a dead father, a dead tradition, and a dead innocence; Philip Roth and Joyce Carol Oates present women who cannot free themselves from living fathers, women victimized by the same loss of tradition and innocence. The personal commitment is ultimately more important and potentially more damaging to the individual daughter, they seem to say.

Although the other three novels written by Philip Roth in the 60's focus on the attempts of men to understand themselves and their society (even *Portnoy's Complaint* [1969] despite its fame as an attack on Jewish mothers is more concerned with the Jewish son who would deny responsibility for his own life by blaming Mom), one novel is primarily concerned with a young woman's maturation. *When She Was Good* (1967) has been described by Mary Ellman as a book "in which a pimple of a young woman is created only to be squeezed, interminably, to death."[37] Yet, if another modern-day Frankenstein's monster has been created in Lucy Nelson, at least Roth sensitively examines what ingredients went into her composition. Again we learn what *not* to inherit from parents, as we watch Lucy's ambivalence—for her father especially—lead her slowly but surely to the self-negation of suicide. We find the roots of her depression in self-hate, hate for a heritage she can never hope to escape. Although Ellman objects to "the generally vindictive temper of the novel itself,"[38] the final scene of a young pregnant girl lying dead in the snow on Passion Paradise, the local lover's lane, holding her father's last letter to her cheek, could easily be attacked as sentimental.

Lucy, however, is no sentimental heroine. She is at least as much the product of her parents as Portnoy is of his. Her mother is the living stereotype of self-sacrifice and passivity. Overprotected by her own father, with whom she continues to live, she tries in turn to offer her husband a similar excess. She is "an angel"—hard-working, never complaining, always understanding and accepting the actions of her husband. Lucy's father, on the other hand, remains weak, although he at least tries to change. He was shattered by the depression, he explains, and has never recovered. He can't support his family, periodically abandons them, continually drinks, and guiltily beats his wife when he is home. When she is fifteen, Lucy can tolerate no more of his treatment of her mother and calls the police. She is judged by everyone to be in the wrong; appearances are to be maintained at all costs.

Taught to respect appearances above realities, Lucy feels she must marry immediately when she discovers she is pregnant. Her campus doctor refuses even to discuss abortion, so she sees no alternative even though "she didn't want to marry him. He was the last person in the world she would ever want to marry." She is disappointed that her parents accept her decision: "If only they'd say no, NO. LUCY, YOU CANNOT. NO, LUCY, WE FORBID IT. But it seemed that none of them had the conviction any longer, or the endurance, to go against a choice of hers. In order to survive, she had set her will against theirs long ago—it was the battle of her adolescence, but it was over now." Still young enough to need their support, she even tries to force them to keep her from marrying by admitting that "I'm going to have a baby and I hate Roy and I never want to marry him or see him again."

The damage to appearances that unwed motherhood would entail is rejected by them, but they are willing to offer Lucy an abortion instead. First she is moved by the thought that they would be willing to spend so much money to save her, that her father would get a job to help her. For the first time, she begins to believe that her father loves her, that she is not simply a source of guilt for him. Her insecurity is evident earlier when she tells her mother that "he wishes I'd never been born, Mother. He thinks I'm why everything is so wrong with *him*." Now she is more hopeful: "She was going to cry; they were talking!" But her hope is quickly dissipated when she learns that her mother too has had an abortion, which

her father had arranged for economic reasons. Although her mother
is quick to assure her that "He didn't make me," Lucy is incensed:
"But if only he did his job. If he only stopped being a coward!"
Raised to expect protection and responsibility from men, she finds
her values repeatedly contradicted by her experience. A later conversation with her mother reveals further that the *wife*, not the
woman, gave in:

> "I did what I had to," said her mother mournfully.
> "You didn't! You let him trample on your dignity, Mother! You were
> his doormat! His slave!"
> "Lucy, I did what was necessary," she said, sobbing.
> "That's not always right, though. You have to do what's *right*!"

Searching for values in a world of expediency, searching for
strength in a weak father and a passive mother, Lucy finds herself
frustrated at every turn. Still, she tries to break from the mistakes
of the past; with other daughters of the 50's, she cries: "I refuse—
I refuse to live your life again, Mother, that's what I refuse!"

What should Lucy be like? Self-effacing, self-sacrificing like her
admired—yet pitied—mother? She is not so forgiving. She expects
father to be responsible for what happens to him. Yet her mother
would blame Lucy's vindictiveness for his later incarceration in a
Florida prison: "Because he's where you always wanted him to be!"
Lucy accepts the guilt as most children do and projects her self-
hatred on her equally weak husband Roy whenever she hears of
her father's latest failure.

Lucy lashes out with the violence we have seen in Grau's frustrated women, women who had been taught to live for men and
had turned around to find a world devoid of men. Lucy has inherited
only the empty inadequate traditions and undeserved guilt from
her parents: as Edna St. Vincent Millay wrote for a different generation of lost young women in her poem "The Singing-Woman
from the Wood's Edge" (her tribute to the daughter of a priest and
a leprechaun), "What should I be but just what I am?" Lucy's final
violence, however, is directed toward herself: ironically, she freezes
to death with the cold comfort of a father's letter pressed against
her cheek.

Already in the first novel of what has been a remarkably prolific

career, Joyce Carol Oates begins introducing us to a gallery of
ineffectual fathers, fathers who will slaughter their families, kidnap
or stab their daughters, or less violently demand the sacrifice of
love and life itself from their children. Although these fathers do
not offer protection to their far-from-innocent daughters, they often
manage to stand between them and the world in other ways. As
with the strange children we have met earlier, these daughters often
end up in the parental role instead of the child role, offering what
little protection order can provide to vulnerable parents. Oates
reveals that, in the violence of modern life, neither immediate nor
heavenly fathers can offer dependence, but both can sometimes
destroy independence.

In Oates's first novel, *With Shuddering Fall* (1964), Karen recognizes the sacrifice of self implicit in religion: "Before its brittle
splendor everyone must bow, kneel, forget himself.... Karen
awaited, trembling, the moment at which her individuality would
die." So too she gives up her individual life to return home to her
father, knowing that "he is ignorant and brutal, a killer, he has no
right to my life, and no right to judge it.... But he is my father,
... and I love him." Her last words are "I love you too, Father."

Entering maturity involves leaving the father, but if Oates's
women are representative they suggest that this task is nearly impossible when the fathers fail. Karen physically leaves her father as
sexual awareness leads her to Shar, but the violence of this shift—
Shar's attack which leaves her father in a pool of blood—puts too
much pressure on her. She feels guilty for challenging her role by
maturing:

The fault did indeed lie in her, was of her doing; but it originated not in
her decision to go with Shar but in her deliberately resisting sleep that
morning.... Perhaps she had even understood the price of forcing herself
up from sleep and, in going down to the men, the price of violating her
role.... The rejection of her child's bed would lead, after a series of insane,
vivid scenes, to the picture of her father lying in the cold and, bleeding,
staring up at her—how right was he to judge her, to find her guilty!

Karen accepts the blame for waking up, for not being one of the
many sleepwalking women who fill Oates's pages, and her guilt
proves even stronger than her sexual needs. She goes with Shar,

but only to fulfill her father's orders: "Don't come to me until you get him. Kill him. Kill him." She kills Shar by acting the female role, convincing him that she is totally dependent upon him: "She had always felt her silent, limp passivity to be powerful, a bloodless power she knew was not admirable but could not be matched by real passion."

As Karen's love for Shar is submerged beneath her loyalty to her father, her surface self must conceal the father's daughter within by assuming "a face unrelated to her, to her soul, a mockery of what she knew she was." The tension of the opposing forces within her is strong enough to cause her to miscarry Shar's child and to deny herself to Shar while "she wanted at the same time to embrace him, simply and utterly, as she had imagined she would someday."

When Karen succeeds in driving Shar to suicide, she escapes at least temporarily into insanity. The nature of her madness is revealing: "A delirium of prayer and sexual excitement" followed by protestations that "I'm insane, completely insane. . . . Why don't you believe me? What do I have to do?" and finally by attempts to offer the men patients the love she had denied Shar: "You don't want me! None of you want me! You won't let me make you happy!" Although she tries to escape the self into the anonymity of sex and of religion, Karen finds she cannot return to an innocence she has never known; she can only return to a father who demands a total sacrifice of her own self and binds her by his vulnerability.

Clara Walpole in *A Garden of Earthly Delights* (1967) also manages to leave her father physically (unaware that he has died searching for her), but she has internalized his needs so completely that they still determine her life. Symbolically, the novel is divided into three sections named after the three men in her life—her father Carleton, her lover Lowry, and her son Swan. Never does she exist separate from her men.

Clara shares many traits with Karen: she is her father's favorite child, she has a dead mother, and she is equally unsatisfied with the "sleepwalking of the women" she knows:

Clara felt warm and oppressed. If she could have thought of something else she would have been grateful, but there was no getting around what she had to face up to. This was the way life would be, then. But did all

women have to go through it? . . . It was clear what not to do, but it was
not clear what she should do.

Clara's alternatives are more limited than most women's by her
lack of education, which denies her a career and even the ability to
express herself clearly: "There were times when an idea brushed
against her mind, but she could not seize it . . . when she wanted
to explain something to Lowry words betrayed her and showed
only how stupid she was." Vicarious fulfillment through men seems
to be her only choice.

Clara has two models to choose from, a mother who had borne
five children and who had become more of a child herself with each
one until she died, or a father who clung tenaciously to dreams of
owning a small farm of his own while actually living violently and
out of touch in the world of migrant workers. Clara is attracted to
Lowry because he reminds her of her father; when she leaves him,
her hopeless love for him echoes her hopeless love for Carleton.
When she resists joining Lowry later to go to Canada, it is in order
to fulfill her father's dream of owning property which she could
then pass on to her son Swan. While she comes close to accom-
plishing this goal through her marriage, Swan will reject the past
and destroy the present by murdering his stepfather and himself,
leaving Clara an empty shell watching TV in a nursing home while
another man, her stepson, cares for her.

Oates's other two novels of the 60's deal not with the love of
fathers, but with its corollary, the hatred of mothers. In *Expensive
People* (1968) and *them* (1969), she presents first a matricide and
then a chronicle of one woman's life and that of her mother as was
told to the writer by an ex-student. *Expensive People* is narrated by
the young man who claims to have murdered his mother, and as
such the character of the narrator and his point of view must be
considered. Even his mother's name, Nada, reflects the nothingness
of femininity, which we come to see as a weapon for her as it was
for Karen, a facade adopted when she rejected her original name
and heritage for the more dramatic part she chose to play as her
life. As have other parents, Nada rejects responsibility and forces
her son to assume parental roles: "It was as if Nada, my mother,
had become a kind of embryonic creature stuck in my body, not
in a womb maybe but a part of my brain. How can you describe

a creature that is lodged forever in your brain? It's all impossible, a mess." He tells us that he has killed his mother to keep her from leaving him again, and now he is eating himself to death—a central image in Oates's later novel *Wonderland* (1971) as well. Allowing any appetite full sway is the path to anonymity—to losing the self—and physical glut provides a particularly apt metaphor for American materialism and a visual embodiment of loss of identity, as the flesh eventually obscures individualizing features and buries the kernel of self deep within its weight. Maureen Wendall in *them* will temporarily choose a similar escape.

Although Oates argues in her introduction to *them* that the novel merely repeats what she has been told by the student represented by Maureen and that "so much material had the effect of temporarily blocking out my own reality," the similarities between the women in this and in earlier Oates novels is striking, suggesting that the same personal vision is evident in this pseudohistory as well. And so it should be: *them* as a contemporary chronicle is convincing evidence of the accuracy of Oates's perception of "the moral and social conditions of [her] generation,"[39] her announced interest.

Loretta, Maureen's mother, was favored by her father and had watched her mother deteriorate into madness much as Clara Walpole did. However, she seems to lack a sense of self, the awareness that marks Karen and Clara. Instead, she is a "sleepwalker"; her character ends with its physical reality:

Loretta lived in an eternity of flesh: all week she knew the resistance of muscle, she knew its sad limits, and left to herself she explored her toenails as earnestly as her face, summing everything up, judging and hoping. Her arms, her legs, her stomach and hips, the dipping line of her spine, the rather thick set of her ankles—filled with precious organs and eager blood she leaned a little toward Bernie, waiting.

Such is Maureen's maternal heritage, an "eternity of flesh" in which she can temporarily hide perhaps but which offers her little protection against the penetration of violence. Flesh is vulnerable; nor can men protect these women from life, as Loretta realizes when she looks down at the dead body of her lover: "men always disappointed you, there was no hope in them, nothing. There was no center to men." Loretta survives by flowing with life, moving from man to man as earlier husbands leave or die, and sleepwalking. Her children, therefore, shoulder the burdens of responsibility for her. Jules, Betty and Maureen are all exposed to life early and violently. Maureen is early to reject such a maternal heritage: "It made her angry to think of a future in which she waited in an apartment for a man to come back from whatever it was men did." She acts on her rebellious feelings by becoming a prostitute in order to earn escape money. When her current stepfather discovers the hidden bills and beats her, she retreats into herself, hiding under excess weight and silent passivity: "No man could penetrate this flesh."

Maureen doesn't always associate men with her oppression and unhappiness, but the vulnerability of the flesh—which is somehow her mother's fault—always underlies her frustration. It threatens her in a violent world, even when it appears to protect her. She finally chooses the order of marriage as her protection, although she realizes its artificiality. The end of the novel finds her a suburban, pregnant housewife fulfilling the very role she would have rejected, while her brother Jules reminds her that the violence still surrounds her, that "men can come back in your life. . . . Wouldn't you really want it to happen?"

Maureen denies Jules' suggestion, answering "No, never. Never." Yet her only improvement over her mother's life is that she has picked the man more carefully. Still, she is the "Housewife" described in Anne Sexton's poem of that title who has rebelled and lost, much like the young women in Calisher's fiction, and now knows that "a woman *is* her mother."

UP WITH MOTHERS

"A woman *is* her mother," Sexton tells us, and many father's daughters have been terrified at the prospect. Yet as long as maternal heritage is denied, the personality cannot be integrated nor identity achieved—we cannot become the "radiant daughters" of an equal Lilith. In a few other writers—William Gass, Grace Paley, Hortense Calisher, and Tillie Olsen—our maternal heritage offers more attractions.

William Gass shares Kesey's concern with the destructive effects of modern society on the individual. However, Gass avoids the traditional embodiment of society's evil in women; instead, he encourages individuals, male or female, to turn away from the social orders and rediscover the natural order. In *Omensetter's Luck* (1967), his only novel of the decade, Gass creates an unusual hero who is admired for his " 'unnatural' naturalness, this refusal to take thought or make choices, this 'living by not observing . . . by joining himself to what he knew.' ' The intuitive is recognized as an organic way of knowing, the irrational admired as an identification with the natural world which leads Omensetter to define himself through his actions in harmony with the world around him. A similar insight into the possible relationships between natural order and social order is explored by a woman in Gass's later short story, "Order of Insects," which was collected in *In the Heart of the Heart of the Country* (1969). This woman discovers through the dead roaches in her house her own interest in universal order.

The woman is puzzled by her growing interest in the roaches, telling herself "it's no study for a woman . . . bugs." Even after gaining new insights and self-awareness through this interest, she argues that it is "absurd":

I am the wife of the house. This point of view I tremble in is the point of view of a god, and I feel certain, somehow, that could I give myself entirely to it, were I not continuing a woman, I could disarm my life, find peace and order everywhere; and I lie by my husband and I touch his arm and consider the temptation. But I am a woman. I am not worthy.

"Temptation" is the key word; Eve too was tempted by such knowledge, by a chance to "be as gods." The knowledge of the natural order of life may again offer new beginnings. Meanwhile, however, the wife and mother of this story recognizes the clash between her roles and her desire:

I could go away like the wise cicada who abandons its shell to move to other mischief. I could leave and let my bones play cards and spank the children. . . . Peace. How can I think of such ludicrous things—beauty and peace, the dark soul of the world—for I am the wife of the house, concerned for the rug, tidy and punctual, surrounded by blocks.

The real maternal heritage—an understanding of nature—is buried beneath her inherited roles, and she sees herself as "surrounded by blocks." It is the shell—the bones—which fulfills the roles, while the woman inside explores the natural order and finds there beauty and peace. In the process of exploration, she becomes aware of herself and of life in new and vital ways. Only briefly is she deterred by the ugliness and violence symbolized by the roaches, discovering soon that "it isn't possible to feel disgust toward such an order." An examination of the reality of what had formerly been to her the least attractive aspect of nature offers her insight into the universal order which renews her hope. That a male writer has attributed such a quest for knowledge to a woman character is significant: Gass allows his characters to combine the knowledge of the irrational and the rational, the self and the society, violence and order to resolve the dualism that would put these in opposition rather than combining them to find viable alternatives to the faltering social order presently in effect. Turning to nature for order emerging out of the violence that had deterred earlier explorations, he also turns to women as well as men for the human ability to choose and shape our world. "I don't know which is more surprising," the narrator admits to herself, "to find such order in a roach, or such ideas in a woman."

Another aspect of our maternal heritage is explored in the slim collection of short stories by Grace Paley, *The Little Disturbances of Man* (1959). The title not only refers to the everyday disturbances which absorb the lives of most of Paley's characters; it more specifically refers to the women and children who distract their men from the serious pursuits of life—such as joining an army somewhere, as Virginia's husband leaves to do in "An Interest in Life." But Paley's women are not disturbed much by the exits and entrances of their men; they accept (as did Welty's women) that a man must and will wander and their lives continue much the same way whether or not the men are present. These lower-class, New York City women haven't been exposed to that higher education which so poorly prepares women for the reality of social roles. They have absorbed their knowledge instead from their mothers (because their fathers were seldom present either), and they are able to accept their lives with equanimity precisely *because* the pattern has not changed.

In short, Paley presents an American subculture which, although Margaret Mead has defined America legally as patriarchal,[40] operates along the lines of a matrilineal culture. In matriarchy, Mead explains, "the order and governing of the family . . . are lodged in the women rather than in men" and a society is matrilocal when "house and land are owned by women and pass from mother to daughter, and husbands move in and out."[41] Women may not own the houses in Paley's stories, but they do hold them, while the men do come and go; and childraising is obviously the woman's exclusive responsibility, as is the household governance, even if the current husband or boyfriend may be considerate enough to become—as the title of another story indicates—"The Used-Boy Raiser[s]." Yet, in this woman's world, as in the female communities which govern the Mississippi of Welty's fiction, the man, when present, is always deferred to and is assumed to encompass all intellectual and worldly interests beyond the household. Women are both freed by and confined to their "interest in life"—as Paley both admires and satirizes them.

In a style with, as Roth observes, "new and rich emotional subtleties, with a kind of backhanded grace and irony all its own,"[42] Paley unveils a world of love, warmth and happiness. The best example in this collection is "An Interest in Life," which begins with the husband's desertion. Living with his wife Virginia and their children has become too much for him. When Virginia announces the fourth pregnancy in as many years, he exclaims "I got to get out of here . . . I'm going nuts." Then he kisses his wife and goes "to join the army somewhere," and she looks forward to his eventual return. Meanwhile, she takes as lover a friend who helps raise her sons, but is very careful not to get pregnant because "when my husband comes back, realizing the babies are in school and everything easier, he won't forgive me if I've started it all up again— noisy signs of life are so much trouble to a man."

If the mother complained in Updike's *Of the Farm* that her men held her responsible for everything, she would get no sympathy from Virginia, who accepts this as the simple truth for a wife: "Still, face facts, if my husband didn't budge in life, it was my fault. On me, as they say, be it." Still, she views marriage in romantic terms, as a love match: "Once I met my husband with his winking looks, he was my only interest. Wild as I had been with John and the others, I turned all my wildness over to him and there was no question in my mind."

Virginia accepts the sexual stereotypes completely, knowing that although she is content with her family,

> men are different, they have to own money, or they have to be famous, or everybody in the block has to look up to them from the cellar stairs. A woman counts her children and acts snotty, like she invented life, but men *must* do well in the world. I know that men are not fooled by being happy.

Like Faith in "The Used-Boy Raisers," Virginia is willing to watch her men "set off in pride on paths which are not my concern." She knows that her "interest in life" is all she needs and would be willing to support her children in any way necessary, just as she is willing to accept that support from whatever man or social agency may wish to contribute. She is unconcerned with progress; her life is as cyclical as the seasons. In many ways, "An Interest in Life" reads like an advertisement for the feminine mystique, and we have to remind ourselves that it is written by a woman. Only then do we see the implicit rebellion, which becomes clearer with each collection of short stories that Paley will publish later. While Virginia may not blame her husband, the irony in her situation is clear. Hers is the contentment of the circumscribed life; it can only be maintained as long as she is exposed neither to the mainstream of her society nor to the failure of her support systems. Education, population control, even the need for self-support would change her world drastically. That the mystique can be best maintained only in a dependent subculture reveals how hopelessly impractical it is for modern woman. Virginia "counts her children and acts snotty"; others count them and begin to worry. Certainly a houseful of children, like a litter of kittens, can keep a mother occupied and happy; however, in today's shrinking world, someone else might be paying too high a price for that animal level of contentment to be maintained. Despite the humor and accuracy of Paley's portrayal, Virginia as a role model offers little in her blithe acceptance of life. The picture will grow noticeably darker as the violent realities of today undermine Virginia's and our world in Paley's next two collections, *Enormous Changes at the Last Minute* (1975) and *Later the Same Day* (1985).

A more positive acceptance of maternal heritage, and one much harder to come by, can be found in the fiction of this decade by Hortense Calisher. Calisher leaves behind her fathers' daughters of the 50's who dread becoming like the mothers they see compromising and losing themselves in the feminine mystique. Or rather, she brings them into the 60's and lets them reevaluate that maternal heritage. Her women learn to reject the stumbling blocks of feminine stereotypes; they have grown beyond the limiting protectivity of their fathers and will learn to accept the insights of their mothers so that they can gain a better sense of themselves. They show that if women are able to integrate their fragmented selves by rejecting stereotypes and accepting both their maternal and paternal heritages, they can use the power of their individual perception and freedom of choice to change their world.

Certainly, these changes are not apparent in *False Entry* (1961), Calisher's first novel and first work of the 60's. The women in this novel continue the stereotypes of the 50's. Ruth, whose history will be clarified later in *The New Yorkers* (1969), appears here as an unbelievably passive young woman with a sordid past, although she may not be responsible for it any more than any of us are in such a sordid world. Her relationship with Pierre Goodman is suitably bleak, as he pleads: "Pity us, for we are pitiable. But we dare. . . . The sin is not to try; the illusion is to exalt what we can do." Both Pierre and Ruth have been isolated by their deforming differences; bravely they come together hoping to dissolve into the ordinary. For one who accepts that the world will never improve, that the human condition demands the sacrifice of idealism, Calisher offers the comfort common to the other novelists of the 50's: "and that's company!"

Nor are the other women in *False Entry* more than passive and self-sacrificing. But Ruth is the one to watch: she not only lives the stereotypes; she is the prototype. She inspires Pierre to reflect on the "endless forgiveness" of women: "If they are women they have it, a deep, self-paralyzing sea of trust, an endless remission for some man's sins. And one seeks them for it almost as much as for their sex." Ruth also knows that "a woman's part was to chatter," Pierre tells us, "on whatever would be made to seem harmless, so she did so, but in a way that almost said to me then as she did much later, 'I won't trespass. I will manage—not to!' " Her bravery reminds him of "the congenital bravery of women," who are "bear-

ing within, like a secondary egg, an eager tenderness to be torn.
. . . This is the human condition and she was playing the woman's
part of it." The saving grace is in that last line: surely any woman
conforming to these stereotypes so completely is "playing the
woman's part," and such acting deserves an award! Since this is
Pierre's point of view, and he is similarly traditional in his view of
other women, it is perhaps more indicative of his character than of
theirs.

For instance, Pierre describes Nanette, a woman with a career,
as "ruthless to the eye and lissome to the touch, stony as any
courtesan where her career as vice president of a department store
is concerned, her secret cartilage, appearing in the spot where one
would expect it—in her cleavage, sticky and interminable, to an
indifferent married man." As Dorothy Yost Deegan notes, "the
social attitude toward the woman who remains single, as expressed
by the novelist in America, is far more derogatory than otherwise.
She is at best, as the novelist sees her, an unfortunate member of
society."[43]

Even Pierre's mother doesn't escape his criticism when she dares
to suggest that he adopt the name of his uncle and her new husband,
sacrificing the name of a father who had died ignominiously before
Pierre was born: "How gladly she hurried to annul forever my
father and all the heritage of that other life, hers too, that went
with him." When he signs the petition he chooses another name
out of revenge, although he is sorry to punish his uncle by refusing
his name when "he and I, in our male dreams, were allied. It was
my mother I should be bitter against, who . . . was the natural, the
female guardian of all the philistine." This ambivalence toward
women, exaggerating them in either direction as idealized sufferers
at one end or destructive philistines at the other, not only echoes
judgments in earlier works by Calisher but also reflects a characterization of women which permeates our literature, as Sandra M.
Gilbert and Susan Gubar have shown as they have argued that "a
woman writer must examine, assimilate, and transcend the extreme
images of 'angel' and 'monster' which male authors have generated
for her."[44] Calisher shows that these images have not been confined
to literature; nor will they end with Pierre. Calisher's women must
grow painfully slowly at times into an acceptance of their maternal
heritage and out of the compromising roles.

False Entry was followed by two collections of short stories, *Tale for the Mirror* (1962) and *Extreme Magic* (1964), and one novel, *Textures of Life* (1963), which continued the pattern Calisher had established. In *Tale for the Mirror*, for instance, are the autobiographical stories of the Elkin family discussed earlier. Yet even in this collection the questioning has begun. Although some of the women find fulfillment or fail to as they have or do not have children, some mothers are already feeling less than fulfilled by motherhood. Dorothy in "Saturday Night" has "in her voice, her attitude... the echoing plaint of the other women," her husband discovers. "Nobody seems to enjoy or glory in his children anymore, he thought. We're always plotting, calculating how to have a personal life in spite of them." Dorothy clearly lives in a different section of New York City than do Paley's women! She is a modern woman and she and her friends feel trapped:

Many of them had had careers or talents that marriage and children had interrupted or aborted, and to the memory of those they paid insistent and bitter homage, constantly toting up the frustrations of housewifery in remarks which were like a kind of bleak, allusive shorthand understood by them all.

Disillusionment haunts these women who have tried to fit themselves into their roles. The lonely wife of a senator who invites a pair of newlyweds to "The Night Club in the Woods" merely presages the future for the new wife, who realizes already that "silently, silently, we too have drawn in our horns." Sadder still is the widow in "The Scream on Fifty-Seventh Street" who fears "the sort of disintegrating widowhood, full of mouse fears and softening self-indulgences of the manless." She begins to envy "the simplicity, even the spinsterhood" of Miss Finan because it "had barred her from imagination as it had from experience" and waits for age to free her as well. Even marriages end; the widow is reduced to hearing and finally waiting for the scream of another lonely soul: "waiting for it—for its company." Cold company indeed!

Textures of Life reveals the compromises extracted from a young woman of the 50's in accepting her maternal heritage. Emily Hahn's summary of the story is revealing:

Textures treats of something immediately familiar to everyone, friction between generations. A boy and girl marry. The girl is in violent rebellion against her widowed mother in her snug little uptown flat. She herself, she is determined, will never be caught like the elder woman in a mesh of *things*; she has tremendous scorn of property and security. . . . The young couple compromise, compromise further, until there comes a time when resentment against their elders has been burnt away. They are grown up.[45]

In this bleak picture, the frustrations of the women build up despite the compromises they settle for. David notices this in his young wife:

Her hair was growing again to her shoulders as he had bidden her; she looked the same. He had a glimpse even of how women might live remembering best their losses, feeding on the intangible ones, living their lives by private stations of those very losses—of youth, of infatuation— which men, out in the public world, managed to hold up as gains.

Liz is learning to do "as he had bidden her" because she needs his approval. "Men really ask less of externals, you know," David's father has told Liz's mother, Margot. "Women, on the other hand, have to be conventional. I mean—whether they know it or not, they always are." Margot knows the pain of having a daughter— having someone who rebels against repeating your compromises. "Women who had sons were always coarser-grained—breezier, more accustomed to a claque," she tells David's father. "Not softened, put off their confidence by the lash of daughters." Margot knows that Liz too will be changed by her daughter May, but Liz still struggles:

If Margot's presence would not let her be a mother, then she would be a girl again, rediscovering her need, in all this happy humdrum, to rebel and not forbear, even to shut off from May that new fount of knee-high wisdom May herself had opened in her, and fling up the single hand again— to push against the weave.

Liz becomes "the mother" the first time May makes her suffer, and Calisher has marked it as the onset of puberty, the previous plateau in a woman's life, is marked; as Liz simultaneously realizes "with the certainty of a daughter" that "this is the way it will be, between us" while she also feels "in soft, continuous answer, the wet menstrual blood on her thighs." Against her will, Liz accepts her maternal heritage as an inevitable doom.

Again, in *Extreme Magic*, the Elkins return to tell us that Hester is not happy with mothers, however right they may be. In "The Gulf Between," the practical Mrs. Elkins stands up to her husband, refusing to give him the stock she has bought over the years out of her household money to save for her children. Joseph is shocked by her refusal: "God, what kind of woman are you, to make a man abase himself so? Over *money*!"

Hester, of course, agrees with her beleaguered father: "She aligned her free hand on his shoulder. 'I wonder what I would have looked like,' she said in a hard voice, 'if you had not married her.' " Yet Hester has come to recognize that her father cannot protect her; she must protect him.

Calisher's changing tone is again apparent in Eleanor in "The Rabbi's Daughter," a "thin fair girl whom motherhood had hollowed, rather than enhanced." Eleanor almost envies her cousins because "conformity would protect them," while she is one of "the shriveled, talented women" who have only their premarital *juvenalia* to remember their talents by. "A man, she thought jealously, can be reasonably certain it was his talent which failed him, but the women, for whom there are still so many excuses, can never be so sure." The story ends with Eleanor accepting the role of mother and nursing her baby, but her smile to her husband is "quizzical and false," and previously she has wanted to "warn him standing there, trusting in the devious shadow of her resentment." Even Calisher's women are beginning to resent what before they had been encouraged to accept as inevitable.

One woman in *Extreme Magic* actually rebels—a career woman—and is admired for it by Mrs. Ponthus in "If You Don't Want to Live I Can't Help You." Helen Bonner is "Paul's girl": Paul is Mrs. Ponthus' nephew, a "man with a talent to be nourished, a weakness to be supported." When Helen decides to leave him, she has ironically "achieved wifely status at last, as the person by whom he was most misunderstood." When Paul asks Mrs. Ponthus to bring Helen back, he complains bitterly: "She let me lean on her for years. . . . She got me into this straitjacket. Now she can damn well get me out of it." His tone upsets his aunt, and "for a moment she was rigid with anger, on the part of a woman she had never known well." The first signs of sisterhood, albeit dim and guilty, begin to shine forth in Calisher's fiction.

This glimmer becomes a glow in Calisher's next novel, *Journal from Ellipsia* (1966). Since Calisher has found no exit for her women from the box of their society in her perception of reality, she has stepped outside that reality into speculative fiction to gain perspective in this novel, which presents an incipient rebellion of women against their assigned part in the human condition. They are willing to change places with extraterrestrial beings from Ellipsia who, significantly, are asexual. The Ellipsian who takes the place of Janice Jamison, a young anthropologist who "since the age of six . . . had been a jampot for boys," offers an outsider's perspective on the sex roles of our society, which is contrasted to the traditional viewpoint offered by the other narrator and Janice's ex-lover, Jack Linhouse.

To be male, the Ellipsian soon discovers, is to be "straight"; to be female is to be "curved." She's are the "silly-unsafe" and the "brightly-stupid"; males are "stupidly-bright." Just enough difference to reflect the prejudices it observes, just enough similarity to show how shallow the differences are. The narrator learns quickly to aim for the male while on earth: "But I have high hopes of gender. The straightest." A male "carries its own weight, stands fast and talks short. I intend to fight for my rites."

Coming from the outside and from a "curved" environment itself, the Ellipsian suspects that "maybe the mixture went as far here as even to cause straights and curves both to be present in the same person. Maybe even your straight individuals were partially curved—though not much, of course . . . and your curved ones, partly . . . though in even scantier proportion." The androgynous character of both sexes has finally been suggested in Calisher's fiction—as speculation from an outsider, of course! And the invasion is doomed to be unsuccessful, anyway; only women could be tempted by the concept of "nothingness" because, like Updike's women, they had been taught already the nothingness of femininity: "Use the brightly-stupid ones to get us there; they have more reason to. And trained as they have been to seem humble and amenable, they have more energy for the final arrogance."

Journal from Ellipsia is followed in 1966 by the joint publication of two novellas, *The Railway Police* and *The Last Trolley Ride*. The woman narrator of the first of these is another grotesque whose individuality is a deformity: she is bald. Yet, instead of finding an equally deformed man with whom to share her misery, she bravely breaks the pattern. "I wasn't out to be a heroine—I wasn't serious enough for it," she protests. "I just wanted to be ordinary." She has hidden, therefore, under a magnificent collection of wigs. Her brother, who shares this family heritage which asserts itself at the end of adolescence, profits from it by becoming an actor; the male, operating publicly, again can transform his losses into gains. Perhaps, also, we allow a wider range of differences in men than we do in women: as we had also learned in *Textures of Life,* "women . . . have to be conventional."

But if being an individual requires more courage for women, Calisher's woman is now ready. She ventures baldly into the world, shares a niche in a viaduct with a stanger who had stolen her raincoat, and challenges the authority of society: "Come, you narks, cops, feds, dicks, railway police, members of the force everywhere! Run with us! If the world is round, who's running after who? . . . And so—I was born." Rebirth has again offered new visions for society as well as the individual being "born." Coming out of her closet of wigs, she becomes a subject rather than the decorated object:

And I?—I'm a silly woman—I tripped along mystically, thinking of all the new roles my new head might have in store for me. I thought I saw the pattern of the life it held out to me and all wanderers, a life that was all episodes, through which I was the connecting string. Though these were to fall tangential as snow, it was my fate to unite them. Is *this* ordinary?

Calisher has impelled her women into lives of action, defining themselves and their society by the choices they make, wanderers who weave themselves as "connecting string[s]" into the tapestry of episodic life, helping us see the pattern as well. Such an "ordinary" life *is* special.

To test the strength of her new convictions, Calisher traces the present growth to its roots in the past. *The Last Trolley Ride* introduces the Pardee sisters, Emily and Lottie, who represent our literary heritage of the divided woman—angel and monster/whore, burden and bitch, feminine mystique and isolated feminist. The elder sister Lottie, "round and soft as she was, and always waiting to be told, and pretty in the face as a kewpie doll," is unmistakably the angel. She is properly dependent too, while the younger sister Emily—less attractive with "large eyes that were either farsighted or near, but so vague that they kept you from seeing how neatly her hands were going"—was the businesswoman of the two. Emily is not only efficient; she is also quite liberated, especially for the turn of the century.

Both women (as is fitting since they are aspects of the same woman divided artificially by social stereotypes) marry men named Jim. Emily and her Jim have an affair before marriage, of course. She fits no stereotypes: "And Emily, in her woman's way or merely in Emily's, was left free to expiate herself or approve—whoever knew which with Emily?—what she would *not* do." Nor will Emily judge others: "I can't say what men are, the way you can, or what women are." Although she seems much too independent to succeed, she makes an excellent wife, mother, and helpmate for her Jim.

Lottie, on the other hand, turns out to prefer eating to sex; in fact, she is willing to sell herself for a good meal: " 'It was because I found out—how she *would* do it,' he cleared his throat. 'For a treat,' he said. 'For food. . . . I couldn't stand it. It was like training up a dog!" ' Lottie is an exaggerated symbol of marriage as a bargain in which the men provide support in exchange for sexual compliance. Calisher has successfully ridiculed feminine stereotyping in this novel while offering a wife and mother worthy of admiration in the new, efficient, independent Emily.

Calisher's gift for humor, so richly demonstrated in these two novellas and in *Journal from Ellipsia*, has been used to satirize the very stereotypes which had boxed in her women in the 50's. Unlike Welty and others, she had written no comic novels during that decade—she found nothing funny about the compromising and accommodating—or even the company. Instead, she uses humor to ridicule rather than accept the stereotypes.

Calisher's next and most important challenge in the 60's comes when she returns to a personal past, to Ruth's past, and here the transitional humor is gone and a serious reexamination of maternal heritage reinstates its values for daughters. *The New Yorkers* (1969) provides a startlingly different but obviously related picture of the young woman of *False Entry*. Exorcising the tension between mothers and daughters, Calisher has Ruth Mannix first murder and afterwards learn to accept her mother as a woman and as an individual. Significantly, at least two crucial moments in Ruth's development are accompanied, as in *Textures*, by menstrual blood—the murder itself and Ruth's first sexual experience—underlining not only woman's identification with nature but also her relation to violence, to "nature red of tooth and claw." Blood embodies the seeming contradictions of death and life; menstrual blood specifically symbolizes growth and nurturing. Yet in our society, many young women have been taught, as I was, that this was "dirty blood" that the body had to reject monthly. Mirriam, Ruth's mother, is more realistic in her teachings, telling Ruth that "it's only the body pushing against civilization. . . . When you have a baby, for once they let you walk it as it should be, letting the watery animal drip down." Ruth makes the connection herself in her first words after shooting her mother, delivering the message she had entered the bedroom to give her: "It's come like you said, Mummy. The blood."

Mirriam, unfaithful to her husband and vibrantly alive, is the bitch monster of Ruth's maternal heritage just as surely as Ruth is the angel prototype in *False Entry*. The Judge, Ruth's father, remembers the way Mirriam "stayed in her society, her world, yet slanged it." Ruth remembers that "she only lived when she was moving, acting—she said it herself. Action, she meant. She couldn't *pretend*, not at all. She always had to speak out." Defined through honesty and action, Mirriam herself adds to this composite picture when she tells her son David: "Let no one convince you. Of what you ought to feel. Like they convinced me."

Mirriam tries to pass her female knowledge on to Ruth, talking about childbirth ("You'll want everything they call weird—if you're like me") and men ("Your father's not like us—he can't face the world as we do. It's not allowed him. He has to dream. He's a man."). Although man as dreamer is a cliché, in this context it should remind us, as does Sontag, that the dream is an excuse for abdicating responsibility for one's own thoughts and actions—for irrational realities.

Ruth learns more, perhaps, from observing Mirriam—her model of what a woman is and can be. And what her mother is is frus-

trated, because she "knew almost nothing—she was still finding—
and she knew it was hopeless . . . . Sometimes she talked to me
about the cosmos. 'Imagine me,' she said. 'Talking like that.' "
Like the narrator of Gass's "Order of Insects" or the women who
would journey to Ellipsia, these women discover an interest in
universals alien to their sexual stereotypes. Such behavior and
thoughts in a woman are, as Phyllis Chesler has warned us, considered insanity. The Judge has commented on Mirriam's "lady's
laugh": "All her intensity—or imbalance—was there." Yet Mirriam
envisions a changing world, as Ruth hears her explain to Chauncy
Olney: "Sometimes I felt the world-to-come, the world right outside our door, like an egg inside me. . . . *Me*, who could never stand
a mother's role. Maybe women like me are a new, non-sex to
come." The maternal heritage announces the dawn of a new world,
an androgynous vision born of today's woman. Marge Piercy will
project such a future world, as will other women writers of fantastic
literature, in her fiction.

To share her mother's insights, Ruth must face the violence of
maturity. Even Mirriam had once been her father's daughter first
and admits that "daughters breed daughters." But Ruth escapes the
dependency this symbolizes by escaping innocence; her first step is
murdering her mother.

The Judge is supposedly protecting Ruth by covering up her
crime, but this puts her in his power as well, as cousin Augusta
points out when she says that his "favoring of Ruth was *always*
multiple. Beneath the need to protect and conceal, which was par-
amount, were all those other motives. Ruth is himself." Again we
hear echoes of Strindberg's *The Father* and of Jackson's *Hangsaman*;
the daughter is an extension of the father, perhaps even acting for
him when she acts. Within this cocoon of protection, however,
Ruth is a developing chrysalis.

Ruth's next step toward maturity is her sexual encounter with
Edwin. "It wasn't rape," she tells her father's mistress Ninon afterwards: "I went with Edwin. In my father's house. Daughters
do it all the time." She has in fact repeated her mother's experience,
in the house which had belonged to her mother's father as well.
The cocoon is beginning to crack.

Ruth tells Ninon that Mirriam was like the "assoluta," the dancer
who "is to keep the balance—to which all eyes must now and then

return. It's the wildness, with the truth in it." To claim this maternal heritage, she must tell the story of the murder. Austin Fenno, a warm fatherly protector who wants to relieve her of her suffering, is, as Augusta recognizes, "the right one to have told. And to pass on from." He offers her the strategic retreat in which to unite the self, although he would like to shield her "against the resemblance he saw in her" to her mother. As we have already learned in *False Entry*, their marriage will be brief. Ruth is now ready to make the connections within, accepting her past with her present, her maternal with her paternal heritage, and to face not only the world she has known but even her mother's "world-to-come."

In her single but magnificent collection of short stories published in the 60's, Tillie Olsen explores maternal heritage through the eyes of the mothers rather than the daughters. *Tell Me a Riddle* (1961) articulates the silences between mothers and daughters as well as between women and men. The real silent majority is the working class, and Olsen transforms that silence into music, the poetry of life.

We are within the mother's mind in "I Stand Here Ironing," as she explores her relationship to her teenage daughter. The interaction, and lack of it, between mother and daughter is poignantly documented, and the fabric of their lives so closely interwoven is clearly resistant to the pressing influences of society. While the mother recognizes that her daughter is "a child of her age, of depression, of war, of fear," she also wills her the knowledge "that she is more than this dress on the ironing board, helpless before the iron." Despite the debilitating problems of her life, the daughter has blossomed. Whatever her strengths and weaknesses, she has not only survived but also discovered her unique gift for comedy— a gift constituted out of the pains and pleasures of her growth. Her mother also realizes the responsibility that comes with the discovery of self: "Now suddenly she was Somebody, and as imprisoned in her difference as she had been in anonymity." Yet the daughter has been able to translate her heritage into a gift, and she offers that gift to the world.

Every individual contributes something unique to humanity, as Brooks had reminded us in *Maud Martha*. Olsen shows how the ordinary woman is always special; from the very act of living comes the value of life. In the title story, Olsen offers a portrait at her moment of death of another woman who has fulfilled her roles of wife and mother and is given a brief respite, before cancer claims her, to live for herself. In this short period, the past merges with the present and the woman is complete. Her vitality and perception are not lost; they are lovingly courted and inherited by her granddaughter Jeannie.

Jeannie has appeared in the other two stories of the collection as well. The growth of her appreciation for woman's heritage can be seen as the stories chronicle her resistance. In "Hey Sailor, What Ship?" the youngest Jeannie is embarrassed by the drunken sailor who periodically invades her home on his shore leaves. The stories she loved at four bore her now that she has grown "taller than" her mother. Despite her mother's warnings, she is rude to this man who disturbs her life. She cannot yet absorb the knowledge offered in the kitchen, her mother's insight that "of course he belongs here, he's a part of us, like family. . . . Jeannie, this is the only house in the world he can come into and be around people without having to pay." Patiently, her mother schools Jeannie in the human (often labeled female) values, perceiving beauty and knowledge where the uninitiated see only social censure.

Jeannie begins to differentiate herself from the social attitudes of her peers in the next story, "O Yes." She now observes the conflict between personal insight and social acceptance in her younger sister, who is abandoning her Negro best friend because of peer pressure. She can interpret Carrie's conflict because it reflects her own. She tells her mother that "It's like Ginger and me. Remember Ginger, my best friend in Horace Mann? But you hardly noticed when it happened to us, did you . . . because she was white? . . . Don't you know about junior high? How they sort?" Jeannie's mother might have to be reminded of the signs of prejudice and conformity, but the comprehension she ultimately offers to her daughters is implicit in Jeannie's growing insight. Olsen captures the mother's wisdom in her final loving interchange with Carrie—in the words she never speaks:

Caressing, quieting.
Thinking: *caring asks doing. It is a long baptism into the seas of humankind, my daughter. Better immersion than to live untouched. . . . Yet how will you sustain? Why is it like it is?*

Sheltering her daughter close, mourning the illusion of the embrace.
And why do I have to care?

Armed with her mother's knowledge, Jeannie is ready to accept
and appreciate her maternal heritage in "Tell Me A Riddle." The
subtitle of this story, "These Things Shall Be," reflects Olsen's all-
encompassing vision that each life is a tapestry of glimmering golds
and drab duns whose beauty is never fully perceived until that life
is complete. The dualities of Western society are resolved in the
female vision: synthesis rather than antithesis brings unity within
the self (androgynous and universal) and between self and society
(communal and reciprocal).

Jeannie gains from and gives to her grandmother Eva through
their interchange. When Jeannie's parents come to visit, their dying
mother, "who in her life had spoken but seldom and then only
when necessary (never having learned the easy, social use of words),
now in dying, spoke incessantly." Jeannie listens and absorbs; in
doing so she gives order to her grandmother's reality, uniting the
present and the past as well as carrying both into the future. What
has time to do with life except to order the cycle? The acceptance
and transference of our human heritage allows us to transcend time,
so that all time culminates in the present moment. So too does
death offer a new beginning, which nature—and perhaps woman
as well—has always known. When her grandmother dies, Jeannie
comforts her grandfather:

She is not there, she promised me. On the last day, she said she would go
back to when she first heard music, a little girl on the road of the village
where she was born. . . . Come back and help her poor body to die.

As Eva reminds us, whatever the social realities and oppressions
may be, the human spirit can grow and offer beauty by transforming and ordering the raw materials of its life.

RUNNING THE REVOLUTION

Revolution begins with the self, in the self. The individual, the basic
revolutionary unit, must be purged of poison and lies that assault the ego
and threaten the heart, that hazard the next larger unit—the couple or pair,

that jeopardize the still larger unit—the family or cell, that puts the entire movement in peril.[46]

Speaking of the Black Revolution, Toni Cade discovers the same need for growth "from the dream outward" we have been examining in the fiction, and she too acknowledges in her explanation of the roots of revolution the individual's responsibility for defining the state that Thoreau described in "Civil Disobedience." In the 60's, revolution is in the air, in the historical and literary assertions of the individual. Social stereotypes and discrimination seek, as Betty Friedan warns, to "make [their] own fiction of fact" by mass producing unknown citizens who are little more than vehicles of their society. Conversely, those individuals reborn into an awareness of their own power can begin a revolution which may eventually make society their vehicle—as it should be—serving as what Thoreau has called "reformers in the great sense" who "serve the state with their consciences also, and so necessarily resist it for the most part."

Today, women who have succeeded in overcoming the stereotypes which would limit them, who have faced and survived the violence of maturation, and who have united their own maternal and paternal heritages to meet the violence of life with the integrity of the individual, join with their brothers to define themselves and their world through action. That their model should be handed down, that woman's heritage should finally be preserved from generation to generation, from growth cycle to growth cycle, is the hope of Women's Studies programs. "Each cycle of progress for women seems to end after a decade or two with precious little real advance toward equality," Carolyn G. Heilbrun complains in *Reinventing Womanhood*,[47] blaming this on three failures of women: to support each other, to "imagine women as autonomous," and to resist male protection.[48] Both the women emerging from the cycle we have traced and the world into which they emerge promise change from that pattern if only because neither individual males nor the patriarchal society can offer protection to or withhold autonomy from today's women. Also, the individual woman recognizes that to live for anything demands an involvement in preserving a world in which to live. "To die for the revolution is a one-shot deal," observes Frances Beale. "To live for the revolution means taking on the more difficult commitment of changing our day-to-day life patterns."[49]

In a world shattered by crumbling traditions, by racial and class protests, by violence in war and peace, and by poverty and ecological disasters, the individual woman shares the burden and the responsibility of guiding the state with her brothers. Reexamination of the denigrated "feminine" spheres of knowledge offers alternatives to the inadequate answers suggested by the present social order. The "flight from the feminine" which Dr. Karl Stern had diagnosed as the sickness of patriarchal society can be remedied; society can integrate its maternal and paternal heritage—its rational and irrational sources of knowledge, its thoughts and feelings, its spirit and its humanity—to create a healthier personality by learning from the model of the individual.

However, to accept and learn from the violence of life is not to justify the violence of man, a violence which is so often a product of frustrations and inequality as Grau and others have shown us. Accepting the violence of life, these women yet record their protests against the unnatural violence of "mankind." The violence of nature, whether it be the hurricane in Grau's *The Hard Blue Sky* or the death of roaches in Gass's "Order of Insects," brings out our best as we struggle against it or penetrate through it to an understanding of the beauty and order of the universe. The violence of man, on the other hand, both the self-destructive violence of suicide and the murderous violence of the Oatesian world, benefits no one. Nature is violent but creative; man's violence against man is only destructive.

Olsen has implicitly decried through her fiction the society which limits humanity from the full realization of its potential. By revealing the beauty and strength of the "ordinary" woman, she encourages us to demand more from a world which limits that woman. What possibilities—what brave new worlds—lie beyond those limitations? While Olsen and Paley offer us glory within our society through the female acceptance of life as it is and willingness to create the beauty of the individual commitment to life—the blossoming of the woman rising above her time and place to assert her humanity—both also reveal women in roles if not as violent at least as confining as those which entrap Oates's characters.

Neither all of their contemporaries nor writers of the future accept any need to preserve such a destructive society. Rather, they have already begun to project possible worlds in which humanity might be able to flower more fully—to change the society and let it become a reflection of the new awareness allowed the individual who synthesizes and transcends divisive stereotyping and prejudice. Calisher has called for a world where "children can learn to be bald" so that women will not be tempted to "go elsewhere"—to Ellipsia, perhaps; Gass's narrator in "Order of Insects" considers leaving her bones to social roles while her spirit soars; even Updike's and Kesey's women walk away from traditional roles whether or not they know where they are going. Action, irrational or not, replaces the passivity of the past, and nature rather than society promises values by which to live. The growth cycle has once again brought the female vision to fruition; the fiction of the next decade will push against the external boundaries of time and place to transform the world through the increased perception of the individual.

NOTES

1. Gail Paradise Kelly, "Women's Liberation and the Cultural Revolution," *Radical America*, 4:2 (February 1970), 21.

2. Marlene Dixon, "Where Are We Going?" *Radical America*, 4:2 (February 1970), 27.

3. Martin Luther King, "Letter from Birmingham Jail," in *The Modern Age*, eds. Howard Lief and James F. Light (New York: Holt, Rinehart & Winston, 1969), 520.

4. Philip Roth, "Writing American Fiction," in *Sense of the Sixties*, eds. Edward Quinn and Paul J. Dolan (New York: The Free Press, 1968), 461.

5. Margaret Mead and Frances Balgley Kaplan, *American Women* (New York: Charles Scribner's Sons, 1965), 204.

6. Alice and Kenneth Hamilton, *The Elements of John Updike* (New York: William B. Eerdmans, 1970), 171.

7. Robert Detweiler, *Four Spiritual Crises in Mid-Century American Fiction* (Gainesville: University of Florida Press, Fall 1963), 16–24.

8. Hamilton, *The Elements*, 129.

9. Ibid.

10. Ibid., 130.

11. John Updike, "Museums and Women," *The New Yorker* (November 18, 1967), 58.

12. Hamilton, *The Elements*, 179–80. Cf. also Detweiler, *Four Spiritual Crises*, 21.

13. Charles Thomas Samuels, *John Updike* (Minneapolis: University of Minnesota Press, 1969), 27.

14. Harriet Rosenstein, "Reconsidering Sylvia Plath," *Ms.*, 1:3 (September 1972), 46.

15. Betty Rollin, "Motherhood: Who Needs It?," in *Women's Liberation*, eds. Michael E. Adelstein and Jean G. Pival (New York: St. Martin's Press, 1972), 61.

16. Rosenstein, "Reconsidering," 46.

17. Ibid.

18. William L. Nance, *Katherine Anne Porter and the Art of Rejection* (Chapel Hill: University of North Carolina Press, 1964), 80–155.

19. Louis Auchincloss, *Pioneers and Caretakers* (Minneapolis: University of Minnesota Press, 1961), 141.

20. Barbara Thompson, "An Interview," in *Katherine Anne Porter: A Critical Symposium*, eds. Lodwick Hartley and George Core (Athens: University of Georgia Press, 1969), 21.

21. Theodore Solotaroff, *The Red Hot Vacuum* (New York: Atheneum, 1970), 119.

22. Auchincloss, *Pioneers*, 147.

23. Nance, *Katherine Anne Porter*, 174.

24. Ibid., 176.

25. Susan Sontag, *Against Interpretation* (New York: Noonday Press, 1966), 8.

26. Cf. Solotaroff, *Red Hot*, 262–3.

27. Anais Nin, *The Novel of the Future* (New York: Macmillan, 1968), 5.

28. Solotaroff, *Red Hot*, 262.

29. Ibid., 263.

30. Ibid., 265.

31. Louise Y. Gossett, *Violence in Recent Southern Fiction* (Durham, NC: Duke University Press, 1965), 189.

32. Cf. Ellen Moers, *Literary Women* (Garden City, NY: Anchor Press/Doubleday, 1977), 140–5.

33. Gossett, *Violence*, 192.

34. Leslie Fiedler, *The Return of the Vanishing American* (New York: Stein & Day, 1968), 60.

35. Ibid., 177.

36. Ibid., 181.

37. Mary Ellman, *Thinking About Women* (New York: Harcourt Brace Jovanovich, 1968), 46.

38. Ibid., 70.

39. Quoted on the title page of Joyce Carol Oates's *them* (Greenwich, CT: Fawcett, 1970).

40. Margaret Mead, *Male and Female* (New York: Dell, 1949), 289–90.

41. Ibid., 289.

42. Roth, "Writing," 458.

43. Dorothy Yost Deegan, *The Stereotype of the Single Woman in American Novels* (New York: Octagon Books, 1969), 185.

44. Sandra M. Gilbert and Susan Gubar, *The Madwoman in the Attic: The Woman Writer and the Nineteenth-Century Imagination* (New Haven: Yale University Press, 1980), 17.

45. Emily Hahn, "In Appreciation of Hortense Calisher," *Contemporary Literature* (then *WSCL*), 6 (Summer 1965), 248.

46. Toni Cade, "On the Issue of Roles," *The Black Woman* (New York: New American Library, 1970), 109.

47. Carolyn G. Heilbrun, *Reinventing Womanhood* (New York: W. W. Norton & Company, 1979), 24.

48. Ibid., 30.

49. Frances Beale, "Double Jeopardy: To be Black and Female," in *The Black Woman*, ed. Toni Cade (see above), 99.

4

Afterword on the 70's and 80's

My effort in this study has been to discern the pattern of growth, a pattern which is natural and infinitely repeatable, as it is reflected in American fiction since 1940 and consequently helps us understand coming of age in contemporary America. I have examined women characters because it is their growth as individuals, I believe, that promises to reestablish a balance in our society. I am not alone in that belief. At the end of the 50's William Wasserstrom predicted their leadership; at the beginning of the 70's Carolyn G. Heilbrun explained their heroic commitment to life. At the beginning of the 80's Barbara Hill Rigney further explained that commitment to be to a life of value, a commitment which can transform society as well. In *Lilith's Daughters: Women and Religion in Contemporary Fiction* (1982), Rigney discusses novels by women which "themselves represent a kind of garden wrested from the wilderness of patriarchal language and ideology, expressive of woman's passage through mythology and religion toward a confrontation with existence, responsibility, and freedom. They are both exorcism and celebration. They reclaim women's right to name, if not God, then more importantly the world and the self."[1]

Clearly the insights offered through the eyes of women in this fiction are human perceptions important to all of us. "Texts need not be interpreted as authorial plots for or against women," Margaret R. Higonnet has argued; "critics now stress instead the intersexuality of the forces that operate within the social structures, a commonsense position corresponding to the political argument that women's liberation is really men's liberation."[2] "Our age,"

Rosalind Miles reminds us, "with its increased social, educational, and emotional mobility has seen many casualties, and not all female; . . . we have come, too, to a fuller acquaintance with the problems of internal migration, awkward transitions of personality which may ruin formerly stable relationships or at best render them obsolete."[3]

Nor is the new world envisioned by women one that need be limited by a national literature or society. America today not only has to admit to the multiplicity of the individual and of its own melting-pot society but also must see itself as part of a world society if not a universal reality. The myths of Lilith and Undine defy domination or even definition—demand room for growth and flexibility. Such is the myth which emerges as women reclaim their "right to name" their God and their world. In her study of women's poetry and visual art in the twentieth century, *Women as Mythmakers* (1984), Estella Lauter points to a collective vision that began to emerge in the 70's from women exercising the responsibility and freedom they had earned through the maturation process we have been examining. Particularly, she found that "certain images, themes, and attitudes recur with sufficient intensity to suggest the presence of a myth that is not the product of community life in a particular geographical region so much as the product of women's common 'ground' of experience in patriarchal societies."[4] Furthermore, while she sees the myth arising from a woman's involvement with life itself through her "actual or potential bodily experience," Lauter does not see men excluded. Rather, she argues that "the belief in the permeability of boundaries embodied in the works I have examined here seems to be also an attempt to extend the sphere of the woman without overriding the integrity of others. The female envisioned (or hoped-for) is one with vastly increased responsibility."[5]

"To go outward; to develop a sense of community; to look to the moral rather than to the emotional dimension; to make the right choice and to make it work; these are not only the tasks of women but of all writers," Miles has asserted.[6] Lauter's "fully-conscious adult woman who exercises her agency (her capacity for self-protection, self-assertion, and self-expansion) to move society toward a less repressive condition" could be a description of the composite woman created by a commitment to that task in the writers we have considered. The poets and artists discussed by Lauter have also offered a composite picture of a woman who is "in tune with powerful non-human forces, capable of transforming herself and of collaborating with others to 'save' both herself and the world."[7]

Can the effects of this maturation be seen in the fiction of the 70's and 80's as well? Poetry, free as it is from social definition, has hailed the individuality of woman, while women characters in realistic novels are still striving for even the slightest recognition of their right to such self-definition. Always reflecting the past moment, realistic fiction must necessarily be a step behind. Even its traditional form, for individuals discovering "the permeability of boundaries," can be oppressive. As Ellen Morgan has argued in her projection of a neo-feminist novel:

Neither the psychological nor the sociological novel is a form adequate to express the neo-feminist conception of woman, for she is not only a psyche, but a political being; not only a product and victim of her culture, but also a personal being who transcends it. The stream-of-consciousness novel, with its tendency to equate reality and value with consciousness, cannot sufficiently express her experience, which is political and social as well as personal and psychological.[8]

Consequently, what we often find in the mainstream novels are women characters as trapped in their social restrictions as ever. The major difference, perhaps, is that they are trapped adults, not children—that they are seen in works by male and female writers alike as equal victims with men in a violent and destructive society. In the new fiction by Ann Beattie, for instance, including *Chilly Scenes of Winter* (1977), *Falling in Place* (1981), and *The Burning House* (1983), societal and familial structures continue to disintegrate and no one wants to take responsibility for anyone. This nightmare of material comfort and human vacuity is echoed by most other contemporary writers as well.

On the other hand, many novelists are moving away from the "mainstream" in style in order to say something new in content. While Joyce Carol Oates takes her dismal view of human possibilities to the past (in which her characters have often seemed to be mired) by writing the historical romances of *Bellefleur* (1981) and *A Bloodsmoor Romance* (1983), we have already seen Hortense

Calisher speculate on alternative futures in *Journal from Ellipsia* to gain perspective on the external and internal shackles which held her women to the feminine mystique. She will venture into the future again in *Mysteries of Motion* (1983), and many other women writers share her decision that fantastic literature can offer a more appropriate and flexible form for mythmaking—and distance enough from the present moment to place it in its universal context, as I have discussed elsewhere.[9] Marge Piercy, for instance, has most successfully combined her realistic evaluation of contemporary America with a vision of its possible futures in *Woman on the Edge of Time* (1976).

Other novelists are free of some of the traditional limitations of the mainstream novel because of their minority status in American fiction. These writers, incorporating formal and ideological variety in their fiction, give us some of the most potent statements of the social implications of modern woman's maturation. In Leslie Marmon Silko's *Ceremony* (1977), for instance, the male protagonist confronts myth itself embodied in the women characters until he can discover a new healing ceremony which can unite his native American heritage with his World War II experience. "It isn't easy. It has never been easy," the myth and his aunt both tell him. At the same time, Silko's native Americans realize that individual sickness is a communal problem and that the healing of the individual can reveal the ceremony for the healing of the community as well: "what happened to the girl did not happen to her alone, it happened to all of them." That the healing comes from "feeling" and from being reunited with the natural world around us also echoes insights our women have gained. Similarly, the black community of Claybourne, Georgia, in Toni Cade Bambara's *The Salt Eaters* (1981) heal one of their own and through her heal themselves. Another "Goddess" community, Claybourne's branch of the Seven Sisters also reminds us that the vision is of a world community.

Healing is never easy; nor is growth. "Endless the Medusa, and Perseus endless," Welty reminds us. Yet these writers of fiction still commit themselves to the world, and to a realism which forces them to define their characters in the social context. As they accept their own individuality and responsibility even for this "world [they] never made," the women characters offer insights which

Bibliography

Hortense
In the Absence of Angels. Boston: Little, Brown & Co., 1951.
False Entry. Boston: Little, Brown & Co., 1961.
Tale for the Mirror. Boston: Little, Brown & Co., 1962.
Textures of Life. Boston: Little, Brown & Co., 1963.
Extreme Magic. Boston: Little, Brown & Co., 1963.
Journal from Ellipsia. London: Secker & Warburg, 1966.
The Railway Police and *The Last Trolley Ride*. Boston: Little,
    Brown & Co., 1966.
The New Yorkers. Boston: Little, Brown & Co., 1969.
Mysteries of Motion. Garden City, NY: Doubleday & Co., 1983.

ens, James Gould
The Just and the Unjust. New York: Harcourt, Brace & World,
    1942.
Guard of Honor. New York: Harcourt, Brace & World, 1948.
By Love Possessed. Greenwich, CT: Fawcett, 1957.
Morning Noon and Night. 1968; rpt. New York: Signet, 1970.

ss, William
Omensetter's Luck. New York: New American Library, 1966.
In the Heart of the Heart of the Country. 1968; rpt. New York:
    Harper & Row, 1969.

ordon, Caroline
The Women on the Porch. New York: Charles Scribner's Sons,
    1944.
The Strange Children. London: Routledge & Kegan Paul, Ltd.,
    1952.
The Forest of the South. New York: Charles Scribner's Sons, 1945.
The Malefactors. New York: Harcourt, Brace & Co., 1956.
Old Red and Other Stories. New York: Charles Scribner's Sons,
    1963.

Grau, Shirley Ann
The Black Prince. New York: Alfred A. Knopf, 1955.
The Hard Blue Sky. New York: Alfred A. Knopf, 1958.
The House on Coliseum Street. New York: Alfred A. Knopf, 1961.
The Keepers of the House. Greenwich, CT: Fawcett, 1964.

Jackson, Shirley
The Road Through the Wall. New York: Farrar, Straus & Giroux,
    1948. Published as *The Other Side of the Street* by New York:
    Pyramid, 1956.
The Lottery. 1949; rpt. New York: Avon/Bard, 1960.
Hangsaman. New York: Farrar, Straus & Giroux, 1951.

could change that world. No longer can these stories of women be categorized, as Carolyn G. Heilbrun has done to women's fiction of the past, as only "stories of acceptance, and passivity."[10] "Female authorship," Heilbrun complains, "when it has not projected its dreams of action upon male characters, has contrived either to endow the expected female destiny with terror, wit and passion— the romance or the comedy of manners—or shown the inevitable despair of passivity—the realistic novel."[11]

Changing the form of the fiction is one of the ways novelists try to break with the patterns of the past while acknowledging their hold on the present. As we "proceed from the dream outward" in the magic realism of Shirley Jackson, in the experimental existential forms of Susan Sontag, in the grotesque exaggerations of Carson McCullers and Flannery O'Connor, even in the speculative leaps of Hortense Calisher, these writers keep us firmly rooted in the here and now of their society. Straining the form to gain perspective on that moment, to see through it to understand its rational and irrational realities, they commit themselves to uniting self and society.

The radiant daughters of Lilith and Undine that fill the pages of these novels have voluntarily left Eden to enter the garden that is our world and to give it new definition. They can be seen in the fiction of Toni Morrison as well, as she combines Christian and African myth to find the black experience in *Song of Solomon* (1978), and as she combines Lilith and Undine in the title character of *Sula* (1975), who shocks yet unites her community. While Maureen Wendall has rejected the forms that literature would offer her in Oates's *them*, she soon complains that "I lived my life but there was no form to it. No shape." What will be the shape of the future? With Undine, we can be sure of only one thing—that it will always be changing while we grasp it. The writers who turn to fantastic literature agree with Sam J. Lundwall that it offers "a subversive thing, the prospect of change."[12] Those who stay in the mainstream can flow with Undine as well into new forms and content, redefining "from the dream outward" the social form of our literature as a prelude to redefining our society and our world, because fiction, as Miles has also asserted, "does not only reflect and record experience; it defines and delineates it too."[13]

NOTES

1. Barbara Hill Rigney, *Lilith's Daughters: Women and Religion in Contemporary Fiction* (Madison: University of Wisconsin Press, 1982), 10.

2. Margaret R. Higonnet, Introduction to *The Representation of Women in Fiction*, eds. Carolyn G. Heilbrun and Higonnet (Baltimore: Johns Hopkins University Press, 1983), xviii.

3. Rosalind Miles, *The Fiction of Sex: Themes and Functions of Sex Differences in the Modern Novel* (New York: Barnes & Noble Books, 1974), 197.

4. Estella Lauter, *Women as Mythmakers: Poetry and Visual Art by Twentieth-Century Women* (Bloomington: Indiana University Press, 1984), 213–14.

5. Ibid., 218.

6. Miles, *The Fiction of Sex*, 197.

7. Lauter, *Women as Mythmakers*, 218.

8. Ellen Morgan, "Humanbecoming: Form & Focus in the Neo-Feminist Novel," in *Images of Women in Fiction: Feminist Perspectives*, ed. Susan Koppelman Cornillon (Bowling Green: Bowling Green University Popular Press, 1972), 183.

9. My study, *Worlds Within Women: Myth and Mythmaking in Fantastic Literature by Women*, will soon be released by Greenwood Press.

10. Carolyn G. Heilbrun, *Reinventing Womanhood* (New York: W. W. Norton & Company, 1979), 139.

11. Ibid.

12. Sam J. Lundwall, *Science Fiction: What It's All About* (New York: Ace, 1971), 24.

13. Miles, *The Fiction of Sex*, 198.

Calisher,

Bibliography

Cozz

PRIMARY SOURCES CITED

Baldwin, James
    Go Tell It on the Mountain. 1953; rpt. New Y
    Giovanni's Room. 1956; rpt. New York: Dell,
    Another Country. 1962; rpt. New York: Dell,
    Going to Meet the Man. 1965; rpt. New York:
    Tell Me How Long the Train's Been Gone. 1968;
      Dell, 1969.

Bambara, Toni Cade
    The Salt Eaters. New York: Random House, 1980

Beattie, Ann
    Chilly Scenes of Winter. Garden City, NY: Doubleda
    Falling in Place. New York: Random House, 1980.
    The Burning House. New York: Random House, 1982

Bellow, Saul
    Dangling Man. 1944; rpt. New York: NAL, 1965.
    The Victim. New York: Vanguard Press, 1947.
    The Adventures of Augie March. 1953; New York: Viking,
    Seize the Day. Greenwich, CT: Fawcett, 1956.
    Henderson the Rain King. New York: Viking, 1959.
    Herzog. Greenwich, CT: Fawcett, 1964.
    Mr. Sammler's Planet. New York: Viking, 1964.

Brooks, Gwendolyn
    Maud Martha. New York: Harper Brothers, 1953.

The Bird's Nest. 1954; rpt. in *The Magic of Shirley Jackson*, ed. Stanley Hyman. New York: Farrar, Straus & Giroux, 1966.
The Sundial. New York: Farrar, Straus, & Cudahy, 1958.
The Haunting of Hill House. New York: Viking, 1959.
We Have Always Lived in the Castle. New York: Viking 1962.
Come Along with Me. Ed. Stanley Hyman. New York: Viking, 1968.

Kesey, Ken

One Flew Over the Cuckoo's Nest. New York: Signet, 1962.
Sometimes A Great Notion. New York: Bantam, 1965.

McCarthy, Mary

The Company She Keeps. New York: Harcourt, Brace & Co., 1942.
Cast A Cold Eye. New York: Harcourt, Brace & World, 1950.
A Charmed Life. New York: Harcourt, Brace & Co., 1950.
The Group. 1963; rpt. New York: Signet, 1964.

McCullers, Carson

The Heart is a Lonely Hunter. 1940; rpt. New York: Bantam, 1961.
The Member of the Wedding. 1946; rpt. New York: Bantam, 1966.
The Ballad of the Sad Café. 1951; rpt. New York: Bantam, 1958.
The Mortgaged Heart. Ed. Margarita G. Smith. Boston: Houghton Mifflin, 1971.

Mailer, Norman

The Naked and the Dead. New York: Rinehart & Company, 1948.
Barbary Shore. New York: Signet, 1951.
The Deer Park. 1955; rpt. New York: Berkley, 1967.
Advertisements for Myself. New York: G. P. Putnam's Sons, 1959.
An American Dream. 1965; rpt. New York: Dell, 1970.
Cannibals and Christians. New York: Dell, 1966.
Why Are We in Vietnam? New York: G. P. Putnam's Sons, 1968.
The Prisoner of Sex. Boston: Little, Brown & Co., 1971.

Malamud, Bernard

The Natural. 1952; rpt. New York: The Noonday Press, 1961.
The Assistant. New York: Signet, 1957.
The Magic Barrel. New York: Farrar, Straus & Co., 1958.
A New Life. 1961; rpt. New York: Dell, 1963.
Idiots First. New York: Farrar, Straus & Co., 1963.

Morrison, Toni

Sula. New York: Alfred A. Knopf, 1973.
Song of Solomon. New York: Alfred A. Knopf, 1977.

Oates, Joyce Carol
> *With Shuddering Fall.* 1964; rpt. Greenwich, CT: Fawcett, 1971.
> *A Garden of Earthly Delights.* Greenwich, CT: Fawcett, 1967.
> *Expensive People.* 1968; rpt. Greenwich, CT: Fawcett, 1970.
> *them.* 1969; rpt. Greenwich, CT: Fawcett, 1970.
> *Wonderland.* New York: Vanguard, 1971.
> *Bellefleur.* New York: E. P. Dutton, 1980.
> *A Bloodsmoor Romance.* New York: Dutton, 1982.

O'Connor, Flannery
> *Wise Blood* (1952); *A Good Man Is Hard to Find* (1955); and *The Violent Bear It Away* (1960). In *Three by Flannery O'Connor.* New York: Signet, 1964.
> *Everything That Rises Must Converge.* New York: The Noonday Press, 1965.
> *Mystery and Manners.* New York: Farrar, Straus & Giroux, 1969.

Olsen, Tillie
> *Tell Me A Riddle.* New York: Dell, 1961.

Paley, Grace
> *The Little Disturbances of Man.* Garden City, NY: Doubleday, 1959.
> *Enormous Changes at the Last Minute.* New York: Farrar, Straus & Giroux, 1974.
> *Later the Same Day.* New York: Farrar, Straus & Giroux, 1985.

Petry, Ann
> *The Street.* 1946; rpt. New York: Pyramid Books, 1961.
> *Country Place.* Boston: Houghton Mifflin, 1947.
> *The Narrows.* Boston: Houghton Mifflin, 1953.

Piercy, Marge
> *Woman on the Edge of Time.* New York: Fawcett Crest, 1976.

Plath, Sylvia
> *Ariel.* New York: Harper & Row, 1965.
> *The Bell Jar.* New York: Harper & Row, 1971.

Porter, Katherine Anne.
> *Ship of Fools.* 1962; rpt. New York: Signet, 1963.
> *Collected Stories.* New York: New American Library, 1970.

Powers, J[ames] F[arl]
> *Prince of Darkness.* 1947; rpt. Garden City, NY: Image, 1958.
> *The Presence of Grace.* Garden City, NY: Doubleday, 1956.
> *Morte d'Urban.* Garden City, NY: Doubleday, 1962.

Roth, Philip
>   *When She Was Good.* 1967; rpt. New York: Bantam, 1968.
>   *Portnoy's Complaint.* New York: Random House, 1969.

Salinger, J[erome] D[avid]
>   *The Catcher in the Rye.* Boston: Little, Brown and Co., 1951.
>   *Nine Stories.* Boston: Little, Brown, 1953.
>   *Franny and Zooey.* 1961; rpt. New York: Bantam, 1964.
>   *Raise High the Roof Beam, Carpenters* and *Seymour, An Introduction.*
>   1963; rpt. New York: Bantam, 1955.

Silko, Leslie Marmon
>   *Ceremony.* New York: Viking, 1977.

Sontag, Susan
>   *The Benefactor.* 1963; rpt. New York: Avon/Bard, 1970.
>   *Against Interpretation.* New York: Noonday, 1966.
>   *Death Kit.* 1967; rpt. New York: Signet, 1968.

Stafford, Jean
>   *Boston Adventure.* New York: Harcourt, Brace & World, 1944.
>   *The Mountain Lion.* New York: Random House, 1947.
>   *The Catherine Wheel.* New York: Harcourt, Brace & Co., 1951.
>   *The Collected Stories.* New York: Farrar, Straus & Giroux, 1969.

Styron, William
>   *Lie Down in Darkness.* New York: Signet, 1951.

Updike, John
>   *The Poorhouse Fair.* New York: Alfred A Knopf, 1959.
>   *Rabbit, Run.* Greenwich, CT: Fawcett, 1960.
>   *The Centaur.* Greenwich, CT: Fawcett, 1963.
>   *Of the Farm.* Greenwich, CT: Fawcett, 1965.
>   *The Music School.* New York: Alfred A. Knopf, 1966.
>   "Museums and Women." *The New Yorker* (November 18,
>   1967):65–73.
>   *Couples.* Greenwich, CT: Fawcett, 1968.
>   *Bech: A Book.* Greenwich, CT: Fawcett, 1970.

Warren, Robert Penn
>   *Night Rider.* 1939; rpt. New York: Berkley, 1956.
>   *All the King's Men.* 1946; rpt. New York: Bantam, 1959.
>   *World Enough and Time.* New York: Random House, 1950.
>   *Band of Angels.* New York: Random House, 1955.
>   *The Cave.* New York: Signet, 1960.

Welty, Eudora
>   *A Curtain of Green*(1941) and *The Wide Net*(1943) in *Selected Stories.*
>   New York: Modern Library, 1966.

The Robber Bridegroom. 1942; rpt. New York: Atheneum, 1963.
Delta Wedding. New York: Harcourt, Brace & World, 1946.
The Golden Apples. New York: Harcourt, Brace & World, 1949.
The Ponder Heart. New York: Harcourt, Brace & World, 1954.
The Bride of the Innisfallen. New York: Harcourt, Brace & World,
    1955.
Losing Battles. Greenwich, CT: Fawcett, 1970.

Other References

Auden, W. H. "September 1, 1939" (d. 1973).
Dickinson, Emily. "Much Madness is Divinest Sense" (d. 1886).
Emerson, Ralph Waldo. "The American Scholar" (1837).
Hawthorne, Nathaniel. *The Scarlet Letter* (1850).
Ibsen, Henrik. *The Doll's House* (1879).
Jeffers, Robinson. "The Bloody Sire" (d. 1962).
King, Martin Luther, Jr. "Letter from Birmingham Jail" (1963).
Millay, Edna St. Vincent. "The Singing Woman By the Wood's Edge"
    (d. 1950).
Mill, John Stuart. *The Subjection of Women* (1869).
Plath Sylvia. "Daddy" (d. 1963).
Rossetti, Dante Gabriel. "Eden's Bower" (d. 1882).
Sexton, Anne. "Housewife" (d. 1974).
Shakespeare, William. *King Lear* (1605).
Spofford, Harriet Prescott. "Priscilla" (1894).
Strindberg, August. *The Father* (1887).
Thoreau, Henry David. "Civil Disobedience" (1849).

SECONDARY BIBLIOGRAPHY

Sources Cited

Adelstein, Michael E. and Jean G. Pival, eds. *Women's Liberation.* New
    York: St. Martin's Press, 1972.
Aldridge, John W. *After the Lost Generation.* New York: Noonday Press,
    1951.
Aldridge, John W. *The Devil in the Fire.* New York: Harper & Row, 1972.
Aldridge, John W. *Time to Murder and Create.* New York: David McKay
    Company, Inc., 1966.
Alter, Robert. *After the Tradition.* New York: E. P. Dutton & Company,
    1969.
Appel, Alfred, Jr. *A Season of Dreams: The Fiction of Eudora Welty.* Baton
    Rouge: Louisiana State University Press, 1965.

Auchincloss, Louis. *Pioneers and Caretakers.* Minneapolis: University of Minnesota Press, 1961.

Balakian, Nona and Charles Simmons, eds. *The Creative Present.* Garden City, NY: Doubleday, 1963.

Baumbach, Jonathon. *The Landscape of Nightmare.* New York: New York University Press, 1965.

de Beauvior, Simone. *The Second Sex.* New York: Bantam, 1952.

Bradbury, John M. *Renaissance in the South.* Chapel Hill: University of North Carolina Press, 1963.

Cade, Toni, ed. *The Black Woman.* New York: New American Library, 1970.

Chesler, Phyllis. *Women and Madness.* New York: Avon, 1972.

Clayton, John J. *Saul Bellow: In Defense of Man.* Bloomington: Indiana University Press, 1968.

Cornillon, Susan Koppelman, ed. *Images of Women in Fiction: Feminist Perspectives.* Bowling Green: Bowling Green University Popular Press, 1972.

Detweiler, Robert. *Four Spiritual Crises in Mid-Century American Fiction.* Gainesville: University of Florida Press, 1963.

Deegan, Dorothy Yost. *The Stereotype of the Single Woman in American Novels.* New York: Octagon Books, 1969.

Dixon, Marlene. "Where Are We Going?" *Radical America,* 4:2 (February 1970), 26–35.

Drake, Robert. *Flannery O'Connor.* New York: William B. Eerdmans, 1966.

Eisinger, Chester E. *Fiction of the Forties.* Chicago: University of Chicago Press, 1963.

Ellman, Mary. *Thinking About Women.* New York: Harcourt Brace Jovanovich, 1968.

Evans, Oliver. *The Ballad of Carson McCullers.* New York: Coward-McCann, Inc., 1965.

Fiedler, Leslie. *Love and Death in the American Novel.* New York: Dell, 1960.

Fiedler, Leslie. *The Return of the Vanishing American.* New York: Stein & Day, 1968.

Foster, Jeanette H. *Sex Variant Women in Literature.* New York: Vantage, 1956.

Foster, Richard. *Norman Mailer.* Minneapolis: University of Minnesota Press, 1968.

French, Warren. *J. D. Salinger.* New York: Twayne, 1963.

French, Warren. *The Fifties: Fiction, Poetry, Drama.* Deland, FL: Everett/Edwards, Inc., 1970.

Friedan, Betty. *The Feminine Mystique.* New York: Dell, 1963.

Gilbert, Sandra M. and Susan Gubar. *The Madwoman in the Attic: The Woman Writer and the Nineteenth-Century Imagination*. New Haven: Yale University Press, 1979.

Gordon, Caroline. "Flannery O'Connor's *Wise Blood*," *Critique: Studies in Modern Fiction*, 2 (Fall 1958), 8.

Gordon, Caroline. "With a Glitter of Evil." *New York Times Book Review* (June 12, 1955), 5.

Gossett, Louise Y. *Violence in Recent Southern Fiction*. Durham, NC: Duke University Press, 1965.

Greer, Germaine. *The Female Eunuch*. New York: McGraw-Hill, 1970.

Hahn, Emily. "In Appreciation of Hortense Calisher." *Wisconsin Studies in Contemporary Literature*, 6 (Summer 1965), 248.

Hamilton, Alice and Kenneth. *The Elements of John Updike*. New York: William B. Eerdmans, 1970.

"Hangsaman" (review). *Saturday Review of Literature*, 34 (May 5, 1951), 11.

Hartley, Lodwick and George Core, eds. *Katherine Anne Porter: A Critical Symposium*. Athens: University of Georgia Press, 1969.

Hassan, Ihab H. *Radical Innocence*. Princeton, NJ: Princeton University Press, 1961.

Heilbrun, Carolyn G. *Reinventing Womanhood*. New York: W. W. Norton & Company, 1979.

Heilbrun, Carolyn G. *Toward A Recognition of Androgyny*. New York: Harper & Row, 1973.

Heilbrun, Carolyn G. and Margaret R. Higonnet, eds. *The Representation of Women in Fiction*. Baltimore: Johns Hopkins University Press, 1983.

Hendin, Josephine. *The World of Flannery O'Connor*. Bloomington: Indiana University Press, 1970.

Hyman, Stanley Edgar. *Flannery O'Connor*. Minneapolis: University of Minnesota Press, 1966.

Jessup, Josephine Lurie. *Faith of our Feminists*. New York: Richard R. Smith Publishers, 1950.

Kazin, Alfred. "Heroines." *The New York Review of Books* (February 11, 1971), 28–34.

Kelly, Gail Paradise. "Women's Liberation and the Cultural Revolution." *Radical America*, 4:2 (February 1970), 19–25.

Klein, Marcus. *The American Novel Since World War II*. Greenwich, CT: Fawcett, 1969.

Kraditor, Aileen S. *Up From the Pedestal*. Chicago: Quadrangle Books, 1968.

Lasch, Christopher. *The New Radicalism in America, 1889–1963*. New York: Alfred A. Knopf, 1965.

Lauter, Estella. *Women as Mythmakers: Poetry and Visual Art by Twentieth-Century Women.* Bloomington: Indiana University Press, 1984.

Leeds, Barry H. *The Structured Vision of Norman Mailer.* New York: New York University Press, 1969.

Lief, Howard and James F. Light, eds. *The Modern Age.* New York: Holt, Rinehart & Winston, 1969.

Littlejohn, David. *Black on White.* New York: Viking, 1966.

Lundberg, Ferdinand and Marynia F. Farnham. *Modern Woman: The Lost Sex.* New York: Harper & Brothers, 1947.

Lundwall, Sam J. *Science Fiction: What It's All About.* New York: Ace, 1971.

Lutwack, Leonard. *Heroic Fiction.* Carbondale: Southern Illinois University Press, 1971.

McKenzie, Barbara. *Mary McCarthy.* New York: Twayne, 1966.

Malin, Irving, ed. *Saul Bellow and the Critics.* New York: New York University Press, 1967.

Mead, Margaret. *Male and Female.* New York: Dell, 1949.

Mead, Margaret and Frances Balgley Kaplan, eds. *American Women.* New York: Charles Scribner's Sons, 1965.

Miles, Rosalind. *The Fiction of Sex: Themes and Functions of Sex Differences in the Modern Novel.* New York: Barnes & Noble Books, 1974.

Miller, James E., Jr. *J. D. Salinger.* Minneapolis: University of Minnesota Press, 1965.

Millet, Kate. *Sexual Politics.* Garden City, NY: Doubleday, 1970.

Moers, Ellen. *Literary Women.* Garden City, NY: Doubleday, 1977.

Morgan, Robin, ed. *Sisterhood is Powerful.* New York: Vintage, 1970.

Mussell, Kay. *Fantasy and Reconciliation: Contemporary Formulas of Women's Romance Fiction.* Westport, CT: Greenwood Press, 1984.

Nance, William L. *Katherine Anne Porter and the Art of Rejection.* Chapel Hill: University of North Carolina Press, 1964.

Nin, Anais. *The Novel of the Future.* New York: Macmillan, 1968.

Noble, David W. *The Eternal Adam and the New World Garden.* New York: Grosset & Dunlap, 1968.

O'Connor, Flannery. *Mystery and Manners.* New York: Farrar, Straus & Giroux, 1969.

O'Connor, William Van. *The Grotesque: An American Genre.* Carbondale: Southern Illinois University Press, 1962.

O'Neill, William. *Everyone Was Brave.* Chicago: Quadrangle Books, 1969.

Opdahl, Keith M. *The Novels of Saul Bellow.* University Park, PA: Southern University Press, 1967.

Papashvily, Helen Waite. *All the Happy Endings.* New York: Harper & Brothers, 1956.

Patai, Raphael. *The Hebrew Goddess.* New York: KTAV Publishing House, Inc., 1967.

Philip, R. L. "Shirley Jackson: A Chronology and a Supplementary Check-list." *Bibliographical Society of America Papers*, 60:2 (1966), 209–13.

Pratt, Annis with Barbara White, Andrea Loewenstein, and Mary Wyer. *Archetypal Patterns in Women's Fiction*. Bloomington: Indiana University Press, 1981.

Quinn, Edward and Paul J. Dolan, eds. *Sense of the Sixties*. New York: The Free Press, 1968.

Rigney, Barbara Hill. *Lilith's Daughters: Women and Religion in Contemporary Fiction*. Madison: University of Wisconsin Press, 1982.

Rogers, Katherine. *The Troublesome Helpmate*. Seattle: University of Washington Press, 1966.

Rosenstein, Harriet. "Reconsidering Sylvia Plath." *Ms.*, 1:3 (September 1972), 44–51, 96–99.

Rovit, Earl. *Saul Bellow*. Minneapolis: University of Minnesota Press, 1967.

Samuels, Charles Thomas. *John Updike*. Minneapolis: University of Minnesota Press, 1969.

Schneir, Miriam, ed. *Feminism: The Essential Historical Writings*. New York: Vintage, 1972.

Shinn, Thelma J. "Flannery O'Connor and the Violence of Grace." *Contemporary Literature*, 9 (Winter 1968), 58–73.

Shinn, Thelma J. "Women in the Novels of Ann Petry." *Critique: Studies in Modern Fiction*, 16 (1974), 110–20.

Shinn, Thelma J. *Worlds Within Women: Myth and Mythmaking in Fantastic Literature by Women*. Westport, CT: Greenwood Press, 1986 expected publication date.

Smith, Margarita G. (ed.). *The Mortgaged Heart*. By Carson McCullers. Boston: Houghton Mifflin, 1971.

Solotaroff, Theodore. *The Red Hot Vacuum*. New York: Atheneum, 1970.

Sontag, Susan. *Against Interpretation*. New York: Noonday Press, 1966.

Spacks, Patricia M., ed. *Contemporary Women Novelists*. Englewood Cliffs, NJ: Prentice-Hall, Inc., 1977.

Stern, Dr. Karl. *The Flight From Woman*. New York: Farrar, Straus & Giroux, 1965.

Stock, Irvin. *Mary McCarthy*. Minneapolis: University of Minnesota Press, 1968.

Stone, Merlin. *When God Was A Woman*. New York: Dial, 1976.

Waldmeir, Joseph J., ed. *Recent American Fiction: Some Critical Views*. Boston: Houghton Mifflin, 1963.

Wasserstrom, William. *Heiress of All the Ages*. Minneapolis: University of Minnesota Press, 1959.

Witham, W. Tasker. *The Adolescent in the American Novel 1920–1960*. New York: Frederick Ungar, 1964.

Wylie, Philip. *Generation of Vipers*. 1942; rpt. New York: Pocket Books, 1958.

Related Sources

Alexander, Maxine, ed. *Speaking for Ourselves: Women of the South*. New York: Pantheon Books, 1984.

Auerbach, Nina. *Communities of Women: An Idea in Fiction*. Cambridge: Harvard University Press, 1978.

Barr, Marleen S., ed. *Future Females: A Critical Anthology*. Bowling Green: Bowling Green University Popular Press, 1981.

Berg, Stephen and S. J. Marks, eds. *About Women: An Anthology of Contemporary Fiction, Poetry & Essays*. Greenwich, CT: Fawcett, 1973.

Christ, Carol P. *Diving Deep and Surfacing: Women Writers on Spiritual Quest*. Boston: Beacon Press, 1980.

Davidson, Cathy N. and E. M. Broner, eds. *The Lost Tradition: Mothers and Daughters in Literature*. New York: Ungar, 1980.

Earnest, Ernest. *The American Eve in Fact and Fiction*. Bloomington: Indiana University Press, 1975.

Fleischmann, Fritz, ed. *American Novelists Revisited: Essays in Feminist Criticism*. Boston: G. K. Hall & Company, 1982.

Fryer, Judith. *The Faces of Eve: Women in the Nineteenth Century American Novel*. New York: Oxford University Press, 1976.

Goldenberg, Naomi R. *The Changing of the Gods: Feminism and the End of Traditional Religion*. Boston: Beacon Press, 1979.

Griffin, Susan. *Woman and Nature: The Roaring Inside Her*. New York: Harper & Row, 1978.

Hall, Nor. *The Moon and the Virgin: Reflections on the Archetypal Feminine*. New York: Harper & Row, 1980.

Harding, Esther. *Woman's Mysteries: Ancient and Modern*. New York: Bantam, 1973.

Kaplan, Sydney Janet. *Feminist Consciousness in the Modern British Novel*. Urbana: University of Illinois Press, 1975.

Kelley, Mary. *Private Woman, Public Stage: Literary Domesticity in Nineteenth-Century America*. New York: Oxford University Press, 1984.

Klein, Viola. *The Feminine Character: History of an Ideology*. New York: International University, 1948.

Kolbenschlag, Madonna. *Kiss Sleeping Beauty Good-Bye: Breaking the Spell of Feminine Myths and Models*. New York: Doubleday, 1979.

McCarthy, Mary. *On the Contrary: Articles of Belief*. New York: Noonday Press, 1962.

Merchant, Carolyn. *The Death of Nature: Women, Ecology, and the Scientific Revolution*. San Francisco: Harper & Row, 1979.

Pearson, Carol and Katherine Pope. *The Female Hero in American and British Literature.* New York: R. R. Bowker, 1981.

Rigney, Barbara Hill. *Madness and Sexual Politics in the Feminist Novel: Studies in Brontë , Woolf, Lessing and Atwood.* Madison: University of Wisconsin Press, 1978.

Rosinsky, Natalie M. *Feminist Futures: Contemporary Women's Speculative Fiction.* Ann Arbor: UMI Research Press, 1984.

Showalter, Elaine. *A Literature of Their Own: British Women Novelists from Brontë to Lessing.* Princeton: Princeton University Press, 1977.

Spacks, Patricia Meyer. *The Female Imagination.* New York: Avon, 1976.

Staicar, Tom, ed. *The Feminine Eye: Science Fiction and the Women Who Write It.* New York: Frederick Ungar, 1982.

Index

About the Author

THELMA J. SHINN, Associate Professor of English and Women's Studies, Arizona State University, is the author of *Worlds Within Women: Myth and Mythmaking in Fantastic Literature by Women* (Greenwood Press, forthcoming). She has contributed to *American Women Writers* and *Contemporary Literary Criticism* and such journals as *Modern Drama, Literature and Psychology, Critique,* Contemporary Literature, *The Nathaniel Hawthorne Journal,* and *Colby Library Quarterly.*